animals

AN ILLUSTRATED A-Z

This is a Starfire Book
First published in 2002
This edition published 2006

07 09 10 08 06

3 5 7 9 10 8 6 4 2

Starfire is part of
The Foundry Creative Media Company Limited
Crabtree Hall, Crabtree Lane, Fulham, London, SW6 6TY

www.star-fire.co.uk

ISBN 1 84451 462 5

A copy of the CIP data for this book is available from the British Library

Printed in China

Special thanks to: Lisa Balkwill, Sarah Goulding, Julia Rolf and Richard Walker

animals

AN ILLUSTRATED A-Z

GENERAL EDITOR: GERARD CHESHIRE

STAR
FIRE

CONTENTS

THEMES

Each A–Z entry is tagged by themes which can be followed as threads throughout the book

 Birds

 Invertebrates

 Reptiles and Amphibians

 Fish

 Mammals

INTRODUCTION

It is believed that life on Earth began an estimated 3.5 billion years ago. Since then life has thrived around the globe as living organisms have competed with one another to survive, promoting the evolution of new, more sophisticated species along the way. With the arrival of humans came the first evolved minds able to wonder about the origins of life on earth. In 1735 a Swedish naturalist called Carolus Linnaeus (1707–78) became the first person to classify species according to their similarities and give them scientific names. Then, in 1859, the English naturalist Charles Darwin (1809–82) explained to the world how living things have managed to evolve into the bewildering number of species that comprise the animal, plant, fungal, protistan, eubacterial and archaeobacterial kingdoms today. Since then scientists have learned much about the finer details of evolution – in particular the working mechanism behind evolution, called natural selection. It may well turn out that this intimate knowledge will one day help humans save many of those animal species now sadly in decline.

Living in a twenty-first-century world which is increasingly dominated by human activity, most people are becoming more sympathetic to the plight of the Earth's wild animals. This is partly due to the perceived threat to many species from loss of habitat, pollution, exploitation and general disturbance, which has left many animals vulnerable to extinction. Additionally, many people rarely come into contact with wild animals because they live in urban areas. Learning about animals has therefore become an intriguing pastime that allows people to feel that they are making contact with their own natural beginnings or roots – something that seems more important than ever to people from man-made environments.

For wild animals this can only be a good development: it suggests that conservation issues will thus take more of a centre stage in political arenas world-wide, thus providing the legal measures necessary to prevent humans from destroying what is, after all, their own natural habitat as well as that of other animals. However, surely the best way to ensure that wild habitats are preserved is to educate indigenous human populations of the value of their wild resources. That way local people can take responsibility for overseeing their own conservation projects.

This book is designed to provide a comprehensive view of the animal kingdom. The 500 entries are divided between the two key groupings of mammals – the vertebrates (mammals, birds, reptiles, amphibians and fish) and invertebrates (a massive, varied array of animals including insects, crustaceans, echinoderms and segmented worms). In addition, there are double-page features throughout the book which expand upon the fundamental themes relating to the evolution of the world's animals and how they have been categorized. The entries are arranged alphabetically to make it easy to navigate through the book. However, most entries cover groups of animals rather than specific species, so that the fauna of the planet can be accommodated. For that reason there is also an index and most entries include cross reference tags beneath.

Each entry has been written in an accessible style to provide an interesting and informative read. There is a combination of simple, anecdotal information and more detailed information so that both the general and more knowledgeable reader can use the book with useful effect. Any words that may be considered unusual, because they are specialized terms or not often used, have been included in the glossary that supplies simple definitions, and the feature spreads provide more detail about specific themes, written in the same accessible style as the entries.

Whether you have a passing interest in, or a deep fascination for, the animal kingdom you will not fail to be impressed by the sheer diversity of the world's fauna as described in this book. The more you learn about animal species the more your interest will grow. *Animal Facts* will provide you not only with a useful general understanding of the animal kingdom, it may also spur you on to discover more about areas that particularly you.

GERARD CHESHIRE

AARDVARKS
(Class: Mammalia Order: Tubulidentata)

 These creatures are rather curious, looking like an assemblage of parts from other animals – the body of a badger, the ears of a donkey and the nose of a pig. In fact the name 'aardvark' is Afrikaans for 'earth pig', but aardvarks are not related. They have their own order and family with just one species – *Orycteropus afer*. Aardvarks

are nocturnal animals of the African continent. They live on ants and termites, which they find by burrowing into their nests. The mouth is nothing more than a small opening through which a slender, sticky tongue is slid back and forth.

➟ *Anteaters, Termites*

AARDWOLVES
(Class: Mammalia Order: Carnivora)

Like aardvarks, these animals have an Afrikaans name – this time meaning 'earth wolf'. Although members of the order of carnivores, aardwolves are actually members of the hyena family and not the canine family. They have the front-heavy build of the hyenas, but they are far less robust. Whereas true hyenas hunt and scavenge large prey, aardwolves specialise in far smaller prey. They will take small animals and carrion, but their staple diet is termites, hence their name, for they burrow into termite mounds to find the insects. They also burrow out their own earths, rather like badgers do.

➟ *Hyenas, Termites*

ABOVE The curious-looking aardvark is a nocturnal animal from Africa.
RIGHT Adders, such as this eyelash adder, belong to the viper family.

ACCENTORS
(Class: Aves Order: Passeriformes)

With greyish-brown plumage the accentors are inconspicuous birds characterised by their hopping and shuffling behaviour. They scour the ground under bushes and trees looking for seeds or insects. Males, females and juveniles all share characteristically dull plumage though some species have contrasting markings of orange, black or white. Accentors are found in Asia, North Africa and Europe. There are 13 species, of which the dunnock (*Prunella modularis*) is probably the most familiar. While most accentors form simple pairs, some species, including the dunnock, form polyandrous relationships – where one female mates with several of the opposite sex.

➟ *Finches, Sparrows*

ADDERS
(Class: Reptilia Order: Squamata)

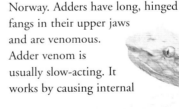 The name 'adder' is applied to several snakes from the viper family, including the common viper (*Vipera berus*) and puff adders. Like other vipers, adders are considered highly evolved snakes. They usually have stocky bodies which are relatively well-adapted to deal with cool temperatures. The common viper is found in Asia and Europe but its habitat extends as far north as Norway. Adders have long, hinged fangs in their upper jaws and are venomous. Adder venom is usually slow-acting. It works by causing internal

haemorrhaging. The bite of some adders, especially puff adders and death adders, is dangerous to humans.
➠ **Snakes**

AESTIVATION AND HIBERNATION IN AMPHIBIANS

Aestivation is the process by which animals enter a dormant phase during summer months. It is similar to hibernation, which is the process by which animals become dormant during the winter. Such processes are common in frogs since they are unable to control their body temperatures by altering aspects of their metabolism, as warm-blooded mammals can. Many frogs in temperate countries over-winter in the mud at the bottom of ponds. This protects them from freezing and increases their chances of survival until springtime, when there is more food available and they can reproduce.

Frogs inhabiting regions that experience hot and arid periods in summer may become dormant in a bid to survive until the next mating season, which begins when wet conditions recur. These aestivating frogs store water within themselves while conditions are wet. When the rainy season finishes and the region becomes arid once more, they dig burrows several centimetres below ground level. The burrows are lined with secreted cocoons and the frogs stay within, dormant, until better conditions prevail. The western spadefoot toad (*Scaphiopus hammondii*) of the Arizona desert and Australian burrowing frogs all aestivate. Australian aborigines can locate burrowing frogs and use them as a source of water.

AGAMAS

(Class: Reptilia Order: Squamata)

The agamas are a group of approximately 60 species of primitive lizard that are found in Asia, Australasia and Africa. They are closely related to iguanids and chameleons and occupy similar habitats. Like most reptiles, they are predators and feed mainly on insects, often inhabiting rocky, desert regions. Agamas are

BELOW Agoutis live in the equatorial zone of the Americas.

30–40 cm (12–18 in) long. They are usually brown or grey but, like the iguanids and chameleons, they are able to change colour. During the mating season male agamas may turn bright red or blue and those of some species have crests that are used in courtship displays.
➠ **Chameleons, Iguanas**

AGOUTIS

(Class: Mammalia Order: Rodentia)

Agoutis are large rodents from Central and South America. They are adapted for running through

undergrowth and have a form somewhat like a small deer or hare, with hoof-like claws. They can also swim very well. There are many species and sub-species over its range. They feed on all manner of vegetation and escape into burrows whenever danger threatens. As agoutis live in the equatorial zone of the Americas they are not subjected to significant seasonal changes in climate. The result is that they can breed all year round and quickly establish large populations, becoming serious pests.
➠ **Mammals, Rodents**

ALLIGATORS

(Class: Reptilia Order: Crocodilia)

Alligators are closely related to crocodiles, caimans and gharials. Together these animals constitute one of the oldest orders of reptiles. They have changed remarkably little since the time – 65 million years ago – when they shared the earth with dinosaurs.

Alligators look very similar to crocodiles although there are two important, visible differences. Alligators have shorter, broader snouts than their cousins and only the upper teeth are visible when the creatures have their mouths closed. Alligators are better able to cope with cool temperatures than crocodiles and are therefore more likely to be found in temperate regions. Alligators are carnivorous and eat fish, frogs, turtles, snails, birds and small mammals. They will attack and kill humans if provoked.

There are two species of alligator. The American alligator (*Alligator mississipiensis*) reaches 6 m (20 ft) in length and is found on the shores of lakes, rivers and swamps in tropical and temperate regions of the Americas. The smaller Chinese alligator (*Alligator sinensis*) is found only on the banks of the Yangtze River.

❧ The Mississippi (American) alligator was declared an endangered species in 1967 and hunting it was made illegal. Since then the population has recovered.

❧ The Chinese alligator is threatened with extinction.

AMPHIBIANS

(Phylum: Chordata Class: Amphibia)

Towards the end of the Devonian Period (408–362 million years ago) some types of fish began to move on to land, following the invertebrates (animals without backbones) to exploit a new habitat. These creatures led to the development of an entirely new group of vertebrates – the amphibians. Some of these animals further evolved into the reptiles.

Amphibians are commonly believed to represent an intermediate stage between fish and reptiles, although millions of years of evolution have produced adaptations that are specific to this group. Amphibians have circulation and respiration systems that allow breathing to occur through their moist skin. Generally, amphibians are able to live in either terrestrial or aquatic habitats although, unlike reptiles, members of this class lay their eggs in water. The eggs lack a shell and amnion. The amnion – a fluid-filled sac in which the embryo develops – is present in the eggs of reptiles, birds and mammals. The eggs are laid in water where they hatch into tadpoles, which undergo considerable transformation as they develop into adults.

There are three orders of amphibian; Caudata, (salamanders and newts), Anura (frogs and toads) and Apoda (the burrowing caecilians). These three groups of animals have had long and separate evolutionary histories. The anurans are the most widespread, numerous and diverse of the amphibians.

❧ The first frogs and salamanders appeared in the Jurassic period – 208–144 million years ago.

❧ Amphibians can produce toxins in their skin that are unique to this group of animals. The arrow-poison frogs of Central and South America, are often brightly coloured as a warning to predators that they have deadly toxins in their skins.

❧ The name 'amphibian' translates as 'double life'. This name alludes to the complex life-cycles of these species, which involve metamorphosis and living in dual habitats – aquatic and terrestrial.

ABOVE The Chinese alligator lives on the banks of the Yangtze River.
ABOVE RIGHT Frogs come from the Anura order of amphibians.

ANACONDAS

(Class: Reptilia Order: Squamata)

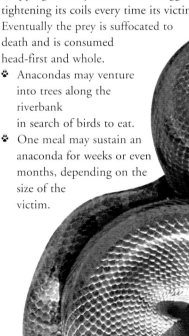 These large snakes, also known as water boas, live a semi-aquatic existence, mainly in the rainforests of South America. Anacondas are closely related to pythons, which are more widely distributed over the world. Both anacondas and pythons kill their prey by constriction and are generally considered to be fairly primitive snakes. Female anacondas are viviparous; they give birth to as many as 75 live young.

There are two species of anaconda in the family Boidae – the yellow anaconda (*Eunectes notaeus*) and the giant anaconda (*E. murinus*). The giant anaconda is the world's largest snake. It can reach 9 m (30 ft) and weigh 250 kg (550 lb). Despite its size, the snake remains remarkably agile by spending much time in water, where its body weight is supported. It lies in wait for passing prey, such as pigs, jaguars or caimans, and then wrapping its body around the struggling prey, tightening its coils every time its victim exhales. Eventually the prey is suffocated to death and is consumed head-first and whole.

❖ Anacondas may venture into trees along the riverbank in search of birds to eat.

❖ One meal may sustain an anaconda for weeks or even months, depending on the size of the victim.

ANCHOVIES

(Class: Osteichthyes Order: Clupeiformes)

There are some 139 species of anchovy. These small fish are of considerable economic significance since they are not only a source of food for humans but represent an important link in the food chain of many other fish. Anchovies consume plankton, which they filter with specially modified mouthparts. They are 10–25 cm (4–10 in) in length and slender in build.

Their large mouths extend beyond their eyes and their snouts are pointed. Most anchovies occupy coastal, marine habitats although they are often found in brackish water, while some species even live in freshwater.

➤ *Fish, Herrings*

BELOW The giant anaconda can grow as long as 9 m (30 ft).

ANEMONES

(Phylum: Cnidaria Class: Anthozoa)

Anemones belong to an invertebrate phylum with the corals and jellyfish called cnidarians. Both corals and anemones are called polyps and they are both

sedentary. Anemones are sometimes known as 'sea flowers' because they resemble the blooms of terrestrial plants, although they are animals. Their mouths are surrounded by hollow tentacles which they use to catch prey or particles of food drifting through the seawater. Most anemones attach themselves to rocks, although they are also found secured to seashells, crab carapaces, turtle shells and so on. All anemones are soft bodied animals, with no internal or external skeleton.

➧ *Corals, Jellyfish*

ANGEL SHARKS

(Class: Chondrichthyes Order: Squatiniformes)

The family Squatinidae contains about a dozen species of shark that are commonly called angel sharks. The species *Squatina squatina*, of the Mediterranean and Atlantic Ocean, is commonly called the monkfish (not

ABOVE LEFT Anemonefish are safe from the sting of their host anemone.
ABOVE RIGHT Marine angelfish are renowned for their bright colours.

to be confused with the unrelated variety of angler fish – see below). An angel shark's body is flattened and its head is wide and rounded. The pectoral fins are very large and appear wing-like. The dorsal surface is normally grey or brown with dark patches and the underneath is white. Angel sharks may reach 2 m (6.5 ft). They live in coastal regions where they lie on the bottom, often covered in gravel and sand, ambushing prey animals they find there.

➧ *Cartilaginous Fish, Sharks*

ANGELFISHES

(Class: Osteichthyes Order: Perciformes)

The term 'angelfish' is applied to groups of unrelated marine and freshwater fishes which characteristically have flattened, deep bodies. The freshwater species, which belong to the family Cichlidae, are native to South America. They are small – up to 15 cm (6 in) – and attractive, making them popular aquarium fish.

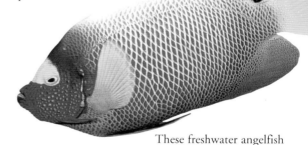

These freshwater angelfish are usually silver in colour with vertical markings. The marine angelfish belong to the family Pomacanthidae. They inhabit tropical coral reefs throughout the world and are renowned for their bold colours and patterns. The young appear dissimilar to the adults. Female emperor angelfish can change sex.

➧ *Fish, Parrot Fish*

ANGLER FISH

(Class: Osteichthyes Order: Lophiiformes)

Angler fish belong to the same group as cod. They are carnivorous, bottom-dwelling, marine fish. They are well-camouflaged and have developed a sedentary method of catching prey. Angler fish, such as the monkfish (*Lophius*), have highly modified spines on their dorsal surfaces. The first spine, or ray, is situated behind the upper jaw and ends in a fleshy lobe. This is dangled in front of the fish's mouth and functions as a lure, attracting prey animals. The monkfish then opens its jaws and sucks in its unsuspecting prey. Some deep-sea angler fish possess a glowing lure to attract prey.

➠ *Cod, Deep Sea Anglers*

ANHINGAS
(Class: Aves Order: Pelecaniformes)

The anhingas belong to one of six families in the order Pelecaniformes. Other members of the order include pelicans, boobies, tropic birds, frigate birds and cormorants. Anhingas or darters are characterised by black and brown plumage and long necks. They also have small heads with sharp, elongate bills and slender bodies. Breeding males may have light-coloured feathers on their heads. Anhingas have surface feathers that quickly become saturated in water, enabling the birds to dive below the water surface. They have to sunbathe to dry their feathers after fishing.

Five fossil species and four living species have been recognized. The American anhinga (*Anhinga anhinga*) is found from the sub-tropical region of North America down to Argentina. Its cormorant-like body is ideally suited to an aquatic life. They live on or near rivers and wetlands, in large nests built from twigs. They swim with most of their bodies underwater; the head and neck stay above water until the bird hunts for prey.

Darters have a useful adaptation that helps them in their hunting. A kink in their neck can be

straightened at speed and with force, enabling the bird to dive towards a fish and spear it with its bill.

➠ *Cormorants, Pelicans*

ANNELID WORMS
(Phylum: Annelida)

Annelid worms are otherwise known as the segmented worms. The phylum includes the earthworms and leeches, although the vast majority of species are worms of marine environments, such as ragworms and lugworms. As their name suggests the bodies of segmented worms comprise a series of segments, more-or-less identical to one another, except for the head and anus. Most species burrow in mud or soil, which they consume to digest its organic content as food. Others remain stationary, filtering particles of food from water. Many leeches actively swim and live off the blood of other animals, including amphibians, reptiles and mammals.

➠ *Invertebrates, Nematode Worms*

ABOVE The neck of the anhinga is specially adapted to aid diving.

ANTBIRDS

(Class: Aves Order: Passeriformes)

There are over 246 species of antbird. They are found in Central and South America in habitats as diverse as tropical rainforest, open grassland and mountains. Antbirds generally have dark plumage, strong legs and stout bills with hooked tips. Physically they are a varied group with species ranging in size from 90–370 mm (8–13 in). They are insect eaters and get their name from their habit of following columns of marching ants. Members of the family include the antwren, antpitta, ant thrush and antshrike. Some antbirds, such as the male barred antshrike and bare-crowned antbird, are strikingly patterned.

➥ *Flycatchers, Shrikes*

ANTEATERS

(Class: Mammalia Order: Edentata)

The term 'anteater' is a generic one used for describing any animals that eat ants or termites, such as aardvarks, numbats, echidnas, pangolins and armadillos. However, there are also true anteaters, belonging to the family Myrmecophagidae, which emanate from Central and South America. The giant anteater (*Myrmecophaga tridactyla*) is a terrestrial animal, reaching 2.4 m (8 ft). It has formidable claws which it uses to rip open termite mounds. Other species are arboreal animals that locate ant or termite nests in the hollows of trees. They include the tamandua (*Tamandua tetradactyla*) and the anteater (*Cyclopes didactylis*).

➥ *Aardvarks, Pangolins*

ANTELOPES

(Class: Mammalia Order: Artiodactyla)

The antelopes are a large group of herbivorous mammals. They are a varied bunch, largely classified as antelopes because they are not deer, cattle, sheep, goats or other clearly identifiable animals. Antelopes include gazelles, wildebeests, hartebeests and duikers. They are found

BELOW LEFT Anteaters have powerful claws to rip open termite mounds.
BELOW The addax is pale to aid camouflage and to keep cool in the desert.

in habitats ranging from tropical forest to savannah to desert. Those that frequent dense foliage live solitarily or in small family groups while other species usually live in herds. This is because strategies against predation change according to the level of visibility and cover.

The antelopes of the African plains are an interesting group because they have evolved sympathetically with one another and other herbivorous animals. The result is that they come in a range of sizes adapted to graze or forage at different heights so that they don't compete directly for the same food sources. Consequently foliage from short grasses up to the lower branches of trees is covered by one antelope species or another. There are also antelopes from North America, the Middle East, Asia and the mountainous areas of Europe.

Antelopes typically possess cryptically coloured hides to provide camouflage. Those of savannah tend to have brown backs to match the dry grasses, but they are also counter shaded, with pale bellies, so that they lose their three dimensional form when seen from a distance by predators. Desert species are very pale to blend with the sand and keep cool. Forest dwelling species are often embellished with stripes and markings to break up their outline in sun scattered clearings.

- The Arabian oryx (*Oryx leucoryx*) is an antelope that can survive for long periods without drinking, because it obtains water by eating succulent plants.
- Typical antelopes have two hollow horns in both sexes, but one species – the chousingha (*Tetracerus quadricornis*) – has four, and many species' females lack horns altogether.

➠ *Deer, Sheep*

ANT-LIONS

(Class: Insecta Order: Neuroptera)

As their name suggests, these insects are ant predators. To be more accurate it is the ant-lion larvae that feed on ants. Adult ant-lions are somewhat similar to dragonflies in appearance, but they are less robustly built. The larvae are squat and bristly, with large, powerful jaws used for piercing their hapless victims to death. They do not hunt, though; instead they lie in wait, buried in the ground at the bottom of conical pits. Passing ants and other small, ground-living invertebrates fall into these pits, where they find the sides too steep and loose to climb to safety.

➠ *Ants, Dragonflies*

ANTS

(Class Insecta Order: Hymenoptera)

Ants belong to a large group of winged insects – endopterygotes – that have separate and distinct phases of development – egg, larva, pupa, imago – rather than developing as nymphs. Although worker ants lack wings, the males and females possess them for a short period of time so that new colonies can be established some distance from their nests of origin. Ants are related to bees, wasps, sawflies and ichneumons which all belong to the order Hymenoptera.

Most species of ant live in colonies and are therefore described as social insects. Colonies are usually housed in nests, which are often hidden below ground or in tree stumps and the like. The nests are divided into galleries and chambers which are used for different tasks, such as nurturing eggs and larvae, processing food and tending the queen. The majority of ants in a colony are worker ants. They are female ants that lack the capacity to reproduce and are responsible for all of the labour inside and outside of the nest; as their name suggests.

Most species of ant are essentially carnivorous, taking all manner of animal matter into the nests as food, although they also take vegetable matter such as fruit pulp and nectar.

➠ *Bees, Wasps*

ABOVE A leaf-cutter ant carries her findings back to the colony.

APES

(Class: Mammalia Order: Primates)

These animals belong to the family Hominidae and are often described as the 'great apes' to distinguish them from gibbons which are sometimes described as 'lesser apes'. There are at least five species of great apes. They are the orangutan (*Pongo pygmaeus*), the gorilla (*Gorilla gorilla*), the common chimpanzee (*Pan troglodytes*), the bonobo (*Pan paniscus*) otherwise known as the Pygmy Chimpanzee and humans (*Homo sapiens*).

Orangutans live in the low-lying and hill forests of Sumatra, Borneo and East Malaysia. There are subtle differences between populations and some scientists regard them as two separate species. They are essentially arboreal animals, rarely descending to the ground unless they have to cross forest clearings. Gorillas live in central Africa and are divided into two geographically separate populations that are seen by many primatologists as being distinct species. Similarly, the bonobo was originally regarded as a dwarf or pygmy race of the common chimpanzee before ultimately earning its own species status.

Gorillas live primarily in dense forest, but they are largely terrestrial as adults, mainly because they grow too heavy for arboreal locomotion to be either efficient or safe. Gorillas live in extended family groups which move on each day to a fresh foraging area. Chimpanzees and bonobos live in larger groups, or troops, which tend to remain in areas marking the transition from forest to savannah, since they are both terrestrial and arboreal in behaviour. They too live in Africa.

❧ The bonobo is regarded by some scientists as the nearest living relative of humans, being similar to the extinct australopithecines.

❧ Chimpanzees have been observed in organized hunting parties, running down monkeys and other animals for fresh meat.

➡ **Gibbons, Monkeys**

APHIDS

(Class: Insecta Order: Hemiptera)

Sometimes known as greenfly or blackfly, aphids are small bugs that derive their nutrition from the sap of plants. Having inserted their tubular mouth parts into the stems of plants they have no need to suck

ABOVE Gorillas are too heavy for the trees and live mainly on the ground.
TOP Orangutan means 'man of the forest'.

because there is sufficient pressure inside the plant for the sap to rise. Many aphids have the ability to reproduce parthenogenetically as well as sexually, which means they can create clones of themselves without a need to mate when conditions are favourable. When aphids multiply in this way their numbers can rise very quickly, with the result that host plants, including food crops, begin to weaken and die.

➠ *Bugs, Insects*

AQUATIC FROGS
(Class: Amphibia Order: Anura)

Frogs belong to an ancient and diverse group of amphibians, inhabiting many different econiches. Most spend their lives both in water and on land, but some are wholly terrestrial and others are totally aquatic. Frogs belonging to the family Pipidae are totally aquatic. The bodies of pipid frogs are well adapted to life in freshwater. Their feet are fully webbed, their skin is slimy and their nostrils and eyes are placed uppermost on their heads. The Lake Titicaca frog and the paradoxical frog are aquatic frogs. The paradoxical frog gets its name from the fact that the tadpole is larger and lives longer than the adult.

➠ *Frogs, Toads*

ARACHNIDS
(Phylum: Arthropoda
Class: Arachnida)

Quite a number of animals fall into the class of Arachnids. They include spiders, harvestmen, scorpions, false scorpions (pseudoscorpions), sun spiders, ticks and mites. All arachnids develop into adults by shedding their skins periodically, having hatched from eggs as miniature versions of the adult form. They are mostly carnivorous with sucking mouthparts which they use to drain their victims' bodily fluids.

Unlike insects, arachnids have just two body sections, instead of three. Their head and thorax is fused together as one and called the cephalothorax. They also have four pairs of legs rather than three, giving them the increased mobility they need to compensate for having no neck. In addition to this, their eyes, of which they may have as many as eight, are often mounted turret-like to provide all-round visibility.

Arachnids have a fifth pair of appendages, in front of their first pair of legs, which are called palps. In most species, such as the spiders, the palps are sensory devices used in feeding and reproduction. In the scorpions and false scorpions however, the palps have been dramatically adapted into pincers for holding and manipulating their prey. Many arachnids use venom for immobilizing their prey. The venom is injected into the victim by a pair of fangs. As well as overcoming the victim the venom contains enzymes that break down the insides of the victim into a soup so that the arachnid can then suck it out as food.

Many arachnids, particularly the spiders, can produce silk from glands called spinnerets. The silk is put to a number of uses, including building nests and protecting eggs and spiderlings, but its most familiar use is as a tool for hunting. Various web designs are used to catch passing prey and the silk is also used for booby traps.

➠ *Scorpions, Spiders*

ARCHERFISH
(Class: Osteichthyes Order: Perciformes)

There are six species of archerfish, all belonging to the family Toxotidae. They are native to the Indo-Pacific region and live in freshwater and brackish water. Their bodies are long, deep and narrow with pointed heads. There is some variety in colouration but most are marked with black spots or stripes. Archerfish get their name from their unique method of catching insects. When an archerfish sees an insect resting on vegetation overhanging the water it shoots a jet of water from its mouth. This knocks the insect off the plant and into the water, where the fish can consume it.

➠ *Bony Fish, Fish*

ABOVE Spiders use their silk for hunting as well as building nests.

ARMADILLO LIZARDS

(Class: Reptilia Order: Squamata)

The armadillo lizard (*Cordylus cataphractus*) of South African deserts is related to the skinks. It is unusual because of the defensive posture it adopts when attacked. It rolls its body into a tight ball and clenches its tail in its mouth. The lizard has hard, horny scales and spines on its back and tail which complete an armoured ball. This is enough to deter all but the most persistent of the lizard's natural predators, including birds of prey. The species is found only in Southern Africa and although it is not an endangered species its status is classed as vulnerable.

➠ *Lizards, Skunks*

ARMADILLOS

(Class: Mammalia Order: Xenarthra)

Armadillos have a rather prehistoric look about them because they are protected by bony plates covered with horn. This armour extends from their nose to their tail and is very effective at deterring predators, especially as the armadillo can burrow or roll up to conceal its soft under parts. Armadillos range in size from the giant armadillo (*Priodontes gigas*) which is 1.5 m (5 ft) to the pink fairy armadillo (*Chlamyphorus truncatus*) at just 125 mm (5 in). They are native to South, Central and North America. Armadillos forage for insects and other invertebrates by using their specially adapted front claws.

➠ *Anteaters, Pangolins*

ABOVE Armour-plated armadillos can avoid danger by burrowing.
ABOVE RIGHT Rainforest tribesmen use these frogs to poison their weapons.

ARROW-POISON FROGS

(Phylum: Arthropoda Class: Amphibia)

Found in the rainforests of Central and South America, these small, brightly coloured frogs are intriguing animals. Diminutive but deadly, these anurans

sport bold patterns and colours in yellow, red, orange, green or pink to signify their potentially lethal killing power. Like many other amphibians, arrow-poison frogs have highly specialised skins that are able to produce toxins.

The toxins belong to the alkaloid group of chemicals and are similar to strychnine, attacking the nervous system very rapidly. Indigenous tribesmen of the rainforest use the toxins for hunting. The tips of spears and arrows are wiped across the backs of the frogs. The weapons then kill quickly, before prey is lost to the forest. Some species from the family Dendrobatidae are known as poison-dart frogs.

Egg fertilization takes place externally, as it does in all amphibians. The eggs are carried on the back of the male until they hatch into tadpoles. The immature tadpoles cling to his back until he manages to locate a stream or pool, where they are left to develop into adults.

🐾 By protecting the young when they are at their most vulnerable, the male frog ensures that more of his offspring are likely to live to adulthood.

➠ *Amphibians, Frogs*

ARTHROPODS

(Phylum: Arthropoda)

This is the term used in describing a large phylum of invertebrate animals that share three characteristics: They all have external skeletons (exoskeletons), segmented bodies and jointed limbs. Arthropods include the insects, arachnids, crustaceans, centipedes and millipedes. The exoskeleton of an arthropod is made from a substance called chitin, which is a tough, fibrous substance comprising various polysaccharides. These are carbohydrate molecules which behave in a similar way to man-made plastics. For an arthropod to grow it sheds its old exoskeleton to make way for a new one underneath, which expands and then sets hard. This is called ecdysis.

➡ *Arachnids, Insects*

AUKS

(Class: Aves: Order: Charadriiformes)

The large order Charadriiformes includes auks as well as gulls, terns and waders. These birds are a common sight near water in many parts of the world. Most are strong and efficient fliers that feed on other animals in or near water. Auks dive underwater for their food. The family of auks, the Alcidae, includes guillemots, puffins and auklets.

Auks or alcids are typically 150–400 mm (6–16 in) in length. They have black and white plumage and have an upright posture. They are dependent on the sea for their diet which comprises fish, crustaceans, sea molluscs and plankton. Auks live in coastal colonies, usually nesting on inaccessible cliffs or islets. They are found in the northern hemisphere, from the Arctic down to northerly temperate regions.

The common puffin (*Fratercula arctica*) is a fairly typical example. It has bright orange feet and a multicoloured bill. It can dive up to 60 m (196 ft) in search of shoaling fish such as herrings, sprats and sand eels. The puffin is a social bird, living in colonies on rocky cliff edges. Nests are made in burrows and lined with soft materials such as feathers. A single egg is laid and then incubated by both parents.

🐾 Auks display clear convergent evolution with the penguins of the southern hemisphere. In fact the

BELOW Puffins are related to penguins and dive underwater for their food.

scientific name for the great auk – *Pinguinus impennis* – demonstrates that it was once called the 'penguin'.

🐾 Now extinct, the great auk reached 75 cm (30 in). It lived in huge colonies along rocky coasts of the North Atlantic.

🐾 Great auks were flightless. Their wings were only 15 cm (6 in) long and were solely used to propel the birds underwater.

🐾 It was mercilessly hunted for oil and food from the early 1800s. The last specimens were collected from Funk Island, off Newfoundland, in June 1844.

➡ *Gulls, Waders*

AXOLOTLS

(Class: Amphibia Order: Caudata)

The name 'axolotl' comes from the Aztec language and means 'water monster'. It is the common name given to the salamander *Ambystoma mexicanum*. This amphibian has been much studied because it possesses a highly unusual quality. It reproduces while still in the immature, or larval, stage. This is known as neoteny or paedogenesis.

Axolotls are physically similar to other salamanders, with long bodies and tails with four legs of similar size. They usually reach 30 cm (12 in) in length. Axolotls retain their feathery gills, unlike other salamanders. Their bodies are plump and black (except in captivity, where albinos are often bred). Once axolotls were found in several lakes in the Valley of Mexico. Now they are found only in Lake Xochimilco, near Mexico City. They are nocturnal animals, feeding mainly on invertebrates. They are preyed upon in turn by waterbirds.

The reason for axolotl neoteny is unclear, but it is possible that conditions outside the lake – arid conditions – are not conducive to life for an amphibian. Maybe the Axolotls have found a way of continuing to exploit the preferred conditions within the lake by reproducing while still in the larval stage of their life-cycle. It is unusual for Axolotls in the wild to ever develop into the adult stage.

- Until 1863 it was not realized that Axolotls were salamanders. Thirty-four were exhibited in the Natural History Museum of Paris. Much excitement was caused when it was noted that the axolotls were beginning to change – metamorphosing into salamanders.
- The ability in these animals to reproduce in the larval stage has continued to fascinate scientists, who believe it provides an insight into evolution.
- It has been suggested that since humans more closely resemble infant apes than adults, it is possible that our own evolution has been influenced by neoteny.

➠ *Amphibians, Salamanders*

AYE-AYES

(Class: Mammalia Order: Primates)

The aye-aye (*Daubentonia madagascariensis*) is a native of the tropical forests on the island of Madagascar. It is a nocturnal, secretive creature, specialised for feeding on the wood-boring grubs of beetles and moths. It has cat-like ears for acute hearing so that it can detect the faint scratching of the grubs hidden inside rotten wood. Having located a grub it gnaws away at the wood with rodent-like teeth to find the chamber. It then uses its specially adapted, wiry middle fingers to hook the grub from its hiding place. The fingers are also used for extracting pulp from fruits.

➠ *Insectivores, Lemurs*

ABOVE Aye-ayes are nocturnal and feed on grubs and fruit.
RIGHT The barbet is a tropical bird which usually lives in treetops.

BABBLERS

(Class: Aves Order: Passeriformes)

 There are over 250 species of these social songbirds, which are also known as 'chatterers' because of their continual and rapid songs and calls to one another. Babblers are found predominantly in Africa, Asia and Australia. They are small- to medium-sized but solidly built birds with a diverse range of habitats and lifestyles. Some scour undergrowth for their preferred diet of insects while others live higher up in trees eating fruits and insects they find living under bark. In some species the non-breeding members of a colony assist breeding members with the incubation of eggs and feeding of chicks.

➡ *Passerines, Songbirds*

BADGERS

(Order: Carnivora Class: Mammalia)

Several badger species live across Africa, Eurasia and North America. They are all squat, robust animals adapted for burrowing, partly for digging earths, but also to unearth food. Badgers live on small animals such as worms and invertebrates, but they will also take carrion and fruits when available, along with reptiles, rodents and birds if they can be caught. The honey badger (*Mellivora capensis*) likes the grubs, pupae and honey of bees. It has a symbiotic relationship with a bird called the greater honey-guide (*Indicator indicator*) which leads the badger to bees nests in exchange for some of the food.

➡ *Honeyguides*

BARBETS

(Class: Aves Order: Piciformes)

Barbets belong to the same bird order as woodpeckers, toucans, jacamars and puffbirds. They are non-migratory, tropical birds that usually live in treetops. They are characterised by bristles at the base of their bills – hence their name. Their bills are used to excavate nesting holes in rotting trees. Barbets are usually green or brown in colour, with flashes of

white or bright colour. Their heads are typically large in relation to their bodies, they have short tails and are weak fliers. They live on insects, other invertebrates, birds' eggs and lizards. Barbets are renowned for their loud, repetitious calls.

➡ *Toucans, Woodpeckers*

BARNACLES

(Subphylum: Crustacea Class: Cirripedia)

Barnacles, otherwise known as cirripedes, are the only sessile crustaceans. Although they look strikingly similar to some molluscs they are very different structurally, having evolved from a crab-like ancestor. The shell is really an adapted carapace, and the abdomen has been reduced to a vestige. The body still has a fine exoskeleton and the limbs have been adapted into feather-like structures for catching floating fragments of food. Barnacles typically secure themselves to solid objects – rocks, shipwrecks, boats and even turtles and whales – as swimming larvae and remain there for the duration of their lives, filtering the water for a living.

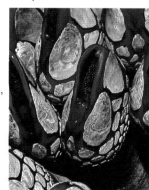

BELOW Barnacles attach themselves to objects and filter the water for food.

➡ *Crabs, Crustaceans*

BARRACUDAS

(Class: Osteichthyes Order: Perciformes)

There are about 20 species of barracuda, all from the family Sphyraenidae. They are all marine carnivores that inhabit temperate and tropical waters throughout the world. The pike-like barracudas have long cylindrical bodies with two dorsal fins. Their large mouths have long jaws and many sharp teeth. Some species are solitary, others hunt in shoals. They mainly feed on other fish but their bold and aggressive nature makes them a threat to humans. There have been fatal attacks on swimmers and divers. Barracudas range in length from 1.2–1.8 m (4–6 ft) and are often prized as sport fish.

➡ *Pike, Sharks*

BASKING SHARKS

(Class: Chondrichthyes Order: Lamniformes)

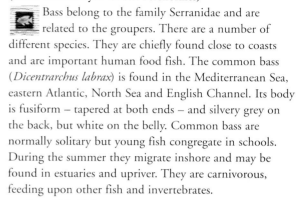 Most sharks are predatory carnivores and scavengers. Basking sharks, however, are harmless filter feeders that eat plankton. Plankton is a mass of tiny organisms, either plant or animal, which floats passively near the surface of the oceans. Basking sharks move slowly through water with their jaws agape, filtering plankton out of the water using their gill-rakers.

About four species of basking shark are recognized. *Cetorhinus maximus* of the North Atlantic Ocean is the second largest fish in the world, after the whale shark. It measures up to 14 m (46 ft) in length. It is normally greyish-brown or greyish-black on its back and light grey underneath. It has five large gill slits on either side of its head. Basking sharks are inhabitants of northern and temperate marine regions. They are found in the Atlantic, Pacific and Indian Oceans and bear live young that are nurtured inside the mother by means of a rich yolk.

❖ Basking sharks typically lead solitary lives, although they may congregate in large groups, of up to 60 members, to feed on large clouds of plankton.

❖ Basking sharks migrate towards coastal areas during the summer and hibernate in winter.

➠ *Sharks, Whale Sharks*

BASS

(Class: Osteichthyes Order: Perciformes)

Bass belong to the family Serranidae and are related to the groupers. There are a number of different species. They are chiefly found close to coasts and are important human food fish. The common bass (*Dicentrarchus labrax*) is found in the Mediterranean Sea, eastern Atlantic, North Sea and English Channel. Its body is fusiform – tapered at both ends – and silvery grey on the back, but white on the belly. Common bass are normally solitary but young fish congregate in schools. During the summer they migrate inshore and may be found in estuaries and upriver. They are carnivorous, feeding upon other fish and invertebrates.

➠ *Bony Fish, Fish*

BATS

(Class: Mammalia Order: Chiroptera)

Bats are divided into two groups – frugivorous (fruit-eating) bats and insectivorous (insect-eating) bats. The first group are often called flying foxes due to their appearance. They feed on fruits and flowers from a variety of trees in tropical habitats. The second group are often called flying mice due to their appearance. Although most of them feed on nocturnal flying insects, several

species have adapted to feed on other foods. Vampire bats feed on the blood of mammals, while another species is able to catch fish. The bats are the only group of mammals that have mastered true, sustained flight.

➡ *Insectivores, Mammals*

BEARS

(Class: Mammalia Order: Carnivora)

In terms of design, the bears are the all-rounders of their habitats. They are classified as carnivores but most are really opportunistic omnivores, feeding on a wide variety of plant and animal matter. Although able to hunt they cannot run at speed for any distance so they rely on stealth and cunning to ambush their prey. Carrion is often won from other predators simply by intimidation. Bears range from the polar north to tropical forests. The Polar bear (*Ursus maritimus*) relies largely on marine mammals for food, while the sloth bear (*Melursus ursinus*) has evolved to eat termites and ants.

➡ *Carnivores, Pandas*

BEAVERS

(Class: Mammalia Order: Rodentia)

There are two species of true beaver: the American beaver (*Castor canadensis*) and the Eurasian beaver (*Castor fiber*). The mountain beaver (*Aplodontia rufa*) is a more primitive rodent from its own family. Beavers are well known for their habit of building dams and lodges on rivers in wooded areas. The purpose of the dam is to

LEFT Fruit-eating bats are also called flying foxes.
ABOVE Polar bears inhabit the Arctic and eat marine mammals.

BELOW Brightly-coloured bee-eaters have curved bills for catching insects.

raise water levels so that the lodge entrance is submerged and therefore protected from predators. Beavers are equipped with chisel-like incisor teeth with which they fell hundreds of trees. They feed on a variety of vegetable matter which they also store as winter food.

➡ *Rats, Rodents*

BEE-EATERS

**(Class: Aves
Order: Coraciiformes)**

The bright and beautiful plumage of bee-eaters distinguishes them as some of the most striking birds in the tropical and sub-tropical regions of the world. Although related to the kingfishers, bee-eaters do not live the semi-aquatic life. Their preferred habitat is woodland, tropical rainforest and open grasslands. They are characterised by their slender, downwards curving bills, ideal for dealing with bees and wasps. They knock off the insects' stings onto branches before swallowing them. They often have elongated central tail feathers and their plumage is typically dominated by greens and browns with flashes of reds, blues and yellows.

➡ *Bees, Kingfishers*

BEES

(Class: Insecta Order: Hymenoptera)

The bees are loosely separated into four groups. These are bumble bees, honey bees, solitary bees, and cuckoo bees. All bees are vegetarian, feeding on nectar and pollen. Bumble bees and honey bees live in colonies as social insects. They have three forms – queens, drones and workers. The queen is the egg-laying female, the drones are the males that fertilize her and the workers are sexually inert females which maintain the nest and forage for food. Solitary bees work alone, as their name suggests, while cuckoo bees lay their eggs in the nests of bumble bees, hence their name.

➡ *Insects, Wasps*

BEETLES

(Class: Insecta Order: Coleoptera)

 There are more species of beetle than any other order of insect. There are over a quarter of a million known to science, all of which vary greatly in size, shape and colouration because they have evolved to suit so many different habitats and econiches. They all share certain characteristics which define them as beetles, the most consistent being their fore-wings which are hardened and thickened into plates of chitin called elytra (the singular is elytron). The elytra are essentially plates of armour which protect the insect from predators. When the insect wants to fly the elytra flip upwards and the hind wings unfold for takeoff.

Some beetles are carnivores, some are vegetarian, while others are omnivores. They all have chewing mouth parts, which means they can consume both solid and fluid foods, unlike bugs, which can only suck fluids. Similarly beetle larvae can eat a variety of foodstuffs, though they often consume different things to adults, such as rotten wood and other detritus.

Species of beetle are generally placed into groups according to their habits and characteristics. For example, there are ground beetles, flower beetles, furniture beetles, weevils, dung beetles, tiger beetles, chafers, longhorn beetles, ladybirds, carpet beetles, soldier beetles, click beetles, rove beetles, stag beetles, scarabs, water beetles and burying beetles.

➧ *Bugs, Insects*

ABOVE There are more than a quarter of a million known species of beetle.
ABOVE RIGHT Remeniscent of their reptilian ancestors, birds still lay eggs.

BIRDS

(Phylum: Chordata Class: Aves)

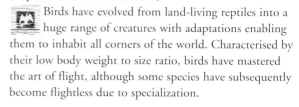 Birds have evolved from land-living reptiles into a huge range of creatures with adaptations enabling them to inhabit all corners of the world. Characterised by their low body weight to size ratio, birds have mastered the art of flight, although some species have subsequently become flightless due to specialization.

As birds evolved from reptiles they developed the ability to maintain their body temperature – they became endothermic, or warm-blooded. They are also characterised by feathers, wings, breathing through lungs and laying eggs to achieve reproduction. In the pursuit of a low body weight the skeletons of birds have become reduced, compact and lightweight. Most birds' bones are hollow and lack marrow. The forelimbs have been modified into wings while the hind limbs are adapted for perching. Hearing and vision are well developed but the sense of smell is usually poor.

Birds exhibit a wide variety of behaviour. Many use song, calls and display to communicate with one another. Reproductive behaviour is often highly complex and this is frequently exemplified by bright and beautiful plumage, especially in males, coupled with courtship flights or dances.

While some birds are largely solitary in habit, many species live and travel in colonies, often migrating long distances to breed or find food. Birds have various methods of navigation. Some are able to measure changes in day length and recognize the position of the sun, moon and stars. It is thought that many birds can also detect changes in the earth's magnetic field, which they use as a built-in compass.

❀ The earliest known fossil bird is Archaeopteryx which lived about 150 million years ago.

❀ Feathers are modified scales, made from the same material as fur and hair – keratin.

➧ *Passerines, Reptiles*

BIRDS OF PARADISE

(Class: Aves Order: Passeriformes)

Birds of paradise belong to the largest group of birds – the passerines or perching birds. There are 43 species of bird of paradise, which are found predominantly in the forested or mountainous areas of New Guinea. They are probably the most spectacular of all bird families. Male birds of paradise possess incredibly ornate and colourful plumage that they use, along with elaborate courtship displays and calls, to attract and entice females for mating. Females are typically drab looking by comparison. They build bulky nests in tree forks, then incubate and rear one or two young unaided.

Birds of paradise feed on fruit and vary in size from 12–100 cm (5–40 in) with an extended and elaborate tail, often accounting for the greater part of their length. The male superb bird of paradise (*Lophorina superba*) possesses an iridescent blue breast shield, while the male Count Raggi's bird of paradise (*Paradisea raggiana*) has a shock of scarlet tail plumes.

❖ The standard-winged bird of paradise (*Semioptera*) was discovered by Alfred Russel Wallace (1823–1913), who became jointly responsible for realizing the theory of evolution with Charles Darwin (1809–82).

➡ *Bowerbirds, Passerines*

BIRDS OF PREY

(Class: Aves Order: Falconiformes)

While many species of bird feed on other animals, the birds of prey, or raptors, are a unique group that have sophisticated methods of hunting. Aided by physical adaptations that enable them to hunt with great accuracy and speed, these predators are killers that reign over the skies of the world. They include eagles, buzzards, hawks, harriers, vultures, falcons, kites and owls (order: Strigiformes).

Birds of prey have extremely good eyesight, enabling them to seek and catch prey on the ground or in flight. Most birds have eyes on the sides of their heads but birds of prey have relatively large eyes that are forward-facing, giving them stereoscopic or binocular vision which provides a precise, three-dimensional image. Together with muscular strength, talons and hooked bills, it enables birds of prey to hunt and kill other animals with efficiency.

Some birds of prey feed almost exclusively on carrion, but most feed on the flesh of freshly killed animals. Depending on their size and specialization they will attack all manner of animals including mammals, reptiles, amphibians, fish, other birds, insects and other invertebrates. There are a few species that have evolved very specialised diets. The secretary bird (*Sagittarius serpentarius*) spends most of its time on the ground, where it runs down snakes with its long legs, while the everglade kite (*Rostrhamus sociabilis*) has a long, downward curved bill adapted for hooking out water snails from their shells.

❖ Birds of prey can see up to four times as much detail as humans.

❖ The peregrine falcon (*Falco peregrinus*) reaches 230 kph (143 mph) as it plunges to strike its prey.

❖ The owls are the only birds of prey that are truly nocturnal. They have relatively enormous eyes to utilize the low levels of light available at night and very acute hearing to detect their prey.

➡ *Eagles, Owls*

ABOVE An eagle's eyes are forward-facing, giving the bird binocular vision.

BITTERLINGS

(Class: Osteichthyes Order: Cypriniformes)

These small, silvery fish are unremarkable except for their method of reproduction. During April and May the males of each species change colour. Some species develop orange bellies and red fins while others turn iridescent blue. The females grow long ovipositors, or egg-depositing tubes, which they insert into the siphons, or air tubes, of freshwater bivalves, such as clams and mussels. Eggs are despatched down the tubes until they reach the gill chamber of the bivalve. The nearby male ejects his sperm into the water near the shellfish. As the shellfish draws more water into its body, through the siphon, the fish's sperm is drawn in too and fertilizes the eggs.

The fish embryos develop within the relative safety of the bivalve's gill chamber. After one month the eggs hatch and fish hatchlings emerge from the shell. This peculiar relationship between fish and invertebrates is not wholly one-sided. As the tiny fish leave their host the bivalve sheds its own larvae which embed in the skin of the hatchlings and remain there while they mature. This is described as a symbiotic relationship.

❧ There are several species of bitterling. Most of them are confined to freshwater streams of central and southern Europe.

➠ *Bivalves, Fish*

BIVALVES

(Phylum: Mollusca Class: Bivalvia)

Bivalves are molluscs with shells divided in two and hinged so they can close or open. The animal itself is much like any other mollusc, being a soft-bodied creature which would be extremely vulnerable to predation were it not for this protection. There are a great many species of bivalve.

ABOVE The Giant clam is an example of a bivalve.
ABOVE RIGHT The male sailfin blenny raises its dorsal fin to appear larger.

Among them are the clams, cockles, mussels, oysters, scallops, razorshells and shipworms, which have modified shells for boring into wood.

Most bivalves are more-or-less symmetrical, but some have a marked asymmetry because they lie flat on the sea bed rather than securing themselves to a solid object or burrowing into substrate. Bivalves generally filter fragments of food from the surrounding water. They have, notably, managed to invade freshwater habitats as well as marine ones and can occur in very high numbers.

Most species are either slow moving or sedentary, but some species can 'swim' by expelling water rapidly from their shells. This is a good way of avoiding predators. Most mobile bivalves use a muscular foot to heave themselves along, although they often remain within a burrow. The foot is drawn in whenever danger threatens so that the two halves of the shell can be closed tightly together.

➠ *Molluscs, Monovalves*

BLENNIES

(Class: Osteichthyes Order: Perciformes)

Blennies are marine fish which typically live in very shallow water. They appear similar to gobies but are placed in their own family, Blenniidae. Blennies have long slender bodies that are scale-less and slimy. There are about 345 species in the blenny family and there is great variation in appearance and lifestyle. Generally, they live in coastal waters, reefs and beds of seaweed. Some eat plant material while others are carnivorous, taking smaller fish and invertebrates. They hide in crevices and holes when alarmed. Some species, such as the tompot blenny, have fringed tentacles on their heads and snouts.

➠ *Fish, Gobies*

BLIND FISH

(Class: Osteichthyes Order: Perciformes)

In an environment devoid of all light there is no advantage in having sight, so a number of species of cave-dwelling fish have, independently, lost the use of their eyes. They are known collectively as blind, or cave, fish. Not surprisingly these fish have compensated for a lack of visual stimulation by becoming hyper-sensitive to other stimuli, especially touch. Evolution has therefore invested in characteristics that are most useful to the blind fish.

Most blind fish are small, reaching a maximum of 100 mm (4 in). They are normally pale in colour and have non-functioning, vestigial eyes that are sometimes covered by skin. Blind fish usually have a keen sense of smell and are able to detect local changes in temperature and pressure by means of their lateral line. The lateral line is a system of sense organs that run in a line down each side of the body. The species *Amblyopsis spelaea* of Mammoth Cave, Kentucky, possesses small tactile organs that are sensitive to touch. These sense organs are arranged over their bodies, heads and tails.

❧ Numerous species of cave-dwelling, blind fish are found throughout the world. Blind fish are found in North America, Cuba, Yucatan, Mexico and Asia.

➠ *Bony Fish, Fish*

BLIND SNAKES

(Class: Reptilia Order: Squamata)

Blind snakes belong to two families; there are 150 species in the family Typhlopidae, which are also known as worm snakes, and 60 species in the family Leptotyphlopidae, which are also known as thread snakes. As their name suggests blind snakes cannot see. Their vestigial or atrophied eyes are covered by head scales. Eyes are not needed by these snakes as they are burrowing creatures. Their bodies are small, cylindrical and smooth. Their heads are blunt to help them dig through soil in search of small invertebrates, such as ants and termites. Blind snakes are found in warm tropical regions.

➠ *Reptiles, Snakes*

RIGHT Boas locate their warm-blooded prey with heat-sensitive organs.

BOAS

(Class: Reptilia Order: Squamata)

Boas belong to the family Boidea and are related to pythons. They vary in size from a relatively diminutive 20 cm (8 in) to an extraordinary 9 m (30 ft). The anacondas, semi-aquatic boas of the South American rainforests, include the longest and heaviest snakes. Boas tend to have stout, broad bodies with short tails. Their scaly skin is often coloured brown, olive-green or yellow and is frequently patterned with blotches or diamonds. They can be found in warm regions of both the Old and New Worlds, although they are most common in South America.

Boas are carnivorous. They eat mammals and birds. Some species are able to locate warm-blooded mammals with heat-sensitive organs. Prey is usually bitten first, then constricted. The snake wraps its coils around the creature and the victim is gradually suffocated by the ever-tightening coils. Each time the victim exhales the coils are constricted round its lungs until, eventually, no breath can be drawn in. The boa's large mouth dilates to engulf the victim's body.

❧ Boas, unlike pythons, do not lay eggs, but bear live young.

❧ Boas usually live a terrestrial life, though some are arboreal and others, such as anacondas, live a semi-aquatic life.

➠ *Pythons, Snakes*

BOMBAY DUCKS

(Class: Osteichthyes Order: Aulopiformes)

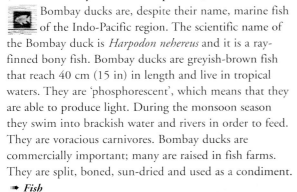 Bombay ducks are, despite their name, marine fish of the Indo-Pacific region. The scientific name of the Bombay duck is *Harpodon nehereus* and it is a ray-finned bony fish. Bombay ducks are greyish-brown fish that reach 40 cm (15 in) in length and live in tropical waters. They are 'phosphorescent', which means that they are able to produce light. During the monsoon season they swim into brackish water and rivers in order to feed. They are voracious carnivores. Bombay ducks are commercially important; many are raised in fish farms. They are split, boned, sun-dried and used as a condiment.
➠ *Fish*

BONITOS

(Class: Osteichthyes Order: Perciformes)

Bonitos are strong swimmers that belong to the same family as the tunnies and mackerel – family Scombridae. Bonitos are predacious hunters and are found worldwide from coastal regions to the open oceans. Their bodies are streamlined – hydrodynamically shaped – for swift movement through water. They have silver bellies and striped dorsal surfaces with deeply forked tails. The Atlantic Bonito has an ultramarine dorsal surface marked with oblique stripes. It is a migratory fish that swims in shoals and reaches 80 cm (3 ft) in length. Bonitos are valued as a source of food and as sport fish.
➠ *Mackerel*

BONY FISH

(Phylum: Chordata Class: Osteichthyes)

Living species of fish are broadly divided into three classes; the jawless fish (Agnatha), cartilaginous fish (Chondrichthyes) and the bony fish (Osteichthyes). The bony fish comprise the largest and most diverse of these classes and live in marine and freshwater environments throughout the world. Bony fish are further divided into two groups; lobe-finned fish and ray-finned fish. The lobe-finned fish are believed to have evolved into the first land-living vertebrates. Most species of fish are ray-finned.

ABOVE Bony fish, such as these moontail bullseyes (top) and barracudas, have swim bladders to control buoyancy.

Bony fish, as the name suggests, have bony skeletons. Their gills are protected by covers and they have internal swim bladders. A swim bladder is a gas-filled sac that controls buoyancy in water and enables efficient vertical movement. Bony fish have good vision and many of them are able to discern colour. They have an acute sense of hearing and chemoreceptors enable them to detect changes in the water around them. They often display complex social and reproductive behaviour. Some species can change the colour of their skin.

Physical and behavioural adaptations in bony fish have enabled this group of vertebrates to expand into virtually every aquatic habitat and exploit a huge variety of ecological niches from tropical waters to polar waters and caves to isolated lakes.

❖ There are believed to be at least 20,000 species of bony fish. There are only 21,500 species of all other vertebrates – mammals, reptiles, amphibians, birds and other fish – put together.
❖ During the Late Devonian Period (374–362 million years ago) a group of air-breathing bony fish, called the rhipidistians, were evolving into the first amphibians.
❖ Bony fish are of great economic importance. They are a significant source of protein, vitamin D and fish oils in both human and animal diets. Fish by-products are used for making glues, fertilizers, fake pearls and gelatin.
➠ *Cartilaginous Fish, Fish*

BOOKLICE

(Class: Insecta Order: Psocoptera)

Despite their common name, most booklice have nothing to do with books. There are around a thousand species of booklice. They are all very small, soft-bodied insects with mouth parts designed for chewing dry detritus. Having hatched from minute eggs they go through about six immature stages, as nymphs, before reaching adulthood. Most species live on trees and shrubs, where they feed on lichens, fungi, pollen and other vegetable matter. They acquired their common name because a few species are found in houses, where they colonize dusty places such as old book shelves. They are hunted by false scorpions.

➠ *Insects, Invertebrates*

BOOMSLANGS

(Class: Reptilia Order: Squamata)

The colubrid family of snakes is not normally considered dangerous to humans. Although some species are venomous, the fangs are set far back in the mouth, which makes it harder for the snake to bite either an aggressor or prey. The boomslang (*Dispholidus typus*) is an exception however. The fangs are set relatively farther forward in these snakes and the venom is so powerful that it can kill prey when delivered in only tiny amounts. The boomslang inhabits dry grasslands of sub-Saharan Africa. It hangs, motionless, in trees and bushes conserving energy while awaiting its prey of lizards or birds.

➠ *Reptiles, Snakes*

BOWERBIRDS

(Class: Aves Order: Passeriformes)

Like their relatives, the birds of paradise, male bowerbirds go to great lengths to attract and mate females, though they typically lack quite such resplendent plumage. Their name comes from their unusual courtship displays which are centred on elaborate structures – bowers – that are made on the ground. Each species has its own bower design.

BELOW A satin bowerbird decorates its avenue, to impress the ladies.

The satin bowerbird (*Ptilonorhynchus violaceus*), for example, constructs an avenue of sticks which it then decorates with bright objects. These birds have even been known to manufacture a type of paint from vegetable matter, charcoal and saliva, which is daubed onto the bower.

Archibold's bowerbird (*Archiboldia papuensis*) creates a mat from a thick pad of plant material which is then surrounded with bright, hanging objects. Feathers, flowers, pebbles and even discarded paper or plastic are used by these bowerbirds to decorate their displays. Once the bower is finished the male sings to attract females before he parades in front of his creation. A good display indicates to the female that her suitor is healthy and fit – potential attributes to be passed to her offspring.

🐾 The 20 species of bowerbird are found in woodlands, and occasionally grasslands, of northern Australia, New Guinea and the surrounding islands.

➠ *Birds of Paradise, Passerines*

BOWFINS

(Class: Osteichthyes Order: Amiiformes)

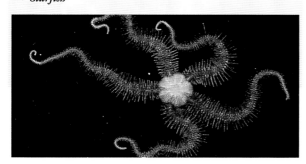 The bowfin (*Amia calva*) is the sole surviving member of an ancient group of fish which had its heyday 180 million years ago. The bowfin is regarded as a primitive ray-finned fish and is placed in the same sub-class as sturgeons, paddlefish, gars and bichirs – the chondrosteans, collectively. The bowfin is a freshwater fish and is found only in North American and Mexican lakes. It is greenish-brown in colour and has a long dorsal fin. The male is smaller than the female, which reaches 75 cm (30 in) in length. The male fish guards the eggs until they hatch.

➡ *Bony Fish, Sturgeons*

BRITTLE-STARS

(Phylum: Echinodermata Class: Ophiuroidea)

These creatures are quite different from familiar starfish. They are primarily adapted for deeper waters and have been recorded at depths of some 6.4 km (4 miles). They have narrow, cylindrical legs made from segments that readily break away when attacked by predators so that the animal itself escapes. Unlike starfish, brittle-stars don't possess tube feet on their legs. This means that they move in a different way, by wriggling their legs. It also means that they cannot cling to rocks easily to avoid being swept away by currents. Instead they wedge themselves into crevices until the turbulent waters calm.

➡ *Starfish*

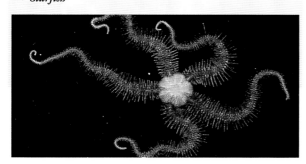

ABOVE The limbs of brittle-stars can be easily broken to escape predators.
ABOVE RIGHT Shield bugs form one group of over 75,000 species of bug.

BUGS

(Class: Insecta Order: Hemiptera)

The term 'bug' has led to some confusion because it is often used as a generic term in the English language to describe insects generally. However, true bugs belong to an order of insects that display defined characteristics. They are similar to beetles, but differ in specific ways. The forewings of bugs are not modified into tough elytra like the beetles, although they are frequently thickened into leathery covers. Bugs also lack chewing mouthparts and are only able to suck fluids by piercing with a needle-like proboscis. Like the beetles, bugs species are adapted to all manner of econiches and diets. There are in excess of 75,000 species recorded.

They are similarly grouped according to habit and characteristics. Thus there are shield bugs, froghoppers, treehoppers, cicadas, assassin bugs, ground bugs, damsel bugs, bedbugs, flower bugs, water surface bugs, aquatic bugs, aphids, plant lice, white fly and scale 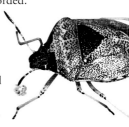 insects. Most feed on the sap of plants, but a good many prey on other invertebrates, sucking them dry of internal fluids. Bugs belong to the group of insects that develop as a series of juvenile stages called nymphs by undergoing incomplete metamorphosis each time they shed their old exoskeleton.

➡ *Beetles, Insects*

BUNTINGS

(Class: Aves Order: Passeriformes)

Buntings belong to the family Emberizidae which contains hundreds of species of bird. They are typically small to medium seedeaters – 10–20 cm (4–8 in) – with large feet that are adapted for rooting out insects and seeds in leaf litter and soil. There are over 35 species of buntings and they are usually characterised by bold markings on their heads while their bodies are often cryptically coloured. The painted bunting (*Passerine ciris*), of the USA and Mexico, is an exception, having a bright plumage in blue, yellow and red. Buntings often have markedly different summer and winter plumage.

➡ *Finches, Sparrows*

BUSTARDS

(Class: Aves Order: Gruiformes)

Over 20 species of bustard are known to inhabit Africa, Southern Europe, Asia, Australia and New Guinea. They are closely related to cranes, rails and gallinules. Bustards are characterised by their long legs which are ideally suited to running. They lack the fourth toe – hallux – which is found in most birds at the rear of the foot. They have compact bodies which are held horizontally while the neck is erect and forward of the feet. The great bustard (*Otis tarda*) of Europe can weigh up to 14 kg (30 lb) and has a wingspan of 2.4 m (9 ft).

➠ *Birds, Cranes*

BUTTERFLIES

(Class: Insecta Order: Lepidoptera)

The word 'Lepidoptera' translates as 'scaled wings' in Latin. That is because butterflies and moths have wings covered in tiny scales, rather like roof tiles. It is these scales that provide their wings with the colours and patterns that characterise these insects. There are some 100,000 species of butterfly and moth known to science.

Butterflies differ from moths in certain ways. For one thing all butterflies are diurnal or day-flying, while moths can be either nocturnal or diurnal. Butterflies rest with their wings held together backwards, whilst moths hold there wings flat, although there are exceptions from both sides. Butterflies also have antennae with club-shaped tips, whereas moths have either thin tapered antennae or feathery ones, depending on their sex. Again there are exceptions.

Butterfly species are broadly divided into families which share particular characteristics. These families include the Papilionidae (swallowtails, birdwings, apollos), Pieridae (whites and yellows), Satyridae (browns), Lycaenidae (blues, coppers and hairstreaks), Hesperiidae (skippers) and Nymphalidae (fritillaries, vanessids, morphos, heliconiids). Butterflies can be found in many environments, from the tropics to the snowline on mountains.

Nectar is the principal food of butterflies. They feed on it by uncoiling a proboscis that comprises two thin, flexible tubes and probing flowers. Most butterfly larvae are vegetarians, feeding on the leaves and flowers of many plants, although a few have developed carnivorous tendencies. The larvae, which hatch from eggs, are called caterpillars. When fully grown, caterpillars shed their skins for a final time to become pupae or chrysalises. Eventually the adult butterfly emerges from its chrysalis after a process called complete metamorphosis. Having stretched out and dried its wings the butterfly can fly away. Butterflies live for between a few days and several months depending on the species, but never for only one day, unless they get eaten.

➠ *Insects, Moths*

BELOW Butterflies inhabit many areas, from the rainforests to the mountains.

CADDIS FLIES

(Class: Insecta Order: Trichoptera)

The larvae of caddis flies are undoubtedly more interesting than the adults, which tend to be drab-coloured moth-like insects. There are approaching 5,000 species of caddis fly. The larvae, which are all aquatic except for one species, often build protective cases for themselves. They produce a sticky silk from their mouth and use it to construct a tubular sock which is then adorned with items of debris for camouflage. The debris may be grains of sand, small pebbles, pieces of leaf or stalk, or fragments of mollusc shell and so on. Caddis larvae may be plant-feeders or carnivores.

➞ *Insects, Stone Flies*

CAECILIANS

(Class: Amphibia Order: Apoda)

The caecilians are related to frogs, toads, salamanders and newts. They are often mistaken for earthworms as they are limbless and live underground. Caecilians are found in Central and South America, Africa and some parts of Asia. They range in size from 10–150 cm (4–60 in) and have slender, cylindrical bodies that are well-adapted to burrowing. They have tiny eyes and small tentacles between their eyes and nostrils that are chemosensory (chemically sensitive). Most caecilians lay eggs which hatch into free-living larvae, but some species bear live young, thus protecting them from predators while at their most vulnerable.

➞ *Amphibians, Newts*

CAIMANS

(Class: Reptilia Order: Crocodilia)

Caimans are closely related to crocodiles and gharials but their closest relatives are the alligators. There are few obvious physical differences between caiman and alligator species. Both alligators and caimans are found in the Americas and have blunter, shorter snouts than crocodiles. Like their relatives, caimans are aquatic, reptilian carnivores that lay leathery eggs. They are laid in nests and vigilantly guarded by the

ABOVE RIGHT The broad-nosed caiman is an endangered species.
RIGHT The dromedary stores water and nutrition in its hump.

females until they hatch. The black caiman (*Melanosuchus niger*) is larger than other caimans and often more aggressive. It has been hunted for its skin and is now considered to be at risk of extinction.

➞ *Alligators, Crocodiles*

CAMELS

(Class: Mammalia Order: Artiodactyla)

The bactrian (*Camelus bactrianus*) and the dromedary (*Camelus dromedarius*) are the two species of camel. To remember which has one hump and which has two, tip the first letters – B and D – on their backs. The reason for camels having humps is to store both water and nutrition – the humps are filled with a fatty tissue which absorbs them and serves as a reservoir whilst camels roam over semi-desert habitats, where another chance to feed and drink may be several days away. All undomesticated camels are thought to be livestock gone feral, so there are no genuinely wild populations left.

➞ *Llamas, Mammals*

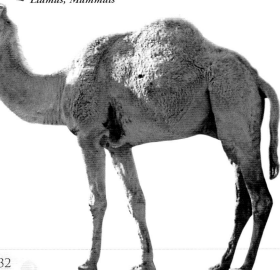

CARNIVORES

This large order of mammals includes dogs, cats, weasels, bears, wolves, foxes, otters, badgers, skunks, racoons, hyenas, pandas, genets, civets, mongooses, aardwolves, sea-lions, walruses and seals. For the most part they are animals adapted for eating flesh, hence their scientific name. They are distinct from other animals described as carnivorous, such as toothed whales and dolphins. All carnivores have stereoscopic or binocular vision, as it is an essential characteristic for being able to hunt prey effectively, by providing a three-dimensional image. This allows the carnivore to assess distance and direction during the chase or ambush.

BELOW LEFT A tiger uses its canine teeth to hold down prey.

The dentition of carnivores is another defining characteristic, being very well adapted for dealing with meat. They typically have long, sharp canine or eye teeth which are designed to hold the prey during its death struggle. The skin of the prey is torn away with the short, clamp-like incisors and the flesh of the victim is sheared from the bone by the scissor-like molars and premolars. The exact number of premolars and molars does vary though between different groups of carnivore.

Carnivores tend to be muscular animals, evolved to overpower their prey. However, they do vary a great deal in size, from the diminutive weasels to the big cats, which catch entirely different prey from one another. Furthermore, some carnivores have adopted social strategies that enable them to hunt large prey by team work. Similarly such carnivores live in extended family groups while the others have solitary lives, except for those periods spent mating and rearing offspring.

❧ The African lion (*Panthera leo*), cape hunting dog (*Lycaon pictus*) and spotted hyena (*Crocuta crocuta*) are all species of carnivore with highly developed and complex social behaviour.

❧ The tiger (*Panthera tigris*), polar bear (*Ursus maritimus*) and giant panda (*Ailuropoda melanoleuca*) are all species of carnivore with solitary behaviour.

➡ *Bears, Cats, Dogs*

CARP

(Class: Osteichthyes Order: Cypriniformes)

The common carp (*Cyprinus carpio*) is a popular ornamental fish. There are several varieties that have been bred for the pet market.

The mirror carp, for example, has been bred to encourage the development of large scales that form reflective surfaces. Carp are native to Asia but have been introduced to Europe and North America. In the wild they are greenish-brown in colour but captive fish are commonly orange – goldfish – or white with dark markings. Carp live in still water such as ponds and lakes, where they forage at the bottom, searching for plants and animals to eat.

➡ *Bony Fish, Goldfish*

CARTILAGINOUS FISH

(Class: Chondrichthyes)

 Once thought of as 'primitive fish' the chondrichthyans are now viewed as a highly successful group of vertebrates that has survived since the Devonian Period (408–362 million years ago). Although it seems likely that bony fish and cartilaginous fish evolved from the same ancestral group – the placoderms – they appear to have evolved quite separately, the cartilaginous fish evolving later. This class of fish includes sharks, skates and rays.

Cartilaginous fish have no bone in their skeletons and this provides them with flexibility. The vertebrae of some larger species are mineralized, thus providing greater rigidity. There are five to seven gill clefts and the teeth, which grow in gums, are renewed throughout life. Scales, which are not present in all species, closely resemble teeth in their structure.

Cartilaginous fish have poor vision. They rely more on their senses of hearing and smell which are believed to be acute. They are all carnivorous and many species, especially the sharks, have a reputation as ruthless predators. They are able to detect vibrations, chemical and temperature changes in the water around them using sensory organs in the skin. These are located in the lateral line system, which runs along the body's sides.

Skates and some sharks lay eggs but rays and most sharks bear live young. Most of these young receive nourishment from their egg yolk while in the uterus, others receive nutrition from the mother as well.

* Unlike bony fish, cartilaginous fish do not have swim bladders and must keep moving to stay afloat.
* Cartilaginous fish can detect weak electrical signals emitted by other animals.
* Sharks can detect incredibly small quantities of blood. A fraction of a part in a million is enough to attract a shark's attention.
* Cartilaginous fish are mostly marine and live predominantly in shallow coastal waters.

➥ *Bony Fish, Sharks*

CASSOWARIES

(Class: Aves Order: Casuariiformes)

Like their close cousin, the emu, cassowaries are large, flightless birds. Three species are recognized

and they inhabit the tropical rainforest regions of northern Australia, New Guinea and the surrounding islands. Cassowaries have reduced wings and strong legs with three toes on each foot. They possess reinforced skulls which protect them when running at speed through the rainforest. Cassowaries live in pairs or small family groups. A clutch of three to eight eggs is laid in winter and incubated by the male. Cassowaries are very aggressive birds. Their inner toes carry sharp claws that can inflict lethal injuries on predators and prey alike.

➥ *Emus, Ostriches*

CATFISH

(Class: Osteichthyes Order: Siluriformes)

The term 'catfish' is applied to a large group of predominantly freshwater fish with about 2,200 species. There are only two marine families – Aariidae and Plotosidae. Catfish are normally active at night and feed by scavenging on the bottom of shallow water. Scientific authorities differ on the taxonomic classification of catfish but certain characteristics can be used to define the group. Catfish have long feelers, or barbels, around their mouths. These resemble cat whiskers and have given the group its name. Many species have several pairs of barbels as well as spines on the dorsal and pectoral fins. The spines may be attached to venom glands and used in defence. Some species use their spines to help them move along the bottom. Catfish do not have scales and are either naked or have bony, armour plates. They all have acute hearing.

* Catfish vary in size, appearance and lifestyle. The smallest – micro cats – are only 40 mm (1.5 in) long. The largest – the wels – are up to 5 m (18 ft) long. Small catfish are popular aquarium fish.
* Larger species are an important source of food, particularly in the Americas where they account for half of all farmed fish production.

➥ *Bony Fish, Fish*

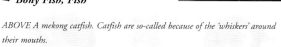

ABOVE A mekong catfish. Catfish are so-called because of the 'whiskers' around their mouths.

CATS

(Class: Mammalia Order: Carnivora)

Cats are divided into two subfamilies: the small cats (Felinae) and the big cats (Pantherinae). Each subfamily has its own distinguishing characteristics. Size is a fairly reliable one, but there are exceptions. The pupils of large cats remain circular, like human pupils, while the pupils of small cats contract to a lozenge shape, or a slit in very bright light, except for those of the puma (*Felis concolor*) which was once classified as a big cat. Also, large cats are unable to purr.

The big cats are the tiger, lion, leopard, jaguar, snow leopard and clouded leopard. There are 30 species of small cat including the caracal, bobcat and marbled cat, plus domestic cats which may or may not originate from a single species, but are given the scientific name *Felis catus*. Finally there are two species that remain undetermined taxonomically. The first is the cheetah (*Acinonyx jubatus*). It is a specialised cat that possesses dog-like limbs, designed for sprinting at high speed. The second is known only by its common name – onza. A single specimen was shot in Mexico in 1986.

🐾 Cats first became domesticated by African tribes over 9,000 years ago.

➡ *Carnivores*

ABOVE The cheetah has dog-like limbs and is not classified with other cats.
RIGHT The bison is an example of wild cattle.

CATTLE

(Class: Mammalia Order: Artiodactyla)

The taxonomy of cattle species has become somewhat obscured as a result of the domestication of many species, so that both wild and tame equivalents exist. The aurochs (*Bos primigenius*), which became extinct in the seventeenth century, is thought to have been the ancestor of all the European domesticates, which are known collectively as *Bos taurus* – European domestic oxen. Similarly the gaur (*Bos gaurus*) of Asia is thought to be the wild oxen stock from which the domestic gayal (*Bos frontalis*) and banteng (*Bos sondaicus*) were derived.

Other wild cattle include the bison or buffaloes, which are very similar to oxen, but tend to be thicker set in the forequarters. All cattle are herbivores, feeding mainly on grasses and low-lying vegetation. They have a complex digestive system that enables them to digest even the most tough and seemingly nutrition-deficient plant matter. They typically live in herds, comprising a bull with a harem of cows and their calves.

🐾 Although it resembles cattle, the musk-ox (*Ovibos moschatus*) actually belongs to the same sub-family as sheep. It is adapted for life on the tundra of Canada and Greenland, where it has no cover from severe blizzards and sub-zero temperatures.

➡ *Herbivores*

CAVIES

(Class: Mammalia Order: Rodentia)

The domestic guinea-pig (*Cavia porcellus*) with all its different breeds is descended from the Brazilian or Peruvian cavy (*Cavia aperea*). It was not domesticated as a house pet, but as a useful source of food. In its wild state it lives in habitats that are fairly barren, eating whatever vegetation is available. It made good sense for the native people of South America to keep guinea-pigs in cages, so that they would convert the indigestible parts of crops into meat. The common name may be a corruption of 'Guyana-pig' with Europeans thinking the animals came from Africa rather than South America.

Other members of the cavy family include the Patagonian cavy or mara (*Dolichotis patagonum*), which looks like a hare, and the capybara or carpincho (*Hydrochoerus hydrochaeris*). The capybara is the largest rodent in the world, reaching 1.2 m (4 ft). It is a thick-set animal with a semi-aquatic lifestyle and is much more deserving of the name 'pig', both in physique and habits.

❧ All cavies make, apparently, good eating, so they are often kept in captivity for that purpose.

❧ In countries other than those in South America guinea-pigs are more often used for laboratory experiments.

➠ *Mammals, Rodents*

CENTIPEDES

(Phylum: Arthropoda Class: Chilopoda)

Some centipedes do have a hundred legs, so their name is quite appropriate. In fact, centipedes have one pair of legs for each segment of their body – usually between fifteen and twenty. All centipedes are predatory, hunting their victims down and seizing them with poisonous fangs before consuming them with three pairs of jaws. The fangs are modified legs. There are between 1,500 and 2,000 species known and they have a worldwide distribution. The largest centipedes live in Central America. They can be 27 cm (10.5 in) long and are able to catch prey as large as lizards and mice.

➠ *Invertebrates, Millipedes*

CEPHALOPODS

(Phylum: Mollusca Class: Cephalopoda)

The cephalopods include octopuses, squid, cuttlefish, nautiluses and vampire squid. They are an advanced class of animals, having evolved from a form of limpet-like mollusc, and they include the most intelligent invertebrate species. Octopuses in particular have been observed solving some difficult problems in laboratory tanks, and they have no problem remembering how to solve them again with considerable speed.

Having evolved from shelled molluscs the cephalopods have an ancestral ability to form a calcium-based shell. In the nautiluses this shell is still put to use as protection from predators and as a buoyancy aid. In the cuttlefish and squid the shell has become an internal structure – the cuttlebone and pen respectively – used as a skeleton to support the body tissues. In the octopuses the shell has been lost altogether. The only other hard part of a cephalopod is its beak or jaws.

Cephalopods eat a variety of animal prey depending on the environments they tend to inhabit. Squid are fast swimming animals of open waters, able to run down fish and the like. Cuttlefish and octopuses tend to frequent

ABOVE The capybara has a semi-aquatic lifestyle.
ABOVE RIGHT The cephalopods include squid.

sheltered areas on the ocean floor and are particularly adept at hunting crabs and other crustaceans. Their beaks need to be strong therefore to break through carapaces.

Locomotion is affected in several ways by cephalopods. Many species use jet propulsion as a means of travel. They squirt water from their breathing siphons causing them to shoot quickly backwards. Cuttlefish and squid have lateral fins which move in a wave motion allowing movement backwards or forwards for very precise swimming. Octopuses use their long tentacled arms to walk and climb along. Most species are also equipped with an ink sac for defence. The ink clouds the water in front of an enemy so that the cephalopod can flee.

➡ *Octopuses, Squid*

CHAMELEONS

(Class: Reptilia Order: Squamata)

Chameleons are related to the iguanas. Like most lizards, chameleons are not aquatic. They live predominantly in trees and have several physical adaptations to suit this arboreal life. Unlike ground-dwelling lizards, chameleons possess prehensile tails that can grasp branches. Their toes are fused into two opposing groups, facing forwards and backwards, for a better grip. Each eye is able to move independently of the other and in all directions. The body is normally narrow and camouflaged. Chameleons have extremely long, slender tongues which they can propel at speed towards an unsuspecting insect. The sticky tip of the tongue adheres to the insect which is then withdrawn to the mouth.

Chameleons are most famous for their ability to change colour. This occurs by the contraction or expansion of colour cells in the lizard's skin. As the colour cells contract they become lighter. Colours include green, yellow, cream and brown. A chameleon does not, contrary to popular belief, change colour to suit its environment. Its colour varies according to temperature and emotion, such as fright.

❖ Male chameleons often sport crests or horns on their heads. These are used in territorial displays or fights, especially during the breeding season.

➡ *Iguanas, Lizards*

CHARACINS

(Class: Osteichthyes Order: Characiformes)

The characins are a large family of freshwater fish that includes the tetras, piranhas and tigerfish. The majority of these fish are native to Central and South America, although some species are found in tropical Africa. There is some disagreement about which fish should be included in this large family, since there are few defining characteristics. Characins tend to be small and attractively coloured fish. They have separate teeth embedded in their jaws, often with replacement rows of teeth waiting behind. Characins also have an adipose fin between the dorsal fin and the tail, which is used for storing fats.

➡ *Piranhas, Tetras*

BELOW Jackson's chameleon is one of the few species to give birth to live young.

CHAR
(Class: Osteichthyes Order: Salmoniformes)

Char are freshwater fish that belong to the same family as trout. They are very similar in appearance to trout but have paler spots on their backs. Their scales are also smaller than those of trout. North American char are sometimes referred to as trout, such as the brook trout and lake trout. The Arctic char (*Salvenilus alpinus*) is the most northerly of freshwater fish. It inhabits both freshwater and marine environments in northern Europe, North America and the Arctic. The Arctic char is a migratory fish and often moves south to breed. Some inhabit entirely landlocked lakes and ponds.

➡ *Bony Fish, Trout*

CHIMAERAS
(Class: Chondrithyes Order: Chimaeriformes)

There are 30 species of cartilaginous fish, known as chimaeras, which are placed in a separate group from their close relatives the sharks, skates and rays. Their long bodies are soft and scale-less, while their large heads have large, iridescent eyes. Chimaeras have long, skinny tails that give them the common name of ratfish. They are found in both temperate and cold marine waters, particularly in the Arctic and Antarctic regions, up to depths of 2,500 m (8,200 ft). Three families are recognized in this group – the rabbitfish, the elephant fish and the long-nosed chimaeras. They eat small invertebrates and other fish.

➡ *Cartilaginous Fish, Sharks*

CHINCHILLAS
(Class: Mammalia Order: Rodentia)

The chinchilla (*Chinchilla laniger*) is a rodent of mountainous terrain in the Andes. Its fur, which is superb at keeping the animal warm in sub-zero temperatures, is prized by humans for the same reason. It is also fine and soft to the touch, with a pearl-grey colour. As a consequence the chinchilla has become rare in the wild, where it is now protected.

BELOW The chinchilla has very dense fur to keep it warm.
RIGHT The shrill song of the cicada is made by organs on the abdomen.

However, chinchillas are now bred in captivity. The viscachas are close relatives of the chinchilla which are adapted for habitats at lower altitudes. They do not possess the same quality of pelt, so are not hunted.

➡ *Mammals, Rodents*

CHONDOSTREANS
(Class: Osteichthyes Infraclass: Chondrostei)

The chondrostreans are an ancient group of primitive ray-finned bony fish. Most modern fish have skeletons made from either bone or cartilage, but chondostreans have skeletons that are made of both cartilage and bone. Living members of the group include sturgeons, bichirs and paddlefish. Fossilized members of the group have been found in rock dating from the Devonian Period (375 million years ago). The living members of this group have developed highly specialised forms and lifestyles and the evolutionary relationship between them has not been ascertained. Since their evolutionary path is unclear there is disagreement over the classification of chondostreans.

➡ *Bony Fish, Cartilaginous Fish*

CHUCKWALLAS
(Class: Reptilia Order: Squamata)

This medium-sized lizard is a resident of south-western North America. The chuckwalla (*Sauromalus obesus*) is unremarkable in its lifestyle, but has developed an extraordinary method of defence. If threatened, the chuckwalla runs for cover in a rocky crevice. It then inflates its lungs to such an extent that its whole body swells and even a determined predator can not extract it from its hole. chuckwallas remain in their crevices during cold weather. They emerge to seek food and bask, but only in very hot weather. Chuckwallas are herbivorous lizards, eating flowers, leaves and fruits that they find on the ground.

➡ *Lizards, Reptiles*

CICADAS

(Class: Insecta Order: Hemiptera)

Cicadas are medium to large bugs of mainly tropical and subtropical habitats. They are responsible for the penetrating calls that typify such places. It is the male who produces the sound, from tymbal organs on the abdomen. They are diaphragms of cuticle which vibrate as fast as 4,500 cycles per second. Both sexes have a well developed sense of hearing, so that the males can keep at a distance from one another and the females can locate the males with the loudest calls for mating.

Cicada eggs are laid in crevices in the bark of trees. The larvae of cicadas burrow into the ground and feed on the roots of plants. They have large front legs designed for burrowing. This is evidently not a particularly nutritious source of food as the larvae of some species can take as long as 17 years to develop, making them the longest-living insects. Consequently adult cicadas tend to emerge in waves, so that some years see far greater numbers than others, depending on the generation for each year. Adult cicadas feed by sucking the sap of trees with a stiff proboscis and they travel between trees by flying on two pairs of wings.

➡ *Bugs, Insects*

CICHLIDS

(Class: Osteichthyes Order: Perciformes)

There are over 600 species of cichlid, belonging to the family Cichlidae. They are predominantly freshwater fish and are inhabitants of tropical regions in America, Africa and Madagascar. The largest number and greatest diversity of cichlids is found in the isolated freshwater lakes of Africa.

Cichlids have rounded tails, deep bodies and rarely reach lengths greater than 30 cm (12 in). They have one nostril on each side of their faces, unlike most fish which have two. They are often brightly coloured in black, white, green, blue, silver or red and are popular aquarium fish. They may be either herbivorous or carnivorous.

BELOW There are many species of cichlid, which are often brightly coloured.

Cichlids display complex behaviour, particularly in courtship and mating rituals. The males and females are often dissimilar in appearance. Males may develop a temporary swelling at the front of their heads during the mating season. A female may mate with more than one male. It is common for cichlids to protect their eggs and newly-hatched young.

Some cichlid species have an effective method of ensuring that their eggs are protected from predators. They keep the eggs in their mouths until they are ready to hatch. This is known as mouth-brooding or oral incubation. Female African cichlids, of the genus Haplochromis, gather their eggs immediately into their mouths having them laid. The males of these species have egg-like spots near their anal fins. The females mistake them for eggs and, as she attempts to scoop them up, the males release their sperm into the water. The sperm enter the female's mouth, so fertilizing the eggs.

❧ In some species of cichlid the mother helps the young fish emerge from their eggs by nibbling the egg membranes.

❧ The male dwarf cichlid helps to take care of the newly hatched young.

❧ Some cichlid angelfish feed their young on secretions from their bodies.

➡ *Bony Fish, Fish*

CIVETS
(Class: Mammalia Order: Carnivora)

Civets are somewhere between cats and badgers on the evolutionary tree. They have the short limbs and long snout of badgers, yet they have a cat-like face, with large, forward-facing eyes. Civets are valued by people for their scent, which is also called 'civet', because it has a pleasant musky perfume. The scent is used in the wild for marking territories. It is produced by anal glands, which the civet rubs against objects, but captive animals have the scent removed with a spatula. Civets are nocturnal hunters, taking all kinds of small animals, including domestic fowl, given the chance.

➠ *Cats, Badgers*

COBRAS
(Class: Reptilia Order: Squamata)

The cobras are highly venomous snakes found in Africa, Asia and Australasia. They are closely related to the mambas and the coral snakes which, like cobras, inject venom through fangs that are located at the front of the upper jaw. The neck ribs of cobras are expanded to form the familiar hood. They are members of the family Elapidae.

The king cobra (*Ophiophagus hannah*) is the largest of all venomous snakes, reaching 3.6 m (12 ft) in length. The deadliest of all cobras, though, is the Indian cobra (*Naja naja*) which is estimated to kill 10,000 people per year.

➠ *Coral Snakes, Mambas*

COCKROACHES
(Class: Insecta Order: Blattaria)

Along with lice and fleas, cockroaches are unpopular insects with humans. That is because some species have taken to living in buildings, where they cause infestations. In fact it is the non-native species from tropical regions that have invaded our towns and cities because they need the warmth to survive. All cockroaches are essentially omnivorous scavengers, so only those buildings with low levels of hygiene can support high numbers of cockroaches. In wild habitats cockroaches are among the animals that keep the place tidy, by helping to recycle the nutrients in detritus.

Cockroaches are generally flat insects, with leathery fore wings, and a brownish colour. The protonum disc of the thorax covers the head for additional protection from predators. Cockroaches are notoriously difficult to catch, being so well able to slip away unharmed. There are some 3,500 species of cockroach, most of which live in warmer regions. They are so well designed that they have changed little in 250 million years. We know this because there have been fossil cockroaches found from the Upper Carboniferous Period. Although cockroaches are often found in swarms they are not social insects by nature, like ants, though some species do live in family groups.

➠ *Fleas, Silverfish*

COD
(Class: Osteichthyes Order: Gadiformes)

The marine fish of the cod family are an economically important human food source. They are found in the North Atlantic and migrate to spawning grounds every spring. Cod are related to hake and pollock. The Atlantic cod (*Gadus morhua*) is the most economically important species. It has dark spots on its dorsal surface and has three dorsal fins. It lives in large shoals on the continental shelves of the Atlantic, feeding on other fish. The Atlantic cod has been caught for many centuries but over-fishing has reduced its populations so much that it is now considered a vulnerable species.

➠ *Hake, Pollock*

ABOVE The Arabian cobra injects poison through its fangs.
ABOVE RIGHT Cockroaches are a household pest in many countries.

COELOCANTHS

(Class: Osteichthyes Order: Crossopterygii)

Bony fish, of the class Osteichthyes, are divided into two groups; ray-finned fish – the largest group – and lobe-finned or fleshy-finned fish. Coelocanths belong to the second group. Their fins are flipper-like and are joined to the skeleton by muscles. This gives them a flexibility and strength more reminiscent of limbs than fins. Coelocanths have robust, heavy bodies with an average length of 1.5 m (5 ft) and weight of 45 kg (100 lb). They live along deep rocky slopes of the ocean and lead a predatory lifestyle.

Commonly referred to as 'living fossils' the coelocanths (*Latimeria* spp.) were believed to have died out 65 million years ago, until discovered in the Indian Ocean in 1938. It later transpired that the inhabitants of the Comoros Islands, west of Madagascar, were familiar with these fish and caught them for food. In the 1990s a second population of coelocanths was discovered in Indonesian waters. It is believed that this second group was separated from the first between four and six million years ago.

There are therefore two coelocanth species, but they may still be able to interbreed.

The fossil record suggests that coelocanths first lived 350 million years ago and were a successful and populous group of fish for over a hundred million years. Fossil coelocanths have been found worldwide. Both populations of modern coelocanth are small and in danger of extinction as their habitats are disturbed by the fishing industry.

❧ Coelocanths are related to the rhipdistians, an ancient and extinct group of air-breathing fish that are believed to be the ancestors of amphibians and therefore all land vertebrates.

❧ Coelocanths use their limb-like fins to move around the ocean floor and to manoeuvre themselves into crevices.

❧ Coelocanths probably evolved first in freshwater, then moved by degrees towards a marine lifestyle.

➠ *Bony Fish, Fish*

BELOW Thought to be extinct, living coelocanths were found in the 1930s.

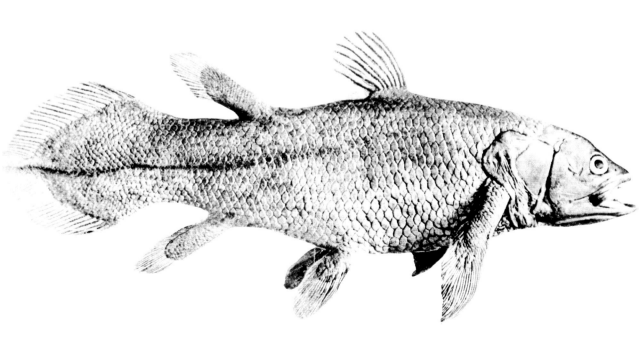

COLUBRID SNAKES

(Class: Reptilia Squamata)

Colubrids belong to the largest group of snakes, with over 1,500 species. They are found in many habitats worldwide and they are the only snakes to be found in cold regions. Colubrids are characterised by the complete absence of hindlimbs and the possession of only one functional lung. They also lack a bone in the lower jaw that is found in other snakes. Colubrids are able to open their jaws to an unusually wide extent and this enables them to swallow large items of food whole. The upper surface of a colubrid's head is covered with large scales and this is a unique feature of the group.

Some species of colubrid possess fangs at the rear of the mouth that are connected to venom-producing glands. Unlike the elapids (true venomous snakes) the fangs are solid but have a groove down which the venom flows. Generally the venom is weak and the fangs are set too far back in the mouth for colubrid snakes to be considered particularly dangerous to people. Some colubrids kill by constriction.

- Most colubrid snakes lay eggs although some, especially semi-aquatic species, bear live young.
- The European grass snake (*Natrix natrix*), boomslangs and ratsnakes are all colubrids.

➡ *Reptiles, Snakes*

COPEPODS

(Subphylum: Crustacea Class: Maxillipoda)

This is one of the most difficult groups of animals to describe generally. There are many thousands of species of copepod and they vary so much in design that they share few consistent characteristics. They are all small aquatic crustaceans and have colonized both marine and freshwater environments. None of them possesses a carapace shell, but some species have fused segments.

Broadly speaking copepods fall into two groups. There are free-living copepods and parasitic copepods. Those that swim in marine environments often comprise part of the plankton alongside other animals, which is an important food source for fish and other large predators.

➡ *Crustaceans, Zooplankton*

CORAL SNAKES

(Class: Reptilia Order: Squamata)

This family of venomous snakes is confined to the tropics. The true coral snakes are found only in the New World, although similar species inhabit warm or hot regions of Africa and Asia. There are 65 species of coral snake and they are related to cobras, vipers, mambas and sea snakes.

Coral snakes are similar in appearance and size to the less dangerous colubrid snakes although they are usually brighter in colour and pattern. The most common pattern is one of wide red and black rings, interspersed with narrow rings of yellow or white. The bold colours warn potential predators that the snake is venomous. Most coral snakes are rather docile and loathe to attack, but when they do a number of species may inject venom that can kill large mammals, including humans. Coral snakes are usually burrowing, nocturnal creatures that prey upon other snakes.

- The Eastern coral snake (*Micrurus fulvius*) is native to North America. It is 76 cm (30 in) long and has wide bands of red and black that are separated by narrow bands of yellow.

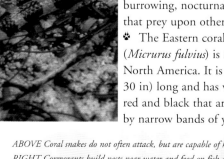

ABOVE Coral snakes do not often attack, but are capable of killing a human. RIGHT Cormorants build nests near water and feed on fish and squid.

❖ The warning colouration of coral snakes has been copied by other less dangerous or harmless snakes that are described as 'mimics'.

➟ *Colubrid Snakes, Sea Snakes*

CORALS
(Phylum: Cnidaria Class: Anthozoa)

Corals are animals called polyps that usually live in colonies and are related to sea anemones. Unlike anemones they have an ability to produce a calcium-based, skeleton-like framework in which they

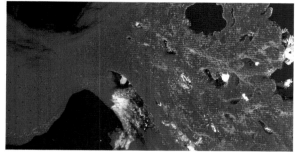

live out their lives, generation after generation. In this way they manage to build enormous reefs over thousands of years. Each polyp usually fends for itself by filtering the surrounding water for particles of food with short tentacles. However it pays to live communally as it enables the polyps to construct all manner of tree-like, dome-like or fan-like corals that elevate new polyps into better feeding positions.

➟ *Polyzoans, Sea Anemones*

CORMORANTS
(Class: Aves Order: Pelicaniformes)

Cormorants and shags are related to pelicans and darters. Similarly, cormorants live close to water, often building nests of seaweed and guano on rocky cliffs at the sea edge. They may alternatively build nests of sticks in trees beside lakes and rivers. There are about 30 species of cormorant. They are characterised by possession of long bills with hooked tips and patches of bare skin on their

BELOW LEFT Corals, such as this one with a sponge, live communally in reefs.

faces and throat pouches. They live on a diet of fish and squid which they hunt by diving. In China cormorants have been trained to catch fish commercially and their guano is sold as fertilizer.

The common cormorant (*Phalacrocorax carbo*) is the largest and most widespread of all cormorants, inhabiting Europe, North America, Asia and southern Africa. It is found in all types of aquatic habitat but prefers to hunt in shallow water, although it can dive to depths of 30 m (100 ft) in search of food.

❖ On the Galapagos islands there lives the flightless cormorant (*Phalacrocorax harrisi*). With no natural predators, before the arrival of humans, it had no need of flight so evolution allowed its wings to become atrophied. It also has no natural fear of people unlike most birds.

➟ *Anhingas, Pelicans*

COTINGAS
(Class: Aves Order: Passeriformes)

Like other passerines, the cotingas are fairly intelligent birds with complex behaviour and song. There are 90 species in this family, which share the characteristic broad bill with slightly hooked tip, rounded wings and short legs. Cotingas are forest birds and are found particularly in the Andes. They are solitary animals and feed mainly on fruits. Male cotingas often exhibit bizarre courtship behaviour and may have unusual calls which sound like bells ringing or hammers tapping. Some males have bright plumage and crests that they use to attract females.

➟ *Passerines*

COWFISH

(Class: Osteichthyes Order: Tetraodontiformes)

Cowfish, also known as trunkfish or boxfish, are inhabitants of shallow marine water regions in the Pacific and Indian Oceans and the Red Sea. They live at

the bottom of coastal areas in tropical and warm seas, especially coral reefs. Cowfish are covered in thick rigid scales that are fused together to form a protective armour. This 'carapace' covers most of the body. Some species have horns that project from the front of the head above the eyes, hence the name 'cowfish'. Cowfish are often brightly coloured and sometimes dried and sold as ornaments as part of the tourism trade.

➠ *Goatfish, Pufferfish*

CRABS

(Subphylum: Crustacea Class Malacostraca)

Crabs, along with lobsters and crayfish, are decapods. This name alludes to their having ten legs. Crabs typically have a wide carapace covering the whole of the upper surface of the body, with a small abdomen tucked beneath. Like all crustaceans they have to undergo a process of shedding their old skins to grow bigger, called ecdysis. This is because their tough shells are made from an inflexible material called chitin. They have to hide immediately after ecdysis until their new shells have expanded and hardened.

A few species of crab lack the characteristic carapace – the hermit crabs – but have found a means of protecting themselves by living inside old mollusc shells. There are over 4,000 species of crab. They are all dependent on marine environments to some extent, especially to breed. Some remain submerged for all of their lives, but many live on the shoreline and some have become terrestrial as adults. Crabs greatly vary in size. Tiny pea crabs live inside the shells of bivalves, whilst spider crabs may attain a leg span of 244 cm (96 in).

❧ The robber crab (*Birgus latro*), a land crab of the tropics, can climb trees in search of food.

➠ *Crustaceans, Lobsters*

CRANES

(Class: Aves Order: Gruiformes)

These tall, elegant birds inhabit wetlands worldwide, except South America. They are an ancient group of birds. The earliest fossils – found in North America – date from the Eocene epoch (56–35 million years ago). Cranes are related to bustards, rails and trumpeters. They are similar in appearance to herons but are usually larger. They have partly

naked heads, heavy bills, compact plumage and a raised hind toe on each foot. Most species of crane migrate, often travelling long distances between their winter homes and breeding areas. In flight cranes stretch their necks ahead and trail their legs.

➧ *Herons, Storks*

CRESTED NEWTS

(Class: Amphibia Order: Caudata)

While most newts are well camouflaged, some species do have elaborate patterning and bright colours to advertize the toxic secretions that are produced by their skin. Others, such as the great crested newt (*Triturus cristatus*) sport crests on their dorsal surfaces during the breeding season. Great crested newts are found throughout Europe and Central Asia. They measure 10–13 cm (4–5 in) and live a mainly terrestrial life, though close to water. The male develops a crest during the breeding season and he uses it to display to females during his courtship ritual. The females do not have crests.

➧ *Newts, Salamanders*

CRICKETS

(Class: Insecta Order: Orthoptera)

There are two groups of crickets – bush crickets and true crickets. They both differ from grasshoppers in having long antennae instead of short, being essentially nocturnal instead of diurnal and rubbing their wings together to sing instead of using a leg against a wing. They are often carnivorous rather than vegetarian. Bush crickets are usually greenish and tend to frequent the foliage of shrubs, as their name suggests, where they hunt other small invertebrates. Females possess a sabre-like ovipositor for inserting eggs into the stems of plants. True crickets are creatures of the ground. They are usually brownish and have domed heads.

➧ *Grasshoppers, Katydids*

CROCODILES

(Class: Reptilia Order: Crocodilia)

There are about 14 species of crocodile and they all live semi-aquatic lives in lakes, lagoons, rivers and occasionally estuaries or oceans. Crocodiles are related to

BELOW Crocodiles are more of a danger to humans than alligators are.

alligators, caimans and gharials. They inhabit tropical regions in Asia, Africa, Madagascar and America. Like alligators, crocodiles have long muscular and lizard-like bodies. They are carnivorous and feed mainly on birds, turtles, fish, small mammals and carrion. Crocodiles are believed to be more aggressive than alligators and more likely to attack humans. Their snouts are longer and more slender than those of alligators and the fourth tooth on each side of the lower jaw is visible when the mouth is shut – unlike alligators.

Crocodiles are able to bask in water for a long time with their eyes and nostrils just protruding above the water surface. Here they can wait until an unsuspecting animal passes by. Then the crocodile propels its huge body forward with thrusts from its strong tail and legs. The jaws close firmly on the prey, which is then dragged below the water to be drowned and eventually consumed.

Male crocodiles are very territorial and mate with more than one female if possible. The females lay their eggs in nests of vegetation or a prepared burrow. They guard their nests until the eggs hatch, often helping the young crocodiles as they emerge. The females often then carry the hatchlings down to the water's edge in their mouth. They continue to protect them for several months afterward.

❧ 'Maneater' crocodiles have been hunted down and discovered to contain various recognizable parts of people in their stomachs.

❧ Sometimes a crocodile may store its prey underwater until it rots, making it easier to dismember.

❧ Crocodiles shake their prey to loosen the joints. They then twist off pieces of the body to acquire bite-size portions.

➧ *Alligators, Caimans*

CROWS

(Class: Aves Order: Passeriformes)

This is one of the most ubiquitous and successful of bird groups. Crows inhabit all parts of the world, apart from the Arctic and Antarctic. They are omnivorous opportunists, eating almost anything, including seeds, fruit, berries, insects, reptiles, small mammals, amphibians, carrion and other birds. They are catholic in their choice of habitat too. They can be found in urban and rural areas, as well as wilderness.

Crows do not migrate but often move around locally according to the season. Crows typically have black plumage but some species are brightly coloured. Many species of crow are gregarious. Nests may be isolated or located in a colony. They are messy collections of twigs, built in bushes or trees. Crows, magpies, ravens, jays and choughs are all members of the family.

❖ The common raven (*Corvus corax*) is the largest member of the crow family. It frequents mountainous regions of the northern hemisphere, reaching 65 cm (26 in) in length.

❖ The entirely black carrion crow (*Corvus corone*) is a familiar western European bird, though its range is extended northwards and eastwards by the hooded crow (*Corvus cornix*) which is a sub-species that has a grey body with black wings, tail and head.

➡ *Passerines*

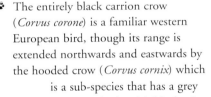

CRUSTACEANS

(Phylum: Arthropoda Subphylum: Crustacea)

This is a huge subphylum of animals that includes crabs, lobsters, shrimps, crayfish, copepods, woodlice, water-fleas, fish lice and barnacles. Crustaceans are an extremely successful class of arthropods, having succeeded in colonizing land, marine and freshwater environments. The Latin name alludes to the fact that crustaceans have a crust or exoskeleton. In the smallest crustaceans the exoskeleton is nothing more than a thin, transparent layer, but in the crabs and lobsters it becomes a tough, thick armour for protection from predators. Crustaceans also have segmented bodies and jointed, paired limbs.

The larvae of aquatic crustaceans often look quite different from the adult form, because they display the characteristics of evolutionary origin rather than any specialization. Many are called nauplii (singular – nauplius) and have an unsegmented body with a single eye. The larvae of terrestrial crustaceans hatch as miniature adults. They develop into adults by moulting their old exoskeleton periodically to grow larger. Crustaceans have exploited a great many food sources. Some are active predators, whilst others are herbivores. The majority though are opportunist scavengers, cleaning away all kinds of organic material to create an omnivorous diet.

LEFT The common raven is the largest member of the crow family.
ABOVE RIGHT Crustaceans get their name from their exoskeleton, or crust.

To cope with the demand for their flesh crustaceans have developed survival strategies. Firstly crustaceans produce prodigious quantities of eggs so that enough larvae survive into adulthood to maintain each species. Crustaceans are also masters of disguise, using camouflage to conceal themselves against their natural background. Some crustaceans bury themselves from view, whilst others hide beneath solid objects or swim off very quickly when danger threatens. Most large crustaceans have armoured shells and defence weapons in the shape of powerful claws which any predator would be wise to avoid.

❧ Crustaceans have many enemies, as they are an important food source for other animals.

❧ Most crustaceans have separate sexes, but a few are hermaphrodite.

➠ *Crabs, Lobsters*

CUCKOOS

(Class: Aves Order: Cuculiformes)

Cuckoos are well known for their parasitization of other birds. By leaving their eggs with other species they avoid having to invest any effort in rearing their offspring and can produce many more eggs. Not all cuckoos do this, nor do they all make the characteristic 'cuckoo' call of the common cuckoo (*Cuculus canorus*). There are about 15 species. Most are fairly drab in colour, although the emerald cuckoo (*Chrysococcyx cupreus*) is predominantly iridescent green.

Cuckoos live throughout the world in both tropical and temperate regions. They prefer thickly vegetated areas and are more likely to be heard than seen. Parasitic species lay as many as 25 eggs into 25 nests, each time removing a genuine egg to help fool the host birds. Cuckoos are able to lay eggs that mimic the colouration of the hosts'. The cuckoo chick further aids its own survival by ejecting the other eggs and chicks from the nest.

❧ The common roadrunner (*Geococcyx californianus*) is a North American member of the cuckoo family. Although it can fly the roadrunner prefers to stay on the ground where it can reach considerable speeds – 30 kph (19 mph) – in pursuit of lizards, snakes, birds and small mammals.

➠ *Passerines, Warblers*

BELOW The young cuckoo rids the nest of chicks and is fed by the host bird.

CUTTLEFISH

(Phylum: Mollusca Class: Cephalopoda)

Like the crabs and lobsters, cuttlefish and squid have ten limbs and are called decapods, but they are not related. Four pairs of a cuttlefish's limbs are normal arms used for manipulating objects, but the fifth pair are retractable weapons, equipped with suckers on club-shaped tips. They use these very accurately to strike and seize their prey, which is usually crustaceans and small fish. They have very good eyesight and stalk their prey in shallow waters. Cuttlefish communicate their moods by means of rapid fluctuations in the colour and pattern on their skin. This also provides camouflage while hunting.

➠ *Cephalopods, Squid*

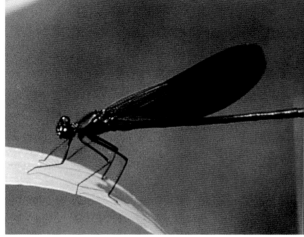

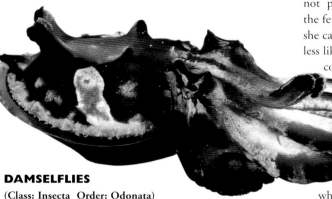

DAMSELFLIES

(Class: Insecta Order: Odonata)

Damselflies are closely related to dragonflies, but they have their subtle differences. Perhaps the most obvious difference is that damselflies fold their wings above and behind them when resting, rather than holding them flat as dragonflies do. Damselflies tend also to be more delicately built than dragonflies. Both are carnivorous hunters, preying upon other flying insects, but different species have evolved to take advantage of various food sources.

As a general rule, damselfly species tend not to stray too far from water, where they prey on slow-flying airborne insects such as caddis flies, stone flies, midges and mayflies. This is because damselflies themselves are not particularly strong flyers. Egg laying often involves the female becoming completely submerged so that she can reach water weed, with the tip of her tail, that is less likely to dry out if water levels should fall over the course of the summer months. The larvae – called nymphs – are essentially like wingless adults and they prey upon aquatic animals until ready to emerge from the water. This can take one to three years depending on the species.

Damselflies often congregate in considerable numbers above water, where they mate and lay their eggs.

➠ *Dragonflies, Insects*

DECAPODS

(Subphylum: Crustacea Class: Cephalopoda)

The term 'decapod' means to have ten limbs – arms or legs. There are two groups of animals called decapods, but they are not related. One is a group of crustaceans, the other a group of cephalopods. The decapod crustaceans include the crabs, lobsters and crayfish. As a general rule they have four pairs of walking legs and a fifth pair of limbs equipped with claws for seizing and manipulating food. The decapod cephalopods include the cuttlefish and squid. Similarly, they have four pairs of general limbs and a fifth pair that are retractable and equipped with suckered pads for seizing prey.

➠ *Cephalopods, Crustaceans*

ABOVE Cuttlefish can change colour to express their mood or to camouflage.
ABOVE RIGHT Damselflies stay near water in order to breed and find food.

DEEP-SEA ANGLERS

**(Class: Osteichthyes
Order: Lophiiformes)**

Many fish that live in deep ocean waters have developed unusual strategies for survival in the harsh conditions. Light cannot penetrate the inky depths of the oceans and this reduces the food available to animals that live there. Consequently fish life in this habitat is amongst the most specialised in the world. Deep sea fish are characterised by having huge mouths and eyes. Many species are able to produce light – an ability known as bioluminescence. Angler fish, for example, have extended dorsal fin spines that appear luminescent at the tip and are dangled above the fish's heads as lures for prey. Organisms attracted to the light swim straight into the path of the predator's mouth.

- Kroyer's deep sea angler has another, extraordinary, adaptation to life in the deep. The small male attaches himself to the larger female by his mouth. The tissue of his mouth fuses to her body and his body degenerates, except for his reproductive organs.
- This is an example of a symbiotic relationship, because both parties benefit from the arrangement. In this instance both male and female can ensure regular reproduction occurs without having to find a partner, which is a difficult task in the deep ocean.

➡ *Angler Fish*

BELOW The male red deer grows and sheds its antlers each year.

DEER

(Class: Mammalia Order: Artiodactyla)

Deer are even-toed, hoofed herbivores. They graze and browse on a variety of grasses, mosses, herbs and shrubs.

There are many species worldwide and they vary considerably in size. The largest species is the Alaskan moose (*Alces americanus*), which measures an incredible 2.4 m (8 ft) at the shoulder. The smallest are the various mouse-deer, which are no more than 30 cm (1 ft) at the shoulder. Sexual dimorphism is common among deer, with the males growing considerably larger than the females. In most species it is also only the males that grow antlers. They are grown and then shed each year.

➡ *Antelopes, Cattle*

DESERT LIFE

There are various types of desert, but they can all
be broadly described as hot or cold deserts. Their
most defining characteristic is very low moisture
levels, making them largely barren environments
where animals cannot survive without particular
adaptations. In some deserts it never rains at all,
so any moisture has to be obtained from the air
by condensation. Deserts tend to grow larger over
time because soils get blown away where there are
insufficient plants to hold them in place.

The most obvious adaptations in desert-living
animals are seen in their ability to both obtain
water and conserve it. Nocturnal habits are a
clear advantage because it means that animals
can avoid the desiccating sunshine. In addition
many animals have impermeable skins or shells
to prevent water loss. They often derive their
moisture from their food alone, so that water
is actually passed up the food chain.

RIGHT The 'wild' camel population today is probably livestock turned feral.
FAR RIGHT The desert spiny lizard often basks on rocks and in trees.
ABOVE RIGHT Fur on the fennec fox's paws protects it from the hot sand.
MAIN Gemboks use their horns in fights over crowded watering holes.

DESERT REGIONS

ARCTIC

ASIA

NORTH
AMERICA

EUROPE

Sonoron Desert

Gobi Desert

Tropic of Cancer

Sahara Desert

AFRICA

Arabian Desert

Equator

SOUTH
AMERICA

Tropic of Capricorn

AUSTRALIA

Atacama Desert

Kalahari Desert

Great Sandy Desert

Major deserts

ANTARCTICA

DESMANS

(Class: Mammalia Order: Insectivora)

These are essentially semi-aquatic moles. They are adapted for swimming in rivers and streams, with webbed feet for propulsion. They also have long, tubular snouts for searching out freshwater invertebrates, on which they feed. Desmans make their homes in the soft banks of watercourses. There are two species: the Pyrenean desman (*Galemys pyrenaica*) and the Russian desman (*Desmana moschata*). The Russian desman is twice the size of the other species, at 25 cm (10 in) body and tail. The tails of desmans are partly compressed, laterally, for use as rudders and to provide additional propulsion whilst their forelimbs are busy.

➠ *Moles, Shrews*

DIPPERS

(Class: Aves Order: Passeriformes)

Most passerines are perching birds that live in bushes and trees, but the dipper family follow a semi-aquatic way of life. They live near water, building their nests of moss in crevices, often behind waterfalls. All five species of dipper search for food in fast-flowing streams. They forage for insect larvae and other small invertebrates beneath pebbles and small rocks. Dippers will also dive into water in pursuit of prey, propelling themselves along with their wings. They are small, plump birds, 15–20 cm (6–8 in) long, with stub tails. They frequent Europe, Asia, and North and South America.

➠ *Birds, Passerines*

ABOVE The dipper lives a semi-aquatic life, diving for food in streams.
RIGHT The dingo was introduced to Australia by settlers in prehistoric times.

DIVERS

(Class: Aves Order: Gaviiformes)

Also known as loons, divers are streamlined, aquatic birds that are ideally adapted to movement through water. They are 60–90 cm (24–36 in) long. Divers have tapered bills, small pointed wings, and legs that are placed far back on the body to facilitate swimming and diving. Plumage is typically grey or black on the back and white underneath. During the breeding season the back is marked with white patterning. The red-throated diver (*Gavia stellata*) has a northern circumpolar range, while other species are restricted to particular regions. Divers feed primarily on fish, but they will also take aquatic invertebrates.

➠ *Auks, Grebes, Gulls*

DINOSAURS

(Class: Reptilia Super-order: Dinosauria)

Dinosaurs are extinct reptiles that lived between 230 million and 65 million years ago. What is known about them has been gleaned from an incomplete fossil record and the examination of evolutionary relationships between their modern relatives – the birds and reptiles. Dinosaurs dominated the planet for many millions of years and they showed a huge diversity in size, form and lifestyle. Most were terrestrial but some were aquatic and others airborne. The cause of the dinosaurs' demise is uncertain and a subject of scientific contention, but it does coincide with a meteor strike and the expansion of the mammals.

➠ *Lizards, Tuatara*

DOGFISH

(Class: Chondrichthyes)

The term 'dogfish' applies to three families of small sharks – Scyliorhinidae (e.g. the spotted dogfish), Squalidae (e.g. the spiny dogfish) and Triakidae (e.g. the smooth dogfish). Generally, dogfish are widely distributed, mostly inhabiting coastal waters where they roam about the sea bed. They prey on crustaceans, fish and any other small creatures they find on the sea bed. They are often nocturnal and some species migrate to deeper water to mate, then return to shallow water to spawn. Dogfish are greyish-brown with paler under parts. They often have blotches or spots of brown or black on the dorsal and ventral surfaces.

➠ *Cartilaginous Fish, Sharks*

DOGS

(Class: Mammalia Order: Carnivora)

The domestic dog belongs to the same genus – Canis – as various wolves and jackals. They are so closely related that they can be cross-bred to produce fertile, hybrid offspring. There are other wild dogs that have not been domesticated, such as the cape hunting dog, Siberian wild dog, bush dog and maned wolf. Most dog species are fundamentally pack animals, but they are quite proficient at living and hunting alone when necessary. This happens when young adults are expelled from social groups to establish themselves elsewhere. The dingo (*Canis dingo*) is a half-domesticated species introduced to Australia by prehistoric settlers.

➠ *Carnivores, Wolves*

DOLPHINS

(Class: Mammalia Order: Cetecea)

The term 'dolphin' is not a specific one, as it is used in describing some of the smaller, toothed whales, but by no means all. The killer whale, grampus or orca (*Orcinus orca*) is among their number. In the same family are the pilot whales (*Globicephala* spp.), the false killer whale (*Pseudorca crassidens*) and the common dolphin (*Delphinus delphis*). Another family comprises the beaked and bottle-nosed dolphins, while a third family contains the river dolphins.

Dolphins are all aquatic hunters. They feed on a variety of animals, especiallly fish, squid and cuttlefish. Many live in social groups called schools and are known

BELOW The bottle-nosed dolphin belongs to one of three dolphin family groups.

to be relatively intelligent, with their own communication systems of gestures and noises. Marine species will often ride the bow waves of boats, partly to save energy but also out of sheer curiosity, peering as they leap from the water.

❧ The river dolphins are specialist fish eaters with long, slender snouts. They have small, more-or-less redundant eyes because they live in large rivers with murky waters, where echo-location and touch are far more useful senses.

❧ There are two species of marine fish called dolphins (*Coryphaena* spp.); otherwise known as dorados, and a third, freshwater fish (*Salminus maxillosus*).

➠ *Porpoises, Whales*

DORIES

(Class: Osteichthyes Order: Zeiformes)

Dories are marine fish with deep but laterally flattened bodies, tall dorsal fins and large eyes and mouths. They are found worldwide, in moderately deep waters. The best-known species in this family is the John dory (*Zeus faber*), which is a delicacy in many countries. The John dory has a row of armour scales with spines on the belly and on each side of the dorsal and anal fins. It is grey with a characteristic round black spot on each side of the body, behind the gills. The John dory is a solitary, carnivorous feeder which frequents European coastal waters.

➠ *Bony Fish, Fish*

DORMICE

(Class: Mammalia Order: Rodentia)

Dormice are about halfway between mice and squirrels. They are small, mouse-like rodents, with bushy tails and arboreal habits. The species from temperate climates typically fatten themselves up during the summer and autumn months so that they can hibernate. This has led to a long tradition of eating dormice as a delicacy in southern European countries. The edible dormouse (*Glis glis*) was kept in earthenware jars for this purpose by the Romans and was introduced into new areas by them. Some species of dormouse are found in Africa and Asia too, but they are globally confined to the Old World region.

➡ *Mice, Rodents*

DRAGONFLIES

(Class: Insecta Order: Odonata)

Dragonflies and damselflies are closely related to one another, in a similar way to butterflies and moths. Dragonflies are more robustly built than damselflies and rest with their wings folded down instead of behind them. This is because their wings are fixed in position, being adapted for stronger flight. While damselflies tend to stay near to water, dragonflies tend to fly considerable distances in search of food. Some species even migrate thousands of miles to find suitable places for dispersing their eggs. In this way they are better able to colonize new habitats.

Dragonflies have extremely good eyesight and can spot prey insects tens of metres away. They out-fly their prey with aerobatic skills unrivalled in the insect world, except perhaps by hoverflies. As they approach their prey for the kill they bend their legs forwards to make a basket shape in which to cradle their victim as it struggles. Dragonflies have changed little over millions of years such is the perfection of their design. Fossils have been found which show that dragonflies were once the largest insects ever to have lived on earth.

❧ During the age of dinosaurs, dragonflies reached wingspans of 70 cm (27.5 in).

➡ *Damselflies, Insects*

EARWIGS

(Class: Insecta Order: Dermaptera)

The origin of the name 'earwig' has become confused over time. The name is a contraction of 'ear-wiggler'. Earwigs do indeed wiggle when picked up, but the 'ear' in their name refers to the seed heads of plants, where earwigs like to conceal themselves for hibernation, and not human ears. The insects are scavengers of organic matter and can be found on the ground as well as on plants. There are some 13,000 species recorded over the world. They develop into adults as nymphs which look very like the adult form but smaller. Different species often look very alike.

➡ *Cockroaches, Insects*

ECHIDNAS

(Class: Mammalia Order: Monotremata)

Also called spiny or porcupine anteaters, echidnas are monotremes, along with platypuses. They represent a link between reptiles and therian mammals (marsupials and placentals) as they lay eggs, so they are sub-classed as prototherians. Echidnas have worm-like or vermiform tongues which they use for licking up ants, having burrowed into their nests. The eggs of the echidna are not laid in a nest, but in a rudimentary pouch which grows in response to hormonal changes. The young remain in the pouch once hatched, where they feed on milk secreted by mammary glands. They live in Australia, Tasmania and New Guinea.

➡ *Monotreme Mammals, Platypuses*

ABOVE TOP For dragonflies, mating can be a tricky business.
ABOVE Egg-laying echidnas form a link between mammals and reptiles.

EDIBLE FROGS

(Class: Amphibia Order: Anura)

The edible frog (*Rana esculenta*) belongs to a group of frogs known as the 'green frogs'. This group includes the marsh frog (*Rana ridibunda*). Edible frogs are vivid green with black spots on their backs and yellow spots on their sides. They have a yellow back stripe and white bellies. Edible frogs are found throughout Europe except the Iberian Peninsula and northern Scandinavia. It is the legs of the edible frog that are regarded a delicacy in some countries, particularly France. The creatures are reared in pools for the restaurant trade. They have balloon-like vocal sacs for emitting their loud calls.

➡ *Amphibians, Frogs*

EELS

(Class: Osteichthyes Order: Anguilliformes)

Eels comprise a large and diverse group of fish. There are about 600 species in the order and they are found in both marine and freshwater habitats. Eels have elongate, slender bodies and more closely resemble snakes than fish. They normally lack scales, but their bodies are covered in a protective mucus instead. The pectoral, pelvic and tail fins are either reduced or absent but the dorsal and anal fins are usually greatly extended along the fish's back and are used to thrust it forwards.

Eels have adopted a variety of lifestyles. Some are carnivorous predators, others are scavengers and several species are filter-feeders. Most species are marine, but members of the family Anguillidae are freshwater inhabitants that return to the sea to spawn.

The European eel (*Anguilla anguilla*) lives its adult life in freshwater streams and lakes. It stores fat in its body in preparation for its long migration, which takes it across the Atlantic Ocean to the Sargasso Sea. After swimming for 6,400 km (4,000 miles) it spawns and dies. The young hatch in the sea and are carried back to coastal

BELOW A giant moray, assisted by a cleaner wrasse.

waters by the ocean currents in a journey that takes three years. By the end of the journey they have been depleted in number since they are preyed upon by all manner of sea creature. Nevertheless, countless millions of elvers – young eels – enter European estuaries and begin travelling upriver, where they will spend several years developing into adult eels.

❧ Eels have a transparent larval stage that is very different to the adult stage. They are called leptocephali.

❧ Conger eels can grow up to 3 m (9 ft) in length.

❧ Freshwater eels can absorb oxygen directly into their skin.

❧ Gulper eels have enormous jaws that enable them to swallow fish as large as themselves.

➡ *Hagfish, Lampreys*

EFTS

(Class: Amphibia
Order: Caudata)

The term 'eft' is believed to be an Old or Middle English word for newt. It now has two separate, though related, meanings. An eft may be any member of the family Salamandridae, which contains 40 species of warty-skinned salamander that live terrestrial lives. Alternatively the term 'eft' may be applied to the juvenile stage of any newt or salamander that has a terrestrial stage in its lifecycle. The eft stage begins when the larval newt or salamander loses its gills and begins to breathe through its skin and lungs. The eft enters adulthood when it becomes sexually mature.

➡ *Newts, Salamanders*

EGG-EATING SNAKES

(Class: Reptilia Order: Squamata)

There are only five species of these slender snakes that eat a diet entirely of eggs. They inhabit sub-Saharan Africa and northeastern India and are typically arboreal. They belong to the family Colubridae.

Although relatively small at only 76 cm (30 in) these colubrids are able to consume whole birds' eggs. Other reptiles are able to feed on the soft-shelled eggs of their own kind but it is much more difficult to consume a hard-shelled bird's egg. This is achieved by several modifications to the head. Their teeth are either reduced or absent and the jaws can be opened wide enough to allow a whole egg to pass through to the flexible throat. Once in the throat the egg is crushed. This is achieved by specially adapted neck vertebrae that cut into the shell. They have spines that extend into the throat for the job. The contents of the egg progress through to the stomach while the eggshell is regurgitated.

❖ Egg-eating snakes, such as the common egg-eating snake (*Daspeltis scabra*) of Africa, may fast for months until the birds' breeding season begins. They then gorge themselves on the huge supply of available eggs.

➡ *Reptiles, Snakes*

ELECTRIC EELS

(Class: Osteichthyes Order: Gymnotiformes)

Despite its name the electric eel (*Electrophorus electricus*) is not a member of the eel family. It is more closely related to characins and catfish. The electric eel is a native of the Orinoco and Amazon rivers in South America. It is long and cylindrical in shape, reaching a length of 2.75 m (9 ft) and a weight of 22 kg (49 lb). The dorsal and tail fins are reduced but the anal fin extends along most of the underside of the body and this propels the eel forward. It rises to the surface of the water to gulp air from which it absorbs the oxygen.

Electric eels are slow-moving carnivores that have poor eyesight. They rely upon the emission of weak electric pulses from their body to detect their prey. These electric pulses may also be used in navigation and defence. Electric eels are also able to produce large emissions of electricity that stun, or even kill, prey. They have electricity-producing organs that consist of groups of compacted nerve endings. These organs are concentrated

TOP LEFT The red eft is a warty-skinned, terrestrial species of salamander.
LEFT The egg-eating snake's jaws and neck are apadted to suit its diet.
RIGHT African elephants have larger ears and have two 'lips' on their trunk.

in the tail, which constitutes most of the fish's length. They can produce a discharge of 450–650 volts – easily sufficient to kill humans.

➡ *Catfish, Characins*

ELECTRIC RAYS

(Class: Chondrichthyes Order: Torpediniformes)

Many fish with skeletons made of cartilage emit weak electric signals. It is believed that they do this to detect prey and navigate. In some species, such as electric rays, the electricity – generated by specialised nerve endings – is sufficient to stun, and even kill, prey. Electric rays lie buried in sand, so their disc-shaped, flattened bodies are camouflaged and only their eyes remain visible. They emit powerful electrical discharges, from electric organs placed on either side of the head, which disable other fish and invertebrates before they can escape. Electric rays inhabit shallow coastal waters in temperate and warm regions.

➡ *Sharks, Rays*

ELEPHANT BIRDS

(Class: Aves Order: Aepyornithiformes)

When explorers first returned from their journeys around the east African coast they brought with them stories of gigantic birds, many times the size of man. To support their stories the explorers exhibited huge eggs, up to 1,000 mm (40 in) in circumference. They were the eggs of birds that would later come to be known as the elephant bird, vouron patra or roc-bird (*Aepyornis maximus*).

This flightless bird is now extinct but was believed to have been 3–4 m (10–13 ft) in height and weighed nearly four times as much as an ostrich. Evidence from Madagascar shows that the elephant bird was not the only species of *Aepyornis* to have lived. It is thought that between three and seven different types of elephant bird lived beyond the Pleistocene Period, which ended 10,000 years ago.

The island of Madagascar was probably first populated by humans only 2,000 years ago. When Europeans visited the island in the sixteenth century the elephant birds had already become quite rare because the Malagasy people valued their flesh and eggs as food. They were probably

fearless of people and relatively easy to kill, so their extinction was only a matter of time.

➡ *Moas, Ostriches*

ELEPHANTS

(Class: Mammalia Order: Proboscidea)

The two species of elephant are the African elephant (*Loxodonta africana*) and Indian elephant (*Elephas maximus*). They are very similar to one another, barring a few minor characteristics. African elephants are about one metre taller at the shoulder, at 3–3.6 m (10–12 ft). They also have larger ears. Indian elephants have a single 'lip' at the end of the trunk, while their African counterparts have two. African elephants are creatures of scrub and savannah while Indian elephants tend to live in more densely forested areas. The extinct woolly mammoth (*Mammuthus primigenius*) was an elephant adapted for cold habitats.

➡ *Hyraxes, Mammals*

EMUS

(Class: Aves Order: Casuariiformes)

The Emu is the last surviving member of its family, the others having become extinct after being hunted for food by aboriginal settlers to Australia and Tasmania. Like its close relatives, the cassowaries, the Emu is a large, flightless bird with a long neck, long legs and small wings covered by shaggy plumage. After the Ostrich, the Emu is the largest bird, with a height of 1.5 m (5 ft). It can weigh as much as 45 kg (100 lb). Like many terrestrial, flightless birds, Emus are built for running and can reach speeds of up to 50 kph (31 mph).

➡ *Cassowaries, Rheas*

FEATHER-STARS
(Phylum: Echinodermata Class: Crinoidea)

 Feather stars and sea-lilies – crinoids – belong to the same class of animals. Along with starfish, sea urchins, sea cucumbers and brittle stars, they belong to the phylum of animals known as echinoderms (*Echinodermata*). Larval feather-stars are free-swimming creatures known as doliolaria. They swim about for a few days and then settle on objects where they develop into the adult form. Feather-stars are feathery looking, delicate starfish that filter particles of food from sea-water. Sea-lilies are similar, but they are stalked animals that 'root' themselves to the spot, while feather-stars are able to move about, albeit rather slowly.

➠ *Sea Urchins, Starfish*

FINCHES
(Class: Aves Order: Passeriformes)

This is a large group of songbirds found throughout the temperate regions of the northern hemisphere, South America and Africa. Finches tend to be small – 10–20 cm (4–8 in) – with compact bodies and conical bills that are well-adapted to their diet of seeds. They also take insects and fruits. The name 'finch' is used for many species from other seedeater families. Finches typically display marked differences between male and female plumage. Additionally, their plumage varies between the winter and summer periods, no doubt relating to camouflage from predators. Finches roam in mixed flocks during the wintering season.

➠ *Buntings, Sparrows*

ABOVE Feather-stars move about freely and filter food from the water.
ABOVE RIGHT Glands behind the fire salamander's eyes produce a toxin.

FIRE SALAMANDERS
(Order: Amphibia Class: Caudata)

The fire salamander (*Salamandra salamandra*) is a largely terrestrial salamander that is found in north-west Africa, Europe and western Asia. It inhabits woodlands and forests and spends most of the winter buried underground. The fire salamander has a variable appearance; its skin may be black with yellow spots or yellow with black spots, or even striped. This bright colouration warns potential predators that the salamander carries a foul-tasting toxin, which is produced by glands located behind the salamander's eyes. The fire salamander is an active hunter at night. It eats small invertebrates such as slugs, snails and insects.

➠ *Newts, Salamanders*

FISH LICE
(Subphylum: Crustacea Class: Branchiura)

A fish louse is a crustacean that has evolved to become a parasite. There are about 100 species recorded. They inhabit both marine and freshwater environments where they typically attach themselves to the skin or gills of fish, where they feed on blood. One species can grow to 25 mm (1 in) and parasitizes the alligator garfish. Fish lice have flattened bodies to enable them to slip between the scales or gills of fish and prevent them from being knocked away from their anchorage. They hang on to their hosts with special hooks or suckers, depending on the species.

➠ *Crustaceans, Gars*

FISH

(Phylum: Chordata)

Fish are vertebrates that live an aquatic way of life, usually breathing via gills. They typically have fusiform bodies – tapered at both ends – which facilitates their movement through water. Fish bodies normally have scales, and fins are present rather than limbs. However these are generalizations about a group that is so large and diverse that exceptions are abundant.

The term 'fish' does not necessarily reflect strong evolutionary or physical relationships between all members of the group; it is an informal name for up to five classes of aquatic vertebrates that are listed below. There is considerable dispute over the classification of fish, which is continually changing as the fossil record reveals more evidence about the evolution of modern species.

The fish group is enormous. There are approximately 41,000 species of vertebrates, the majority of which are fish. This diversity may be partly attributed to the size of habitat available to them as over 70 per cent of the Earth's surface is covered by water. That equates to about 95 per cent of the total three-dimensional living space on the planet.

There are five classes of extant and extinct fish:

- Class Agnatha: Jawless filter-feeding fish that first appeared 500 million years ago and are now extinct, except for the hagfish and lampreys.
- Class Acanthodii: Early jawed fish that appeared 400 million years ago. All members are extinct.
- Class Placodermi: Early jawed fish with armour-plated skin. They appeared 390 million years ago and are possible ancestors of bony and cartilaginous fish. All members are extinct.
- Class Osteichthyes: Bony fish – teleosts – that appeared 390 million years ago and now form the largest group of fish. At least 20,000 species are recognized.
- Class Chondrichthyes: Cartilaginous fish, which probably appeared later than the bony fish. Includes all modern skates, rays and sharks. About 800 species are recognized.

➠ *Bony Fish, Cartilaginous Fish*

BELOW Flamingos use their specially adapted bills to sieve food from the water.

FLAMINGOS

(Class: Aves Order: Ciconiiformes)

These elegant birds are closely related to herons and storks. Flocks of flamingos live near water, mainly in tropical and sub-tropical regions. They have long slender bodies and necks, large wings and short tails. Flamingos have bare faces and plumage that varies in colour from white to cerise. The colour comes from algae and shrimps which constitute a large part of their diet. Flamingos wade in shallow water, stamping the mud to disturb their food. They sieve it from the water using their adapted bills, designed specifically for use upside down.

➠ *Herons, Storks*

FLATFISH

(Class: Osteichthyes Order: Pleuronectiformes)

There are over 600 species of flatfish, such as flounders, turbots, halibuts, dabs and soles. They are bottom-dwelling, marine fish that mainly inhabit coastal waters of moderate depth from tropical to polar regions. Some species spend all or part of their lives in freshwater. Flatfish are camouflaged on their upper surfaces where pigmentation is patchy and resembles the sandy substrate. In most species this upper surface can change colour to suit the surroundings. Their ventral surfaces – lower – are white. Flatfish swim by undulating their bodies and fins but most of their adult lives is spent on the sea-floor, hidden below a thin layer of sand. When small crustaceans or small fish pass by flatfish rush from their hiding places to catch them.

The most unusual characteristic of flatfish is their asymmetry. Most other fish are more-or-less symmetrical, but flatfish have evolved from them to become bottom dwellers. The larvae hatch from their eggs with an eye on each side of their head as usual. However, they rapidly metamorphose into the adult form and one eye migrates to the other side. The body then twists until the blind side lies flat on the seabed. Further distortion in the fish's skull brings both gills and the mouth onto the dorsal – upper – surface.

Flatfish are commercially important as food fish and are heavily exploited by the fishing industry. The plaice (*Pleuronectes platessa*) is Europe's most important commercial flatfish and over-fishing has led to a depletion of stocks. Its populations may be vulnerable.

* Flatfish can be as small as 100 mm (4 in) or as large as 2 m (6.5 ft).
* All flatfish have evolved from bilaterally symmetrical fish, but some flattened to the right side, while others have flattened to the left.
* Female flatfish may lay hundreds of thousands of eggs at a time.

➠ *Bony Fish, Fish*

FLATWORMS

(Phyla: Platyhelminthes and Nemertina)

This is a large collection of worms, including flukes, tapeworms and ribbon worms. They vary greatly in size and shape but generally speaking they tend to have flattened bodies. All-in-all there are perhaps

ABOVE *Peacock flounders spend most of their adult life on the sea-floor.*
RIGHT *A vermillion flycatcher keeps a look-out from its perch.*

10,000 species. They have colonized land, marine and freshwater environments and become parasites on or in other animals. Flukes are parasitic flatworms that typically use fish and amphibians as their hosts. Tapeworms parasitize the intestines of vertebrates. Ribbon worms can be extraordinarily long, reaching 27 m (90 ft). Most species live in shallow marine habitats, but some live in freshwater and a few are terrestrial.

➟ *Invertebrates, Roundworms*

FLEAS

(Class: Insecta Order: Siphonaptera)

The Latin word 'Siphonaptera' is derived from 'siphon', because fleas siphon the blood of their hosts for food, and 'aptera' which means 'to have no wings'. There are some 1,500 species of flea. They are typically parasites of mammals and birds. Actually they are described as ectoparasites because only the adult flea is a parasite. The maggot-like larvae of fleas feed on organic detritus in the homes of their hosts before pupating.

Fleas are very well designed for living amongst the fur or feathers of their hosts. They have laterally flattened bodies with short antennae and legs that emerge from beneath so that they can literally run about unimpeded. Having no wings, many fleas have evolved an ability to jump by using their hind pair of legs. This enables them to reach their hosts rapidly without having to climb. Fleas are notorious for their ability to act as vectors for diseases. Bubonic plague, sylvatic plague and endemic typhus are examples. The fleas most frequently encountered by humans are the human flea (*Pulex irritans*), the dog flea (*Ctenocephalides canis*) and the cat flea (*C. felis*).

❀ The jigger, or chigger (*Tunga penetrans*), is a flea that burrows under the skin.

➟ *Insects, Invertebrates*

FLIES

(Class: Insecta Order: Diptera)

Although many insects are called flies, such as dragonflies, butterflies and mayflies, true flies have just one pair of wings rather than two. Their ancestors did have two pairs of wings but the rear pair have been reduced to a pair of small club-like projections called halteres, which are used for balance. True flies include

BELOW True flies, like this stalk-eyed fly, have only one pair of wings.

hoverflies, crane-flies, mosquitoes, midges, horseflies, fruit-flies, blow-flies and house-flies. Fly larvae are typically maggots or maggot-like. Many feed on decaying organic material, although others actively hunt live prey. Adult flies have either piercing mouth parts or a proboscis designed for lapping up fluids from surfaces.

➟ *Insects, Invertebrates*

FLOWERPECKERS

(Class: Aves Order: Passeriformes)

These songbirds live in southern Asia, the western Pacific islands and Australia, in a wide range of habitats from tropical rainforests to gardens. Flowerpeckers have stumpy tails and short bills that are finely serrated. They often have bright and colourful plumage. The pygmy flowerpecker is just 6 cm (2.5 in) long while the largest species reaches only 23 cm (9 in). Diet is varied – some species eat fruit, others insects, while some feed almost exclusively on mistletoe berries. Eggs are laid in domed nests which are suspended from twigs. A clutch of one to four eggs is normally laid.

➟ *Birds, Passerines*

FLYCATCHERS

(Class: Aves Order: Passeriformes)

Flycatchers belong to two, quite unrelated, families, but the Muscicapidae species are known as Old World flycatchers, as opposed to New World or tyrant flycatchers. As their name suggests, flycatchers are adept at catching flying insects. They characteristically use a favourite perch from which to launch sorties whenever prey comes close. Old World flycatchers live in a range of habitats from tropical to temperate. Those that breed in temperate latitudes have to migrate to warmer climes for the rest of the year to find food. Some exotic species have long tail feathers and brightly coloured plumage.

➟ *Tyrant Flycatchers*

FLYING FISH

(Class: Osteichthyes Order: Beloniformes)

Approximately 40 species of the family Exocoetidae are flying fish. They are all inhabitants of oceanic waters and are found most commonly in temperate and tropical regions. Flying fish glide rather than fly; their movement through air is dependent upon horizontal wind currents.

Flying fish are small with maximum lengths of about 45 cm (18 in). Their pectoral fins are greatly enlarged and wing-like. In some instances the pelvic fins are enlarged too. As a flying fish swims underwater it builds speed, keeping its fins close to its body to create a torpedo-like body shape. As the fish approaches the surface of the water its tail undulates and pushes it into the air. The pectoral fins open out and catch the wind current; this provides lift and the whole body is raised from the water. The pelvic fins now spread out and a gliding motion is achieved. Movement through air can be faster than through water since it offers less resistance and can offer a flying fish a means of escaping predators. The common flying fish (*Exocetus volitans*) uses only enlarged pectoral fins to glide over water. However, it can attain speeds of 65 kph (40 mph), gliding for 15 seconds at a time.

➠ *Bony Fish, Fish*

FLYING FROGS

(Class: Amphibia Order: Anura)

Flying frogs belong to the family Rhacophoridae and come from forested regions of southeast Asia. These frogs do not actually fly but glide from one tree to another to escape predators or find food. By flattening

ABOVE In flying fish, the pectoral fins are enlarged and resemble wings.
RIGHT When disturbed, the flying gurnard takes off through the water.

their bodies and spreading their limbs, flying frogs increase their lower surface area, so creating maximum air resistance. This technique, combined with partial webbing between their toes, enables flying frogs to glide distances of 15 m (50 ft), although they need to start from a high vantage point. Wallace's flying frog (*Rhacophorus nigropalmatus*) is one of several species that glide through the rainforest.

➠ *Amphibians, Frogs*

FLYING GECKOES

(Class: Reptilia Order: Squamata)

An ability to escape predators quickly offers a better chance of survival. Some species of reptile have developed the ability, not to fly, but glide away from danger. Kuhl's gecko (*Ptychozoon kuhli*) comes from southeast Asia where it lives in tropical rainforests. It is an arboreal lizard that hunts small invertebrates such as insects. The body of a Kuhl's gecko is camouflaged by cryptic colouration. When threatened it leaps into the air, spreading its limbs out and flattening its body. The gecko has strong webbed feet and a flattened tail that create the air resistance it needs to glide effectively.

➠ *Lizards, Reptiles*

FLYING GURNARDS

(Class: Osteichthyes Order: Dactylopteriformes)

There are several species of small, marine fish known as flying gurnards. They are characterised by their having large heads and wing-like pectoral fins, which are often marked with blue stripes. The heads and bodies of flying gurnards are grey or brown with spots or similar markings. These fish normally live at the bottom of the sea

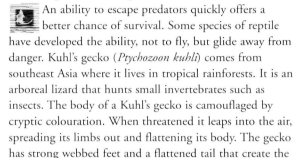

where they feed on crustaceans and other small animals. The pectoral fins are normally folded against the body but when disturbed the fish open them and 'fly' through the water. There are unsubstantiated reports that these fish can also take to the air.

➡ *Bony Fish, Fish*

FLYING LEMURS

(Class: Mammalia Order: Dermoptera)

 The name 'flying lemur' is misleading in two ways: firstly these animals are not lemurs, despite their resemblance, and secondly they cannot fly, but merely glide. There are two species of flying lemur, otherwise known as colugos (*Cynocephalus* spp.). They have

membranes between their forelimbs and hindlimbs which they use to glide from one tree trunk to another, losing height in the process. True lemurs live only in Madagascar, while flying lemurs live in southeast Asia. They are nocturnal creatures that hang upside down, bat-like, during the day. They have carnivore-like teeth, but they are plant and fruit eaters.

➡ *Lemurs, Phalangers*

FLYING LIZARDS

(Class: Reptilia Order: Squamata)

While no lizards can truly fly there is a group of lizards from southeast Asia and the East Indies that can glide. They do this with membranes of skin that

BELOW Paradoxically, flying lemurs are not lemurs; neither can they fly.

protrude from the sides of the body between the forelimbs and hindlimbs. The skin membranes are reinforced and held rigid by five or six elongated ribs. When at rest the membranes and ribs are folded back against the body, enabling the lizards to remain fully mobile. The flying dragon (*Draco volans*) is a typical member of this group. It glides to escape predators and find food among the trees of the rainforest.

➡ *Lizards, Reptiles*

FLYING SQUIRRELS

(Class: Mammalia Order: Rodentia)

There are two families of arboreal creatures known commonly as flying squirrels. The Sciuridae comprise real squirrels but the Anomaluridae are a group of rodents otherwise known as scaly-tailed flying squirrels. Evidently it is an advantage to be able to glide from tree to tree while escaping predators, since the flying lemurs and phalangers have the same skills as flying squirrels. Like most rodents, they are vegetarian feeders. Those from the Sciuridae family come from Southeast Asia, northern Eurasia and North America, while those from the Anomaluridae family live in Africa. They are born with their gliding membranes.

➡ *Phalangers, Squirrels*

FOAM-NESTING TREE FROGS

(Class: Amphibia Order: Anura)

Most frogs mate and lay their eggs in water but some species have developed alternative methods of reproduction. Grey foam-nesting tree frogs (*Chiromantis rufescens*) of central Africa, congregate on branches overhanging freshwater pools. As a male grasps a female she produces a viscous, white secretion. The male then whips it into a frothy mass with his hindlimbs. The female then lays her eggs into the foam and the male squirts his sperm onto them. The foam adheres to the branch and hardens externally, but stays moist within. When the eggs hatch the tadpoles drop into the water.

➡ *Amphibians, Frogs*

FOREST LIFE IN THE NORTH

The fir forests of Russia, Scandinavia, Canada and Alaska cover vast areas of wilderness, where few people live or even visit. These northern forests follow the Arctic Circle around the globe and are subject to extremes of weather. In the height of summer the sun never sets and temperatures rise considerably as the dark land absorbs the solar radiation. In the height of winter, however, the sun never rises and for months on end the temperatures plummet to well below freezing point.

Even farther north the deeper ground remains constantly frozen and is called permafrost. Here only shallow-rooted plants can grow, so the forest gives way to terrain known as Arctic tundra. In these hostile and uncongenial environments making a living is a tough business for all animals, not least because nutrition is hard to come by where plants – the foundation of food chains – find it difficult to grow.

RIGHT The bobcat population has declined due to the fur trade
FAR RIGHT The grizzly bear's name refers to its grizzled coat.
ABOVE RIGHT Reindeers' hair traps air, providing insulation.

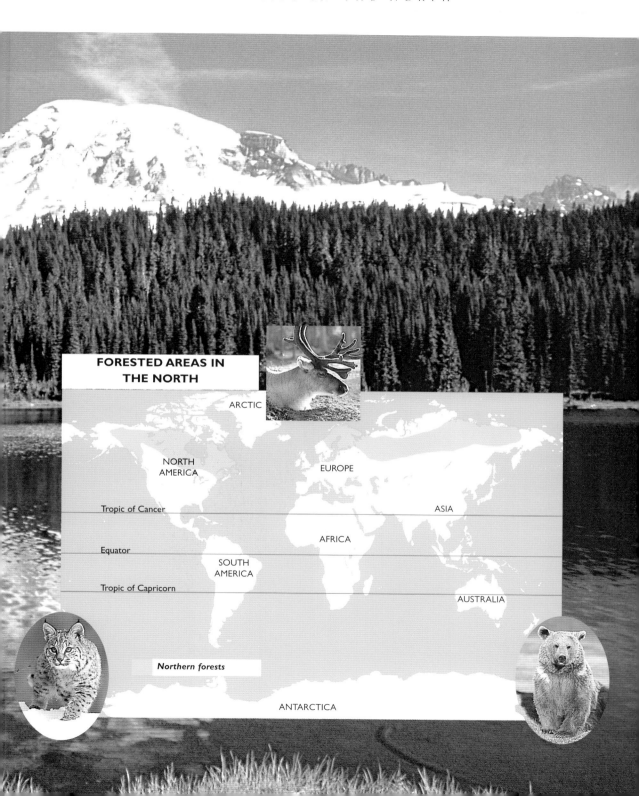

FORESTED AREAS IN THE NORTH

ARCTIC

NORTH
AMERICA

EUROPE

Tropic of Cancer

ASIA

AFRICA

Equator

SOUTH
AMERICA

Tropic of Capricorn

AUSTRALIA

Northern forests

ANTARCTICA

FOREST LIFE IN TEMPERATE REGIONS

The temperate regions contain forests comprising a mixture of deciduous and evergreen, broadleaf trees. Temperature ranges from summer to winter are notable, but they are not generally extreme. They are sufficient however to dictate a seasonal cycle in the forests, characterised by the growth and loss of foliage on most plants. Consequently all life in temperate forests follows an annual rhythm governed by the availability of vegetation, as with forest life in the north.

Leaves provide nutrition for plant feeders, also known as vegetarians or herbivores. They, in turn, become prey for meat eaters – predators or carnivores. In addition there are the omnivores – scavengers or opportunists of the forest that feed on all kinds of foodstuffs, whether they be plant or animal, dead or alive. Most temperate forest species hibernate over winter, but some migrate to warmer places and a few remain active all year round.

RIGHT Tawny owls take small mammals, birds and worms for food.
FAR RIGHT Hedgehogs living in temperate forests hibernate for the winter.
ABOVE RIGHT In Northern America, racoons live alongside humans.

FORESTED AREAS IN TEMPERATE REGIONS

ARCTIC

NORTH
AMERICA

EUROPE

Tropic of Cancer

ASIA

AFRICA

Equator

SOUTH
AMERICA

Tropic of Capricorn

AUSTRALIA

Temperate forests

ANTARCTICA

FOREST LIFE IN THE TROPICS

The most telling characteristic of tropical forests is their relative lack of temperate variation. This is because they lie within the two tropics – Capricorn and Cancer – and close to the equator, where seasonal change is virtually non-existent, apart from rainfall levels. The result is forest with an ecological profile largely influenced by availability of water and resulting in wet and dry seasons. This is not the case, though, in forests described as rainforests, because they generate a constant level of moisture.

Broadly speaking, there are two types of tropical forest, perhaps best described as jungle and rainforest. Although different in respect of rainfall levels and distribution, both are characterised by evergreen, broadleaf trees and animals species that generally remain localized. Those of the jungle generally time their reproduction with the flush of greenery following the rains, while those of rainforests tend to breed all year round.

RIGHT Toucans' large bills may be designed to reach for fruit.
FAR RIGHT Varied lorikeets are attractive birds and make popular pets.
ABOVE RIGHT The orangutan's Malayan name translates as 'forest man'.

FORESTED AREAS IN THE TROPICS

ARCTIC

NORTH
AMERICA

EUROPE

Tropic of Cancer

ASIA

AFRICA

Equator

SOUTH
AMERICA

Tropic of Capricorn

AUSTRALIA

Tropical forests

ANTARCTICA

FOWL

(Class: Aves Order: Galliformes)

The terms 'fowl' and 'poultry' are used to describe many birds that are raised specifically for their meat, eggs and feathers. They are of significant agricultural and commercial importance. Domestic chickens are descended from the jungle fowl (*Gallus gallus*) of India. It is believed that these birds were first domesticated over 4,000 years ago and centuries of selective breeding have produced the modern birds. They have been bred in Europe since the Medieval era.

Similarly, domestic turkeys are descended from the wild turkey (*Meleagris gallopavo*). They were first domesticated by the indigenous peoples of Mexico. Explorers took them back to Spain in 1519, from where

The partridge (RIGHT) and pheasant (ABOVE) are two examples of fowl. FAR RIGHT One of the more familiar species of fox is the red fox.

they spread throughout Europe and were mistakenly believed to have originated in Turkey. Domesticated turkeys were introduced into North America in the seventeenth century. Wild turkeys may weigh as much as 10 kg (22 lb) but selective breeding to encourage a greater proportion of meat has resulted in domestic turkeys that weigh much more.

Pheasant, partridge, quail, peafowl, guineafowl and grouse have also been bred for centuries. They are often released to be hunted for sport as well as food, hence the term 'gamebird'. Gamebirds are ground-dwelling species and are found worldwide in many different habitats, including woodlands and mountainous regions. The common quail (*Coturnix coturnix*) is one of a few gamebirds that migrate long distances – from Europe to Africa and vice versa. Other members of the group are the ptarmigan (*Lagopus mutus*), the capercaillie (*Tetrao urogallus*), snowcocks, francolins and the prairie chicken (*Tympanuchus cupido*).

❖ Male fowl often possess brightly coloured plumage in order to attract the females which are typically cryptically coloured.

❖ Mallee fowl (*Leipoa ocellata*) do not incubate their eggs by sitting on them. Instead they build large mounds of vegetation which slowly decompose, so generating adequate warmth for the developing eggs.

➡ *Birds*

FOXES

(Class: Mammalia Order: Carnivora)

Foxes are members of the dog family. They are typically lighter in build than jackals, with relatively long bodies and short limbs. Their snouts are pointed and they have bushy tails, sometimes known as brushes. Foxes specialise in catching smaller prey than their relatives, often taking rodents and birds. They also consume carrion when it's available. Foxes have colonised a broad range of habitats from the Arctic tundra to the African deserts. There was once a fox called the warrah (*Dusicyon australis*) indigenous to the Falkland Islands. Charles Darwin saw it in 1833, but it was extinct 40 years later.

➡ *Dogs, Wolves*

ABOVE Arctic foxes follow polar bears in the hope of eating their leftovers.

FRESHWATER LIFE

The term 'freshwater' can mean anything from ponds to lakes, or streams to rivers. It is any water that doesn't contain salt. By their very nature, freshwater habitats tend to be isolated from one another. The result is that species have evolved which belong to a single place, so they are extremely vulnerable to extinction should the habitat be disturbed or polluted. Indeed, a number of species have already declined in number or gone extinct in this manner.

Lake Baikal in southern Siberia, Russia, (pictured here) is the largest freshwater lake in Europe and Asia. By volume it is the largest body of freshwater in the world, reaching a depth of 1,743 m (5,714 ft). It has become so isolated that it has many indigenous species of fish and even its own species of seal. The river dolphins of Asia are increasingly under threat due to habitat loss, human disturbance and pollution.

RIGHT The exotic-looking mandarin duck is originally from the Far East.
FAR RIGHT African peacock cichlids can be found in Lake Malawi.
ABOVE RIGHT The platypus uses its beak-like mouth to search for food.

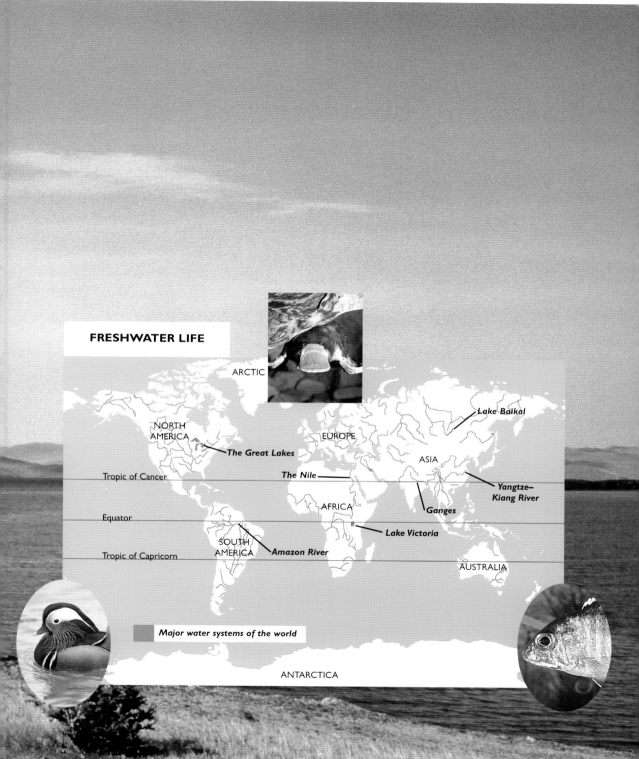

FRESHWATER LIFE

ARCTIC

NORTH
AMERICA

EUROPE

Lake Baikal

ASIA

The Great Lakes

Tropic of Cancer

The Nile

Yangtze–
Kiang River

Ganges

AFRICA

Equator

Lake Victoria

SOUTH
AMERICA

Amazon River

Tropic of Capricorn

AUSTRALIA

Major water systems of the world

ANTARCTICA

FRIGATE BIRDS

(Class: Aves Order: Pelecaniformes)

Frequenting the coasts of tropical and semi-tropical areas, these large birds are among the world's best fliers. With long, slender bodies, long forked tails and wingspans that can reach 2.3 m (7.5 ft) these birds fly with acrobatic prowess. Frigate birds rarely land, except to sleep and tend their nests. A single egg is incubated by both parents. They rarely stray farther than 160 km (100 miles) from the coast. Frigate birds are pirates; they attack other seabirds and rob them of their catches. They also fly close to the surface of the water and grab fish swimming close to the surface.

➠ *Gulls, Skuas*

FRILLED LIZARDS

(Class: Reptilia Order: Squamata)

The frilled lizard (*Chlamydosaurus kingii*) of Australia and New Guinea belongs to the family Agamidae. This large lizard has a stocky grey or brown body that reaches 85 cm (33 in). It possesses a large neck frill that it raises behind its head when threatened. The effect is to make the lizard appear larger than it really is, thereby intimidating any predator from attacking. As it raises its neck frill the lizard also opens its mouth and hisses aggressively. The frilled lizard has another unusual attribute – it can run bipedally, with its forelegs and tail held above the ground.

➠ *Lizards, Reptiles*

ABOVE The magnificent frigate bird steals food from other sea-birds.
RIGHT Frogs, such as this gold frog, can breathe through their skin.

FROGS

(Order: Amphibia Class: Anura)

There is no clear distinction between frogs and toads, although it is broadly agreed that species with warty skin, a terrestrial lifestyle and a crawling, rather than jumping, movement should be called toads. Frogs usually live near water, in moist and warm habitats. The greatest diversity of species is found in the tropics.

Adult frogs are characterised by squat tail-less bodies, broad heads and protruding eyes. Their hind legs are longer than the front ones and modified, with strong muscles and webbed feet, for swimming and jumping. The moist skin of a frog is used as a respiratory surface – in effect the frogs can breathe through it. The frogs' skin may be camouflaged to provide protection from predators. Alternatively, the mucus-producing glands of the skin, which keep the skin moist, produce poisons to deter predators. The presence of these toxins is often displayed by bright and bold skin colours. Frogs are predominantly aquatic. However this group is the largest of all amphibians and its members display a wide range in lifestyle and diversity of preferred habitats.

Fertilization is external in frogs and usually takes place in water. The smaller male climbs on to the female's back and grasps her tightly. As she produces eggs his sperm washes over them. The eggs are laid in strands or clumps, attached to plants or free floating. When the eggs hatch

tadpoles emerge. Tadpoles are aquatic larvae that possess external gills, plump bodies and tails. They gradually metamorphose into the adult form. In some terrestrial species of frog the eggs hatch to reveal froglets – partially developed adults – rather than tadpoles.

❖ The mating embrace between male and female frogs is called 'amplexus'.

❖ Many male frogs make calls to attract females during the mating season. Vocal sacs may be used to increase the volume of calls.

➠ *Amphibians, Toads*

FROGS, COMMON
(Class: Amphibia Order: Anura)

The common frog (*Rana temporaria*) is a familiar visitor to gardens and ponds throughout all of northern Europe and can even survive extreme cold inside the Arctic Circle. It is 50–90 mm (2–4 in) in length and has a mottled colouration of green, brown and black. The adults live a terrestrial life but always in moist habitats. They return to water for the mating season which takes place in spring. Many large clumps of frogspawn may litter a pond but relatively few tadpoles survive to adulthood since they are a source of food for other animals, especially fish.

➠ *Frogs, Toads*

GALAPAGOS FINCHES
(Class: Aves Order: Passeriformes)

The Galapagos Islands are a volcanic archipelago of 19 islands in the Eastern Pacific, lying 1,000 km (620 miles) west of mainland Equador. Their geographical isolation has provided biologists with a useful insight into how species evolve into new species.

In 1835 the English naturalist Charles Darwin (1809–82) visited the Galapagos Islands and found the evidence that inspired his theory of evolution. Darwin noticed that there were many different types of finch that appeared to be sufficiently similar to one another as to have had a common ancestor. Yet they displayed adaptations that allowed each type of finch to exploit a slightly different econiche, thereby avoiding direct competition for resources. The Galapagos finches, also known as Darwin's finches, thus became famous as the animals that helped Darwin support his theory.

There are 14 species of Galapagos finch. They are all 10–20 cm (4–8 in) long, with brown to black plumage. Although similar, the variety in bill shape and size is their telling characteristic. The bills differ according to the

BELOW Galapagos finches gave Darwin the inspiration for his theory.

birds' feeding habits. Some birds possess delicate bills for probing bark in search of insects. Others have broad bills for breaking seeds. Some species have something in between and are more generalist in diet.

❖ The woodpecker finch (*Cactospiza pallidus*) uses cactus spines to search for grubs – an interesting and relatively rare example of tool use in birds.

❖ The tree finch (*Camarhynchus parvulus*) takes small insects, while the ground finch (*Geospiza magnirostris*) eats hard-shelled seeds.

❖ There is even a species nicknamed the vampire finch because it has been observed sipping blood from the ankles of seabirds.

❖ Darwin proposed that a common ancestral bird must have evolved into the current 14 species in response to the different vacant habitats. This is a phenomenon now described as 'adaptive radiation'.

➠ *Finches, Passerines*

GALAPAGOS TORTOISES

(Class: Reptilia Order: Chelonia)

The Galapagos Islands lie 1,000 km (620 miles) west of Equador and have ranges of unusual flora and fauna that are found nowhere else on earth. Galapagos giant tortoises (*Geochelone nigra*) are examples of how these islands have provided isolated habitats leading to the evolution of various sub-species. The tortoises reach 120 cm (4 ft) in length and their great size is believed to help them store food in a harsh environment where food supplies are unreliable. These tortoises are herbivorous and spend much of their day grazing or lying in mud. They can live for over 100 years.

➠ *Reptiles, Tortoises*

GANNETS

(Class: Aves Order: Pelecaniformes)

Gannets and boobies belong to the same order as pelicans and cormorants. There is no difference between gannets and boobies, except that gannets are migratory and boobies frequent warmer regions. There are nine species and they range over most of the world's oceans. They typically have white bodies with dark wingtips and brightly coloured feet. Nests are made of seaweed and mud and laid in dense colonies on cliff ledges. When fishing gannets and boobies dive into the water from the air like darts, with their wings pulled back. They will also follow ships in order to seize flying fish.

➠ *Cormorants, Pelicans*

GARS

(Class: Osteichthyes Order: Lepisosteiformes)

Gars are placed in the same subclass (Actinopterygii) as bowfins, bichirs, sturgeons and paddlefish. They are bony fish that have lost some ossification and have skeletons that are, at least partly, made up of cartilage. They are regarded as primitive fish. There are eight species of gar and they are mostly freshwater inhabitants. Gars are characteristically long and slender fish. They bask at the water's edge, breathing air. Their bodies are covered in thick scales. They lie in wait for prey, such as small fish, which they catch in their long beak-like jaws that are lined with small but sharp teeth.

➠ *Bony Fish, Sturgeons*

GECKOES

(Class: Reptilia Order: Squamata)

The name 'gecko' is applied to any member of the lizard family Gekkonidae. There are over 750 species of gecko and they are found in warm regions throughout the world. This large and successful group has been able to adapt to many habitats, from deserts to towns. Geckoes are typically small, nocturnal lizards that feed primarily on insects. Their digits end in 'suction' pads – pads covered in microscopic hooks – that enable the agile creatures to

climb vertical surfaces adeptly. Geckoes are able to detach their own tails when trapped and regenerate new ones. Geckoes are oviparous – egg-laying.

➠ *Lizards, Reptiles*

ABOVE LEFT The Galapagos tortoise and hawk are examples of subspecies
ABOVE Geckoes need to lick their eyes to keep them clean and moist.

GENETS
(Class: Mammalia Order: Carnivora)

Genets are very like civets, but smaller and with longer tails. They are cat-like in appearance, with blotches and stripes on their coats for camouflage. Genets are nocturnal carnivores which specialise in catching small mammals and birds. The small-spotted genet (*Genetta genetta*) has a range extending from Africa into Arabia, Spain and southern France, but it is rarely seen by people because it is so secretive. It hunts only under cover of darkness and hides during the day. Genets are prized for their fur in some areas, which probably accounts for their shyness of humans. They live largely solitary lives.

➠ *Cats, Civets*

GHARIALS
(Class: Reptilia Order: Crocodilia)

The gharial or gavial (*Gavialis gangeticus*) is a close relative of the crocodile and the alligator. It lives in the rivers of northern India. The gharial looks similar to a crocodile but its jaws are very slender and edged with small, sharp teeth, ideally suited for dealing with its diet of fish. These reptiles have weak limbs and move very slowly across land but are efficient predators in water. Gharials catch fish by sweeping their jaws from side to side underwater. When a gharial catches its prey it tosses it in the air so that it can be swallowed head first.

➠ *Alligators, Crocodiles*

GIANT SQUID
(Phylum: Mollusca Class: Cephalopoda)

This is the largest invertebrate on the planet. Dead specimens, washed up on beaches, have measured in excess of 10 m (33 ft) in length. However, evidence has shown that there are specimens in the deepest oceans that measure 24 m (80 ft). The evidence is found on the skin of sperm whales. The whales hunt squid for their food, and when they attack giant squid they become scarred by the suckers on the squids' tentacles as they fight for their lives. It is the size of these sucker marks that betray the dimensions of the squid. At that size a giant squid has eyes 1.8 m (6 ft) across.

Despite their enormous size, giant squid remain one of the mysteries of the deep because no one has ever managed to study one alive. Being cephalopods they are intelligent creatures. Coupled with their speed the only animals able to outwit them are sperm whales. Little is known of their life history consequently, but they too are predators of other marine animals, especially fish. They probably rise to the oceans surface at night to hunt under cover of darkness.

➠ *Cephalopods, Squid*

BELOW The gharial hunts in water as it cannot move quickly on land.

GIANT TOADS

(Class: Amphibia Order: Anura)

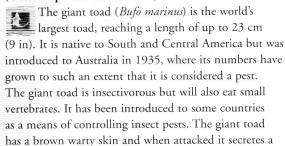 The giant toad (*Bufo marinus*) is the world's largest toad, reaching a length of up to 23 cm (9 in). It is native to South and Central America but was introduced to Australia in 1935, where its numbers have grown to such an extent that it is considered a pest. The giant toad is insectivorous but will also eat small vertebrates. It has been introduced to some countries as a means of controlling insect pests. The giant toad has a brown warty skin and when attacked it secretes a potent milky venom, from glands on its shoulders, to deter predators.

➡ *Frogs, Toads*

GIBBONS

(Class: Mammalia Order: Primates)

Gibbons are sometimes described as the 'lesser apes' to distinguish them from their relatives, the 'great apes'. They are obviously smaller and are far more arboreal too. In fact, gibbons rarely bother to descend to the ground, unless they decide to cross a clearing in the forest or if they fall, which happens quite often. A study of gibbon skeletons has shown that many suffer fractures and breaks to their bones as a result of accidents.

The reason is that they have evolved for a specialised form of locomotion, known as brachiation. It involves the animals swinging from one handhold to the next like a pendulum. Gibbons have relatively long arms with hook-like hands and squat bodies for the job. They can travel at remarkable speeds but it is inevitable that occasional

errors of judgement will occur. All it takes is a weak branch or a missed handhold and the animal is in trouble.

* At full momentum gibbons can hurl themselves across gaps up to 10 m (33 ft) wide.
* Gibbons are unable to swim as a result of their specialised design, so they are deeply afraid of water.
* To communicate through the canopy gibbons emit very loud calls to one another.

➡ *Apes, Primates*

GILA MONSTERS

(Class: Reptilia Order: Squamata)

 Named after the Gila River basin in Mexico, this lizard is a distinctive inhabitant of south-western USA and northern Mexico. The gila monster (*Heloderma suspectum*) is one of only two lizards that produce venom, so that they can incapacitate prey quickly, before it escapes into the desert. Gila monsters live in semi-desert and scrub habitats. They feed at night in warm weather and store up fat in their tails and bodies. When winter comes they hibernate in burrows, living off their stored fat.

The Gila monster has a stout, heavy body that is boldly patterned in black and pink with shiny, bead-like scales to warn off its own potential predators. It reaches 50 cm (20 in). It has large muscular legs for digging burrows, where it lays its eggs or hibernates. The teeth of a Gila monster have grooves that carry venom from the lower jaw, where it is produced, into the body of a victim.

LEFT The gibbon's long arms and small body make travel in the canopy easy.
ABOVE Gila monsters can poison their prey to prevent it from escaping.

❖ The venom is a nerve poison that will kill the gila monster's normal prey of small mammals and birds. It is not thought to be fatal to humans.

❖ The gila monster is considered a vulnerable species and its future in the wild is uncertain.

➠ *Lizards, Reptiles*

GIRAFFES

(Class: Mammalia Order: Artiodactyla)

Giraffes fall between deer and cattle in evolutionary terms. Were it not for their long necks and legs the similarities would seem more obvious. They are creatures of the scrub and savannah in Africa and have evolved to browse on the highest tree branches to avoid competing with other herbivores for food. The giraffe (*Giraffa camelopardalis*) is a single species, with several sub-species from different areas – distinguished by different patterns on their hides. The okapi (*Okapia johnstoni*) is a near relative that lives in dense forest. Giraffes were once thought to be a cross between a camel and a leopard.

➠ *Cattle, Deer*

GIRDLED LIZARDS

(Class: Reptilia Order: Squamata)

The scaly skins of lizards offers some protection from attack. The scales of the girdled lizards are further modified to produce an effective armour. These lizards are characterised by rings of enlarged spiny scales that encircle their tails. In some species these scales extend the whole length of the body, up to the neck. The sungazer (*Cordylus giganteus*), a burrowing girdled lizard, blocks the entrance to its burrow with its armoured tail. If threatened it digs the spiny scales of its neck and back into the burrow sides, anchoring it firmly in place and preventing the predator from extracting it.

➠ *Lizards, Reptiles*

GLASS LIZARDS

(Class: Reptilia Order: Squamata)

The glass lizards are sometimes known as glass snakes. Although they are limbless, and may resemble snakes, these reptiles belong to the same family of lizards as monitors and the gila monster. They are called glass lizards – or snakes – because their tails break away as easily as snapping glass. This is a defence mechanism that leaves a predator holding the wriggling tail while the reptile makes its escape. The European glass lizard (*Ophisaurus apodus*) is common in southeastern Europe and western Asia. It burrows through loose soil and vegetation or lurks beneath stones. It can reach 120 cm (4 ft).

➠ *Lizards, Slow-Worms*

ABOVE Thanks to their long necks, giraffes do not have to compete for food.

GOANNAS

(Class: Reptilia Order: Squamata)

'Goanna' is an Australian corruption of 'iguana'. Also known as the sand monitor, Gould's goanna (*Varanus gouldi*) is native to Australasia. Gould's goannas are large lizards, reaching 100 cm (36 in). Their long and muscular tails are used as weapons against predators but are also used to balance the lizards when they stand upright on their hind legs. Gould's goannas have long forked tongues which they use to taste the air for prey. They eat small mammals, reptiles and birds which they capture with their sharp claws and teeth. These lizards are ground-dwelling and typically shelter in burrows or crevices.

➡ *Iguanas, Lizards*

GOATFISH

(Class: Osteichthyes Order: Perciformes)

The term 'goatfish' is used to describe approximately 50 species of fish in the family Mullidae. They are characterised by four or five barbels – tactile appendages – on the lower jaw. The barbels are used to locate small invertebrates on the sea-floor and are tucked into grooves on the throat when they are not needed. These fish are often brightly coloured in red or yellow and some species are able to change colour. Goatfish are marine and inhabit shallow water in warm and tropical regions, especially near coral reefs. Red mullet (*Mullus surmuletus*) is sometimes simply called the goatfish.

➡ *Bony Fish, Mullets*

GOATS

(Class: Mammalia Order: Artiodactyla)

Mountainous slopes are the ideal habitat for goats. They are perfectly adapted for eking out a living in terrain that would prove too harsh for related animals, such as cattle and sheep. Their stomachs are able to cope with all manner of vegetable matter, which is why they will readily attempt to eat clothing and paper. The wild goat (*Capra hircus*) is believed to be the ancestor of all domestic goats, and still exists in the mountains of Asia

ABOVE Goats are not fussy eaters; they can digest almost any vegetable matter.
RIGHT Some gobies share accommodation with other marine creatures.

Minor. Other wild goats are known as ibex. Two species are the alpine ibex (*Capra ibex*) and pyrenean ibex (*Capra pyrenaica*).

➡ *Cattle, Sheep*

GOBIES

(Class: Osteichthyes Order: Perciformes)

There are over 800 species of fish in this suborder Gobioidei, more than 700 of which belong to the goby family – Gobiidae. There is a wide array of these fish, which inhabit tropical and temperate marine waters, but are also found in estuaries and freshwater. Most species are bottom-dwellers and live in coastal areas or

around coral reefs. Some gobies burrow into the sea bottom, occasionally sharing the burrows of other marine creatures. Gobies eat small crustaceans and invertebrates.

The pelvic fins of some gobies are fused into a shallow, funnel-like disc. This pelvic disc is able to create a weak suction for holding onto rocks. The bodies of gobies are typically long and slender. In some species the body lacks scales. Some species are drab while others are brightly coloured. Gobies are territorial fish and adult males defend their territories, which surround a nest. Females are invited into the territory by means of courtship display. The males guard the fertilized eggs until they hatch. The larvae live among the plankton until they settle to the sea bottom, a few weeks after hatching. Some species act as symbiotic cleaners, by picking parasites from the bodies of other fish as food.

➠ *Bony Fish, Fish*

GOLDFISH
(Class: Osteichthyes Order: Cypriniformes)

Goldfish belong to the same group of fish as the carps and minnows. They are classified as one species – *Carassius auratus* – but over 125 different breeds of this ornamental pet fish exist.

Goldfish are native to south and east Asia but they have been introduced successfully to freshwater regions worldwide. In their native form goldfish are olive-green, brown or grey. They were adopted as pets by the Chinese of the Sung Dynasty at least a thousand years ago. The native species is prone to considerable variation in colour and form and it is this characteristic that led to its being selectively bred. Goldfish can now be found in a huge range of colours and shapes. The most common colour is orange-red but goldfish may be white, black, silvery or patterned. Breeding has produced fish with flowing tails, protruding eyes or swollen masses on the head.

❀ Goldfish were first brought to Britain in the late seventeenth century and are now popular pets. The breeding of goldfish is carried out commercially in many countries to serve the pet industry.

❀ When released back into the wild, goldfish populations eventually resume their natural colouration, with individuals growing to 30 cm (12 in).

➠ *Carp, Minnows*

BELOW The grass snake is a good swimmer and kills its prey with venom.

GOLIATH FROGS
(Class: Amphibia Order: Anura)

The largest frog in world is the goliath frog (*Conraua goliath*) of West Africa. It can grow to an overall length of 40 cm (16 in) and is found in Cameroon and Equatorial Guinea where it inhabits rivers, swamps and ponds in regions of tropical rainforest. It lives an aquatic lifestyle, rarely venturing onto land. If approached it quickly retreats to the relative safety of deeper water. The goliath frog eats small mammals, reptiles and other frogs. It has a smooth, camouflaged skin and muscular hind limbs. Unusually, the male is larger than the female. Mating occurs during the rainy season.

➠ *Frogs, Giant Toads*

GRASS SNAKES
(Class: Reptilia Order: Squamata)

The grass snake (*Natrix natrix*) is one of about 80 species of water snake worldwide. It is also known as the European water snake and, like other members of this group, it spends much of its time either in water or moist habitats. It is an efficient swimmer and hunts in water for its diet of frogs or fish, which it kills with a venomous bite. Grass snakes are dark green to black in colour with small black dots on the dorsal surface. There are white, yellow or orange markings on the neck. They produce a foul secretion when threatened.

➠ *Reptiles, Snakes*

GRASSHOPPERS

(Class: Insecta Order: Orthoptera)

Grasshoppers, ground-hoppers and locusts differ from the crickets in several ways. They have short antennae, they are mostly vegetarian and they are diurnal. In addition, they stridulate or chirp by rubbing their hind legs against their wings, rather than rubbing both wings together. As their name implies, grasshoppers tend to feed on grasses, but locusts will eat any vegetation, especially when they swarm. Grasshoppers are good fliers as adults, launching themselves into the air with their powerful hind limbs. They tend to be cryptically coloured in greens and browns, but their hind wings are sometimes brightly coloured red, pink, orange or blue.

➡ ***Crickets, Locusts***

GREAT WHITE SHARKS

(Class: Chondrichthyes Order: Lamniformes)

The great white shark (*Carcharodon carcharias*) is also known as the 'white death' due to its fearsome reputation. It belongs to the same family as the mackerel shark and the mako – the lamniforms. Its body is robust with a greyish-brown or slate-bluish colour on the back, with a white underbelly. The triangular teeth have the serrated edges that are characteristic of its family. The first dorsal fin is triangular and rigid, the second dorsal fin is much smaller and placed near the tail. The tail fin is shaped like a scythe.

The appearance of the great white shark is familiar to most people since it has a reputation as a fierce and deadly killer. It is certainly an efficient predator of dolphins, seals and other fish. When the shark attacks prey it takes several bites before retreating to safety while the dying animal loses strength. It then returns to finish its meal. Great white sharks do attack humans but it is a relatively rare occurrence.

❖ These sharks are found in tropical and temperate waters worldwide. However, some authorities believe

TOP Locusts, when swarming, are able to destroy entire fields of crops.
ABOVE Although not designed for walking, grebes are exceptional divers.

their numbers are dwindling owing to over-fishing of the sharks' food supply coupled with the capture of these fish as trophies.

➡ ***Cartilaginous Fish, Sharks***

GREBES

(Class: Aves Order: Podicipediformes)

This family of diving birds contains 20 species. Grebes are found throughout the world in tropical and temperate sheltered waters. They have long pointed bills and short narrow wings. Their legs are set back to ease diving and swimming but this makes walking more awkward. Grebes are extremely agile when

swimming. They dive below the surface of the water in search of fish and invertebrates. Many species have bright ear tufts and crests in summer, with dull plumage in winter. Both sexes look alike. Grebes are notable for their complex courtship rituals that involve elaborate dancing and exchange of gifts.

➡ ***Auks, Divers***

GRUNTS

(Class: Osteichthyes Order: Perciformes)

These marine fish are sometimes known as drums. Both names derive from the fish's ability to produce noise in their throats. Grunts are valued as a source of food, although most species are small. They inhabit warm waters in the Atlantic, Pacific and Indian Oceans and over 75 species are recognized. Grunts have short first dorsal and anal fins. Some species have red linings to their lips and others are characterised by an unusual behavioural tendency to approach one another and 'kiss'. Grunts are varied in appearance. They can be striped in blues, yellows or have black markings.

➠ **Bony Fish, Fish**

GULLS

(Class: Aves Order: Charadriiformes)

Some of the most abundant coastal birds are members of the gull family. Unlike their close relatives, the waders and auks, many gulls are not solely dependent on marine habitats for finding food. As well as sea food many species will forage inland, for insects, other invertebrates and even organic refuse. Some species are pirates, scavenging food from other birds, as well as taking eggs and young. Some 80-odd species are recognized. They include about 40 gulls, an equal number of terns and three skimmers. They typically have white bodies with black or grey upperwing surfaces, and bright beaks and legs.

➠ **Auks, Waders**

GUPPIES

(Class: Osteichthyes Order: Cyprinodontiformes)

Guppies (*Poecilia reticulata*) are inhabitants of freshwater regions over the southern Caribbean Sea and northern South America. They are valued locally because they eat the larvae of malaria-carrying mosquitoes. Guppies also have a considerable commercial value as aquarium fish.

Male guppies grow to about 40 mm (1.5 in) and are much brighter than the females. Selective breeding has

BELOW Gulls are primarily coastal birds, but move inland in search of food.

produced a range of pet guppies in various colours. They may be red, yellow, orange, blue, green and purple, and marked with stripes, blotches or bands. No two fish are identical in colour or markings. Guppies are also selectively bred to encourage the development of fancy tails and fins.

Males engage in elaborate courtship rituals but once they have mated the females store sperm for future use. At each spawning a female may produce up to 120 live young in a litter. Up to five litters may be fertilized following one mating and a new litter is produced every four weeks. This prolific output of young is balanced by their low survival rate.

❧ In addition to predators the young are frequently eaten by their own parents.

❧ Those that remain hidden in dense vegetation until they mature are more likely to escape this parental cannibalism.

➠ **Fish, Tetras**

GURNARDS

(Class: Osteichthyes Order: Dactylopteriformes)

The gurnards are marine, bottom-dwelling fish that are found in warm and temperate seas around the world. Their heads are large and armoured with bony scales or plates. The pectoral fins are modified into a fan-shape with several rays separated and used as sensitive feelers. These feelers probe the sea bottom as the fish moves along it, searching for prey such as crustaceans and other invertebrates. The pectoral fins are often brightly coloured, as with the flying gurnard (*Dactylopterus volitans*). Gurnards, such as the sea robin (*Prionotus carolinus*), are able to create sound by vibrating their swim-bladders.

➠ **Bony Fish, Fish**

HADDOCK

(Class: Osteichthyes Order: Gadiformes)

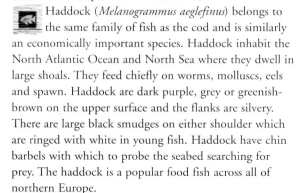 Haddock (*Melanogrammus aeglefinus*) belongs to the same family of fish as the cod and is similarly an economically important species. Haddock inhabit the North Atlantic Ocean and North Sea where they dwell in large shoals. They feed chiefly on worms, molluscs, eels and spawn. Haddock are dark purple, grey or greenish-brown on the upper surface and the flanks are silvery. There are large black smudges on either shoulder which are ringed with white in young fish. Haddock have chin barbels with which to probe the seabed searching for prey. The haddock is a popular food fish across all of northern Europe.

➠ *Cod, Mackerel*

HAGFISH

(Class: Agnatha Order: Myxinidae)

Hagfish and lampreys are the two remaining representatives of an ancient group of fish – the agnathans – which first appeared 500 million years ago. Hagfish have eel-like bodies that lack scales and are covered with mucous, giving rise to the common name 'slime eels'. They lack jaws and have paired barbels at the end of their snouts. Hagfish live at the bottom of the sea, feeding off dead fish. They tie their bodies in knots and, as they feed, movement of the knot enables the hagfish to withdraw its head from within the carcass on which it is feeding.

➠ *Eels, Lampreys*

HAKE

(Class: Osteichthyes Order: Gadiformes)

Hake are usually considered to be members of the codfish family, along with whitings and pollacks. However, they are sometimes placed in a separate family – Merlucciidae – because of slight differences in their skull structure. They are entirely marine fish that inhabit the Atlantic and Pacific Oceans at various depths. Hake typically move to shallow water for spawning. They are usually silvery, reddish-brown or pale brown in colour.

ABOVE The hammerhead's peculiar shape enables it to hunt more efficiently.
RIGHT Hares do not dig burrows and so can run faster than rabbits.

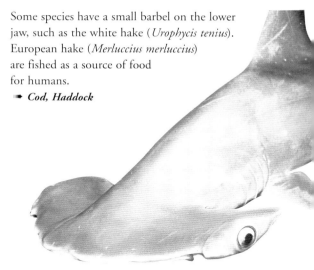

Some species have a small barbel on the lower jaw, such as the white hake (*Urophycis tenius*). European hake (*Merluccius merluccius*) are fished as a source of food for humans.

➠ *Cod, Haddock*

HAMMERHEAD SHARKS

(Class: Chondrichthyes Order: Carchariniformes)

Hammerheads are moderate to large sharks with five gill slits. The upper lobe of the tail is longer than the lower. The first dorsal fin is larger than the second and the round eyes have blinking membranes. Hammerheads have blade-like teeth and the front portions of their heads are flattened and extended into lobes on either side. Eyes and nostrils are placed at the ends of the lobes. It is believed that these projections confer two advantages on the sharks. Firstly, the rudder-shape of the head enables the shark to move more swiftly and easily. Secondly, the position of the eyes and nostrils enables the shark to detect prey more accurately. Like most other sharks, hammerheads give birth to live young.

❧ Hammerhead sharks all belong to the genus Sphyrna.
❧ There are 10 species of hammerhead and they are found in tropical and temperate marine waters. They live in deep water, in coastal regions or even in brackish water. Hammerheads eat fish, stingrays, skates and other sharks.
❧ The great hammerhead poses the greatest threat to humans, having attacked divers. It can reach 4.5 m (15 ft) long. The scalloped, smooth and common hammerhead sharks are also known to have attacked people.

➠ *Great White Sharks, Sharks*

HAMSTERS
(Class: Mammalia Order: Rodentia)

Hamsters are small burrowing rodents. There are some 18 species known. They are characterised by possessing rotund bodies with short hairy tails. Hamsters typically go into semi-hibernation during winter months. They spend the summer and autumn months hoarding foodstuffs so that they can feed periodically from their stores. They have pouch-like cheeks that stretch to accommodate large amounts of food so that they can take fewer journeys to and from their nests. The common hamster (*Cricetus cricetus*) is typical. It feeds on a wide variety of fruits, vegetables, seeds and even small animals, which are all stored in separate chambers.

➡ *Lemmings, Rodents*

HARES
(Class: Mammalia Order: Lagomorpha)

Closely related to rabbits, hares have a different lifestyle altogether. This is reflected by their design. They have longer ears to catch the slightest hint of danger approaching. They are also built for speed with far longer limbs than rabbits, capable of propelling them at 70 kph

BELOW Hamsters hoard food and save it for when they hibernate.

(40 mph). This is because, unlike rabbits, hares do not dig burrows, but remain above ground. So they need to detect and escape predators effectively. Hares tend to be fairly nocturnal for the same reason. During the day they lie in dense vegetation, making a hollow for themselves called a form.

➡ *Mammals, Rodents*

HARVESTMEN
(Class: Arachnida Order: Opiliones)

Along with crane-flies, harvestmen are often known colloquially as daddy-long-legs, although quite unrelated to one another. Harvestmen are similar to their relatives, the spiders, but have a few special characteristics. For one, their bodies are not clearly divided in two. Instead they have a single globular body part which carries the limbs, eyes and mouth parts. Harvestmen lack venom for killing prey and are unable to spin silk for webs. They feed on small invertebrates at night, and will take both live and dead food. There are long-legged and short-legged harvestmen, that live in undergrowth or on the ground respectively.

➡ *Arachnids, Spiders*

HEAVY BILLS

(Class: Aves Order: Ciconiiformes)

 The heavy bills are certain members of the order Ciconiiformes with exceptionally robust bills. They include the boat-billed heron (*Cochlearius cochlearius*), the whalehead or shoebill stork (*Balaeniceps rex*) and the hammerhead (*Scopus umbretta*). Their relatives are the herons, ibises, storks, spoonbills and flamingos. Their bills are not actually very heavy; like those of toucans they are light but strong. The advantage of having a large bill for a waterbird is that large mouthfuls of mud can be scooped up, so that it becomes easier to catch aquatic animals such as frogs. Following a quick rinse, the prey can then be swallowed.

➠ *Herons, Storks*

HEDGEHOGS

(Class: Mammalia Order: Insectivora)

There are two distinct types of animal in the family Erinaceidae. There are those with spines, known as hedgehogs, and those without spines but with tails, called moonrats. All are classified as insectivores. As well as insects they will take many other invertebrates and small vertebrates, such as birds, rodents and reptiles. The common hedgehog (*Erinaceus europaeus*) is noted for its immunity to snake bites, and the desert hedgehog (*Paraechinus aethiopicus*) has an immunity to scorpion stings. Both hedgehogs and moonrats will also eat carrion as well as a variety of fruits. Northern species hibernate for winter to conserve their energy.

➠ *Echidnas, Insectivores*

HERBIVORES

Any animal that mainly eats plant matter is called a herbivore. Vegetarian is another word that can be used. More specifically, an animal that eats mainly leaves or foliage is called a folivore, and an animal that eats mainly fruit is called a frugivore. Caterpillars are folivores and fruit bats are frugivores. There are many, many herbivores. In fact, to be a herbivore is synonymous with being a prey animal, and nearly all classes of animal comprise both herbivore and carnivore species so that a balance between prey and predator is maintained.

Herbivores and carnivores are not necessarily mutually exclusive because many of them actually have an omnivorous diet to a greater or lesser extent when studied in detail. Being a herbivore means that food is usually more readily available than it is for a carnivore. However, plant matter is generally less nutritious than flesh, so a herbivore needs to spend far more time feeding and digesting its food, and this makes it more vulnerable to predation. So there is a clear trade-off.

❧ Deer are typical herbivores. They spend a great deal of time grazing and browsing vegetation, but they have to remain alert to spot predators.

➠ *Carnivore, Omnivore*

HERMIT CRABS

(Subphylum: Crustacea Class: Malacostraca)

Hermit crabs differ from typical crabs in certain ways as a result of having evolved in a peculiar direction. Unlike typical crabs they lack the hard carapace that covers the body because they use the shells of dead molluscs as protection instead. Their bodies are asymmetric as a result because they need to follow the curve of spiralling shell – usually to the right – although some species do live in straight shells. Hermit crabs have rough pads on their abdomens which they use to anchor themselves inside their shells by pushing against the sides. They change shells as they grow.

➠ *Crabs, Crustaceans*

RIGHT Hermit crabs inherit their shells from deceased molluscs.
FAR RIGHT Hippos submerge themselves in water to keep cool.

HERONS

(Class: Aves Order: Ciconiiformes)

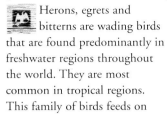 Herons, egrets and bitterns are wading birds that are found predominantly in freshwater regions throughout the world. They are most common in tropical regions. This family of birds feeds on  frogs, fish and other small animals they hunt in shallow pools, swamps and marshes. Herons are typically social birds. They build their large nests on trees, often near the water's edge, in colonies called heronries. Herons have broad wings, long straight bills and 'S' shaped necks. They possess a specialised patch of feathers – the 'powder down' – which disintegrates to form a powder that the birds use for preening.

➥ *Cranes, Storks*

HERRINGS

(Class: Osteichthyes Order: Clupeiformes)

This is one of the largest and most economically important groups of fish. The herring group comprises approximately 200 members worldwide, including the Atlantic herring (*Clupea harengus*), pilchard (*Sardina pichardus*) and European anchovy (*Engraulis encrasicolus*). The term 'sardine' is commonly applied to young pilchards. All these fish are widespread and abundant in the northern hemisphere.

Herring are small, silvery, streamlined fish. Their heads are small and their bodies are covered in iridescent scales. Herrings represent an important stage in the marine food web. They are a principal consumer of the tiny organic life-forms known as plankton. These are sieved from the water using gill rakers. Herrings, in turn, provide a source of food for larger fish, seals, birds, whales and humans. In order to preserve herring populations for the future the fishing industry is now highly regulated and monitored, preventing further over-exploitation.

❧ At spawning time, which is usually in the spring, herrings move closer to coastal regions and the females lay up to 40,000 eggs each on seaweed or rocks.

❧ The eggs hatch after only two weeks and the adults return to the open sea. Herring young reach maturity after four years and may live for around 20 years.

➥ *Cod, Haddock*

LEFT A great blue heron in a cypress swamp in Florida.

HIPPOPOTAMUSES

(Class: Mammalia Order: Artiodactyla)

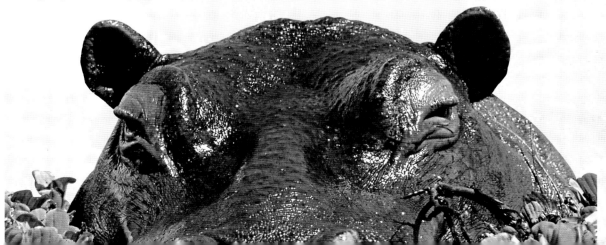 There are two species of hippopotamus or hippo: the common hippopotamus (*Hippopotamus amphibius*) and the pygmy hippopotamus (*Choeropsis liberiensis*). They are both semi-aquatic creatures but they frequent different habitats. The common hippo lives in large rivers and lakes in open areas of Africa. The pygmy hippo inhabits damp, forested areas with freshwater. Common hippos regulate their temperature during the day by adjusting their level of submersion. At night they leave the water altogether to feed on waterside vegetation. They eat little for their size, though, because they use very little energy by floating in water the rest of the time.

➥ *Herbivores, Mammals*

HOATZINS

(Class: Aves Order: Cuciliformes)

This ancient and unusual bird is found only in South America, predominantly in the swamps of the Amazon and Orinoco river basins. The hoatzin (*Opisthocomus hoazin*) reaches 65 cm (25 in) in length, but weighs less than 1 kg (2.2 lb). Unlike most other birds they are able to feed exclusively on plant matter which they digest in a large stomach. They provide a glimpse at bird evolution as they have primitive skeletal characteristics and the young have clawed digits on the wings like the fossil bird archaeopteryx. Hoatzins live in small groups and share the parenting of the young.

➽ *Birds, Reptiles*

HONEYCREEPERS

(Class: Aves Order: Passeriformes)

The name 'honeycreepers' applies to birds from two families. The honeycreepers of the family Thraupidae frequent the American tropics. There are 35 species, also known as 'sugarbirds' because they feed on nectar. They are small birds with brilliantly coloured plumage and long thin bills. The honeycreepers of the family Drepanididae, however, live exclusively in the

ABOVE Hoatzins are a primitive species, giving an insight into bird evolution.
ABOVE RIGHT Most honeycreepers are brightly coloured and feed on nectar.

Hawaiian islands. The Hawaiian honeycreepers are a varied bunch due to their having evolved from a sole ancestor in geographical isolation. Some are nectar feeders while others feed on seeds, fruits or insects. Eight of the 23 species have become extinct. Those remaining are endangered.

➽ *Honeyeaters, Hummingbirds*

HONEYEATERS

(Class: Aves Order: Passeriformes)

There are 170 species of honeyeater. They live in Australia, New Guinea and the western Pacific islands, where they are common birds, frequently seen in woodland areas. Not surprisingly, such a large group of birds show considerable variation in form and lifestyle. They range in size from 10–35 cm (4–14 in) and they are typically dull in colour but there are colourful exceptions. They have slender, downcurved bills with brush tongues that are ideally suited to lapping nectar from deep flowers. Besides nectar, honeyeaters also consume insects and fruit. Generally both sexes are usually quite similar in appearance.

➽ *Honeycreepers, Hummingbirds*

HONEYGUIDES

(Class: Aves Order: Piciformes)

There are 10 species of these small birds – eight in Africa, one in Malaysia and one in the Himalayas. Honeyguides are non-migratory, tropical birds that feed on bees and wasps. Some species are brood parasites. Like cuckoos, they lay their eggs in other birds' nests. The young hatchlings use their temporary bill hooks to kill or injure the hosts' chicks. Honeyguides usually live in pairs or alone, in woodland or open grassland.

Honeyguides get their name from two African species – the black-throated or greater honeyguide (*Indicator indicator*) and the scaly-throated honeyguide. These birds lead honey badgers (*Mellivora capensis*), and tribesmen, to bees' nests by flying ahead and chattering. They wait patiently until the honey is removed from the nest. The birds can then approach and feast on the beeswax and exposed larvae. They possess special bacteria in their guts that enable them to digest wax.

❖ The lyre-tailed honeyguide inhabits lowland forests where it feeds on bees, ants and beeswax. It is renowned for its superb courtship displays, performed by both sexes. The courting birds fly high above the trees, then swoop downwards in a spiralling fashion. As the birds descend the air passing through their wings produces sound.

➥ *Bee-Eaters, Rollers*

HOOPOES

(Class: Aves Order: Coraciiformes)

There is only one species in this family – the hoopoe (*Upupa epops*). It is related to kingfishers, kookaburras, bee-eaters and hornbills. Hoopoes are found in Europe, Asia and Africa. They are 28 cm (11 in) in length and have bold markings in black and white on their wings and tails. The pinkish-brown head is adorned with an erectile black and white crest. The slender, downward-curved bill is used to probe for insects and small invertebrates in the ground. Hoopoes have filthy nests full of rotting food and excrement. It is thought likely that the foul smell deters predators.

➥ *Hornbills, Kingfishers*

HOPPERS

(Class: Insecta Order: Hemiptera)

These insects differ from other bugs and are often put in a separate order, Homoptera. They tend to have their wings held in a roof-like manner over their bodies and they usually have far shorter antennae. There are treehoppers, froghoppers and leafhoppers. They all feed by inserting a needle-like proboscis into the stems of plants and siphoning off the sap. Some species mimic thorns and buds as a form of protection from predators. Others use warning colouration for the same purpose. The nymph larva of the common froghopper is responsible for producing the foamy substance on plants stems known colloquially as cuckoo-spit.

➥ *Bugs, Cicadas*

HORNBILLS

(Class: Aves Order: Coraciiformes)

Birds from this family are characterised by a horny growth mounted above the bill – the casque. There are 45 species of hornbill, all found in tropical areas in forest or woodland habitats. Two species are ground-dwelling. One is the southern ground-hornbill (*Bucorvus cafer*), which is 1.3 m (50 in) long and the largest of all hornbills. Plumage is predominantly dark with white wing flashes. The nest is built inside a tree cavity. After the eggs are laid the male seals the female into the cavity with mud, as protection from predators, and passes food through a slot while she incubates.

➥ *Hoopoes, Toucans*

HORNED TOADS

(Class: Reptilia Order: Squamata)

Despite their name these are lizards, not toads. They have squat, rounded bodies and spiky scales between head and neck. Horned toads – *Phrynosoma* spp – come from dry and hot regions in North and Central America. They are egg-laying, terrestrial lizards anywhere from 75–130 mm (3–5 in) in length. Their bodies are camouflaged with cryptic colours to suit their surroundings. Horned toads are insectivores and they scour the desert looking for insects – particularly ants. If a horned toad senses a predator it remains motionless, relying on its camouflage to conceal its whereabouts, until the threat has passed.

➥ *Lizards, Reptiles*

BELOW Horned toads are actually lizards. They feed on ants and other insects.

HORNED VIPERS

(Class: Reptilia Order: Squamata)

Vipers are among the most specialised and highly evolved snakes. A number of species have developed modifications to the head, such as 'horns' that may help the snake appear more threatening to predators, or they may have other functions as yet undiscovered. The horned viper (*Cerastes cerastes*), of the Old World, has a spiny horn above each eye. It uses a method of locomotion known as 'sidewinding' to move over sand. The sidewinder rattlesnake (*Crotalus cerastes*), of the New World, has adopted the exact same way of travelling, so the two snakes are a clear example of convergent evolution.

➠ *Snakes, Vipers*

HORSES

(Class: Mammalia Order: Perissodactyla)

Like other domesticated animals, there are many types of horse, ranging from the stocky cart horse to the elegant Arabian horse. They all belong to the same species though – *Equus caballus* – which, until recently, lived in the wild in Mongolia. Images of ancestral horses have been found in European caves, where they were painted on the walls by prehistoric people, maybe 20,000 years ago. Przewalski's horses are now being bred in various zoos to keep the subspecies alive.

Other members of the horse family include the zebras and asses. Zebras are typically camouflaged with black and white stripes on their hides, which are effective against the, colour-blind, big cats. There are several species and many subspecies across Africa. There are two species of wild ass: the African wild ass (*Equus africanus*) and the Asian wild ass (*Equus Hemionus*). Like horses, asses have been domesticated successfully as beasts of burden. The donkey (*Equus asinus*) has been bred from the African wild ass.

ABOVE The stripes of this young zebra make it less visible to predators.
ABOVE RIGHT Horseshoe crabs are in fact more closely related to spiders.

✿ Mules and hinnies are sterile hybrids of donkeys and horses – male + female and female + male respectively – while jackasses are male donkeys.

➠ *Herbivores, Tapirs*

HORSESHOE CRABS

(Class: Merostoma)

Although these marine creatures are called horseshoe crabs or king crabs they are unrelated to familiar crabs, as they are not crustaceans but merostomes. In fact they are more closely related to spiders. Fossil merostomes are well known and modern day species are almost unchanged after hundreds of millions of years. There are five species of horseshoe crab. They possess a leathery

horseshoe-shaped thorax with a pair of compound eyes mounted on top. Beneath the body five pairs of legs are concealed. Behind the thorax is a short abdomen armed with a spine-like tail used for righting the animal.

➠ *Crabs, Spiders*

HUMMINGBIRDS

(Class: Aves Order: Apodiformes)

The hummingbirds, famous for their flying prowess, are related to swifts. Hummingbirds' unique wing structure and musculature enables them to hover, fly backwards, sideways and even upside down. They can beat their wings up to 80 times per second. Hummingbirds are usually small birds with bright, often metallic, plumage. They are specialised in eating nectar and pollen from exotic flowers. The bee hummingbird (*Calypte helenae*) is one of the world's smallest warm-blooded vertebrates. It is only 55 mm (2 in) long and weighs 2 g (0.14 oz). Some 320 species are recognized, most are native to South America.

➠ *Birds, Swifts*

HYDRAS
(Phylum: Cnidaria Class: Hydrozoa)

Hydras are small aquatic animals that belong to the coelenterate or cnidarian group, which includes jellyfish, corals and sea anemones. They are tube-like in design, with a mouth at one end and an anus at the other. Surrounding the mouth is a ring of stinging tentacles with which the hydra captures and manipulates its prey. Hydras feed on other aquatic invertebrates, such as small crustaceans. Unlike their relatives, hydras are adapted to live in freshwater habitats, including ponds, lakes and streams, and are found worldwide.

For hydrozoans to live in freshwater rather than saltwater it has taken a considerable evolutionary leap because of the problem of osmosis, which would cause a marine species to inflate until it burst if it were placed in freshwater. Hydras therefore possess a cuticle that is not permeable to water. The name 'hydra' originates from Ancient Greek mythology. The hydra was a snake with an ability to regenerate its many heads when they were lopped off with a sword. Similarly hydras have the remarkable ability to regenerate any body part into an entire organism.

❧ The most common British species is the green hydra (*Chlorohydra viridissima*).
❧ The most common American species is the brown hydra (*Pelmatohyrda oligactis*).
➠ *Corals, Jellyfish*

HYENAS
(Class: Mammalia Order: Carnivora)

Hyenas were once thought to be degenerate evolutionary survivors that were effectively on their way to extinction. This was partly because of their scavenging habits, but also because they seem to have such ungainly proportions, being very front-heavy. In fact they are very well designed for hunting and scavenging in equal measure, demonstrating

BELOW The spotted hyena lives in groups on the African plains.

that being a 'jack-of-all-trades' can be a very effective survival strategy on the African continent. The spotted hyena (*Crocuta crocuta*) is the most familiar species, living on the African plains in social groups. There is also the brown hyena (*Hyaena brunnea*) and the striped hyena (*Hyaena hyaena*).
➠ *Carnivores, Dogs*

HYRAXES
(Class: Mammalia Order: Hyracoidae)

These are small, compact animals that look distinctly rodent-like. In fact they are descended from the same line as elephants, but have obviously evolved in another direction. There are several species, all of which live across Africa and Arabia. They typically frequent hideaways among rocks or trees during the day and venture out to feed at dusk. Their diet is primarily herbivorous but they will also eat insects, lizards and eggs. Most hyraxes live in colonies. All hyraxes are well adapted for climbing, with hoof-like nails and moist soles to their feet which provide an improved grip on dry surfaces.
➠ *Elephants, Rodents*

IBISES
(Class: Aves Order: Ciconiiformes)

Ibises are wading birds like herons, but with long downward-curved bills. They inhabit most warm regions of the world, building their nests at the edges of lakes and rivers. They hunt for fish, amphibians and invertebrates in the shallows. During the breeding season ibises live in vast colonies with thousands of members. Plumage varies greatly. The scarlet ibis (*Eudocimus ruber*) is bright red, while the glossy ibis (*Plegadis falcinellus*) has a greenish metallic sheen. The sacred ibis (*Threskiornis aethiopica*), once venerated as the god Thoth by the ancient Egyptians, has a white body with a black tail and head.
➠ *Herons, Storks*

ICE CAP LIFE

Although the two poles are both characterised by freezing temperatures and ice and snow, they are fundamentally different because Antarctica is a land continent while the Arctic is nothing more than a mass of floating ice, fringed by a few islands. Being on opposite sides of the earth their seasons mirror one another, and this has led to the evolution of some remarkable migratory species. The Arctic tern (*Sterna paradisaea*) breeds on the rim of the Arctic during the Arctic summer. It then flies all the way to the Antarctic to 'over winter' in the Antarctic summer.

Similarly, various baleen whales make the journey from Arctic to Antarctic waters, and vice versa, each corresponding spring in search of plankton blooms. Each polar region also has its indigenous species, in particular species of seabird. The Arctic is home to a family of birds called the auks, whilst the Antarctic has the penguins.

RIGHT Emperor penguins divide the tasks of parenthood between them.
FAR RIGHT Polar bears roll in the snow to prevent overheating.
ABOVE RIGHT The Arctic fox collects food and freezes it in the permafrost.
MAIN The tusks of a walrus can grow up to 1m (3 ft) long.

ICE CAP LIFE

ARCTIC

NORTH
AMERICA

EUROPE

Tropic of Cancer

ASIA

AFRICA

Equator

SOUTH
AMERICA

Tropic of Capricorn

AUSTRALIA

ANTARCTICA

ICEFISH

(Class: Osteichthyes)

The term 'icefish' is applied to several species of fish from two orders – Perciformes and Salmoniformes. These fish are able to survive the sub-zero waters of the Antarctic and southern oceans because their bodies have a number of suitable adaptations. Most notably they lack haemoglobin as well as the red blood cells that normally transport it within vertebrate circulation. However, they have highly efficient circulatory systems with large hearts so they are able to extract extra oxygen from the water via their gills. Some species, such as the Crocodile or Blackfin Icefish (*Chaenocephalus aceratus*), have antifreeze in their bodies.

➡ *Bony Fish, Salmon*

IGUANAS

(Class: Reptilia Order: Squamata)

The term 'iguana' is sometimes used loosely, describing all members of the superfamily Iguania, including chameleons, agamids and iguanids. However, it is used more commonly to denote just the larger iguanids, of which there are a dozen or so species. Like their relatives, iguanas are often brightly coloured. They are considered to be a fairly primitive group of lizards.

Iguanas are found mainly in the Americas and Madagascar, but also on some Pacific islands. They are predominantly terrestrial, except the marine iguana (*Conolophus subcristatus*) of the Galapagos Islands. They occupy a range of habitats – desert, rainforest and grassland. Like the chameleons, iguanas are able to change the colour of their skin, although over

ABOVE The rainforest-dwelling green iguana can grow up to 1.8 m (6 ft).
RIGHT Although not a true insectivore, the slow loris is an insect-eater.

a longer period of time. Males are often brighter in the mating season and the colouring of females may change following mating.

❧ The green iguana (*Iguana iguana*) is a common lizard from South America. It reaches 1.8 m (6 ft) and its green colour is an adaptation to life amidst rainforest foliage.

❧ Unlike most lizards it is almost entirely herbivorous, though immature specimens are likely to eat insects.

❧ Green iguanas commonly roam along branches overhanging water; if startled they drop to the water for safety.

➡ *Chameleons, Goannas*

INDIAN COBRAS

(Class: Reptilia Order: Squamata)

The Indian cobra (*Naja naja*) is one of the world's deadliest snakes. It is a common inhabitant of southeast Asia where it is responsible for as many as 10,000 human deaths yearly. The Indian cobra has fangs at the front of its mouth which it uses to inject lethal venom into its prey. The venom affects the nervous system, causing a rapid death. The high number of fatalities is undoubtedly due to the snake's tendency to live near houses, rivers and paddy fields. Mongooses are immune to the venom of the Indian cobra and are therefore its chief enemy.

➡ *Cobras, Snakes*

INSECTIVORES

The term 'insectivore' can refer to any animal that eats insects, spiders and other invertebrates as the greater part of its diet. Generally speaking though, insectivores tend to be small to medium-sized mammals

with specialised dentition, designed for crunching into the exoskeletons of such prey animals. They will actually take anything within a certain size, so small reptiles, birds and other mammals are counted. Flesh is flesh after all. There are some mammals that almost exclusively eat insects, such as the anteaters, pangolins, the aardvark and the aardwolf, that are not classed as insectivores even though they are insectivorous in habits.

The mammals that actually fall into the order Insectivora include hedgehogs, shrews, tenrecs, moles and desmans. Other mammals that fit the bill, but belong to other orders are the tarsier, aye-aye, lorises, marmosets, tamarins, elephant shrews, tree shrews, colugos and insectivorous bats. The teeth of insectivores are characteristically jagged and sharp. They are somewhat like the teeth of a saw, designed to pierce and cut through both hard and soft-bodied invertebrates, from beetles to worms.

❧ Shrews have such a rapid metabolism that they need to eat their own body weight in food daily to remain alive.

➠ *Hedgehogs, Moles*

INSECTS

(Phylum: Arthropoda Class: Insecta)

There are well over a million species of insect known to science and more are being described each year. They are, by far, the most successful group of arthropods, both in terms of sheer numbers and variety of species. The only significant environment they have failed to colonize is marine. The orders of insect species include Lepidoptera – butterflies and moths, Coleoptera – beetles, Diptera – flies, Odonata – dragonflies and damselflies, Phasmida – stick and leaf insects, Isoptera – termites, Hymenoptera – ants, bees and wasps, Dictyoptera – cockroaches and mantids, and Hemiptera – bugs.

Winged insects are divided into two major groups: endopterygote insects and exopterygote insects. These two scientific names actually refer to the manner in which their wings are formed, but the fundamental difference between the two groups is the way in which species develop into adults or imagoes. In exopterygote insects the eggs hatch into larvae called nymphs, which are essentially miniature versions of the adult form. The nymphs then grow to maturity by shedding their skins periodically to become larger. Each time they do this they undergo a transformation described as incomplete metamorphosis.

Endopterygote insects develop into adults through a series of distinct changes. They hatch from their eggs into larvae that look nothing like the adult form. Once the larvae have grown to capacity they shed their skins to become pupae, an intermediate phase where the components of the adult insect are formed and assembled. Finally the adult insects emerge from the pupae. The transformations from larva to pupa, and then pupa to adult are both described as complete metamorphosis.

❧ Insects cannot grow very large because they use spiracles, located in their abdomens, to breathe and not lungs.

❧ That is why the largest insect ever to have lived was a dragonfly, as it had a body with a high surface to volume ratio.

➠ *Arachnids, Invertebrates*

ABOVE More species of insect are constantly being discovered.

INVERTEBRATES

The animal kingdom is broadly divided into vertebrates and invertebrates. The former have vertebrae which make up a backbone or spine, which carries the spinal cord. The latter have no vertebrae, although they do often have a spinal cord. The invertebrates were the first animals to evolve, as they are more primitive in design than vertebrates, which evolved in turn from invertebrate ancestors. There are around 30 invertebrate phyla and these are further divided into many hundreds of classes, sub-classes, orders and suborders, families and genera. There are millions of invertebrate species, ranging in intelligence from single-celled organisms to octopuses.

Among the invertebrates are insects, arachnids, jellyfish, anemones, starfish, worms, molluscs, crustaceans and corals, to name but a few. Clearly they vary so much in design that it is impossible to describe them in an all-encompassing way. They comprise some 95 per cent of the world's fauna and have colonized just about every environment the world has to offer. Many invertebrate forms have remained virtually unchanged since having first evolved millions of years ago, such is the perfection of their designs in suiting particular habitats. We know this from fossil evidence.

Invertebrates evolved in water first of all. Eventually some lines managed to conquer land and sky, thereby populating the world over with life forms. Another key division in the invertebrates came with the evolution of predator and prey species, which played its part in accelerating change as species evolved to outwit one another for the sake of bettering their chances of survival.

❖ The largest invertebrate is the giant squid (*Architeuthis*) which may grow up to 24 m (80 ft) in length and weigh several tonnes.

❖ Bacteria and cyanobacteria are single-celled or unicellular organisms, but they are classified as prokaryotes, which are neither animal nor plant.

➠ *Vertebrates*

JACAMARS
(Class: Aves Order: Piciformes)

Like their relatives, the woodpeckers and toucans, jacamars have a special adaptation that enables them to perch easily on tree trunks – their feet have two toes pointing forwards and two toes pointing backwards. Jacamars are brilliantly coloured, tropical birds of Central and South America. Their large heads and gently tapering bodies are usually covered in an iridescent blue, green or bronze plumage. Jacamars perch in trees close to streams, waiting for a suitable moment to swoop down on an unsuspecting butterfly or dragonfly. The captured insect is taken back to a branch, beaten against a hard surface and consumed.

➠ *Toucans, Woodpeckers*

JELLYFISH
(Phylum: Cnidaria Class: Scyphozoa)

There are five orders of jellyfish: Semaeostomeae, Rhizostomeae, Coronatae, Cubomedusae and Stauromedusae. All jellyfish have four-rayed symmetry,

ABOVE RIGHT A three-toed jacamar awaits its next meal.
RIGHT Jellyfish consist of a dome-shaped body and numerous tentacles.

which means that they have a radial design, comprising eight sectors, so that a plane cut through them in four places would give a symmetrical result. They typically possess a dome-shaped body, known as a bell, which varies in size and shape from species to species. They have varying numbers of tentacles, armed with stinging cells used for immobilizing prey. The mouth is located in the exact centre beneath the bell. As their name implies, jellyfish are made of a gelatinous substance, called mesogloea, which fills the cavities inside their skins.

True jellyfish are multicellular organisms but single animals or entities. There are other animals described as jellyfish because of their appearance, that are actually called siphonophores. They are in fact colonies of simple animals that work together as one. The Portuguese man o' war is a siphonophore which looks and behaves very much like a jellyfish. Indeed it even has a species name – Physalia physalis – which defines it as a single animal.

✿ Jellyfish have larvae which develop among other drifting plankton until they reach a stage when they can swim about independently.

➠ *Invertebrates*

JESUS CHRIST LIZARDS
(Class: Reptilia   Order: Squamata)

'Jesus Christ lizard' is the popular name given to any of five types of basilisk lizard – Basiliscus species. The basilisks are found

BELOW The Jesus Christ lizard gets its name from its ability to walk on water.

in the tropical Americas, commonly living in trees overhanging water. Their tails are long and slender and the outer scales of their toes have elongated scales. The males typically have crests that extend down their bodies. The plumed basilisk (*Basiliscus plumifrons*) has crests on its head, back and tail. Males are very territorial and may mate with several females during the mating season. Basilisks are able to run, bipedally, across the surface of water, hence their common name.

➠ *Frilled Lizards, Lizards*

KANGAROOS

(Class: Mammalia Order: Diprotodontia)

 Kangaroos are marsupial mammals from Australasia. Most are terrestrial, but there is an arboreal species, the tree kangaroo (*Dendrolagus lumholtzi*) from the tropical forests. Wallabies are simply the smaller species of kangaroo. All kangaroos are grazing and browsing animals. They are an interesting example of convergent evolution, having evolved to fill the econiches otherwise filled by antelopes, deer and so on, on other continents. Like all marsupials they rear their young in a pouch. The largest kangaroos are the red kangaroo (*Macropus rufus*) and great grey kangaroo (*Macropus giganteus*), both reaching 1.5 m (5 ft) from nose to tail root.

➠ *Marsupial Mammals, Wallabies*

KATYDIDS

(Class: Insecta Order: Orthoptera)

'Katydids' is the American name for bush crickets, which are also known as 'wetas' in Australia. Katydids tend to be large, green bush crickets that often belong to the genus Microcentrum. There is a species called the Mormon cricket (*Anabrus simplex*) which is regarded as a serious pest when it decimates crops on the Great Plains region of the United States. Katydids can be either carnivorous or plant-feeding, depending on the species. They all possess, in the female, a scimitar-like ovipositor for cutting into the stems of plants. The eggs are thus afforded some protection from predation while they develop.

➠ *Crickets, Grasshoppers*

ABOVE The red kangaroo can reach 1.5 m (5 ft) from nose to tail.
ABOVE RIGHT A white-breasted kingfisher scours the water for prey.

KINGFISHERS

(Class: Aves Order: Coraciiformes)

Kingfishers are found worldwide, mostly in tropical areas. They have large heads with long, straight bills. Their bodies are small and compact and covered in brightly coloured or patterned plumage.

Kingfishers are usually solitary birds that live in woodlands, near water. They nest in holes in trees or inside burrows at ground level. Kingfishers hunt fish in rivers, streams and lakes. They dive into the water, catch fish in their strong beaks and then quickly kill or stun them by beating them against hard surfaces. The laughing kookaburra (*Dacelo gigas*) is a terrestrial kingfisher from Australia, specialised in eating reptiles.

➠ *Bee-eaters, Rollers*

KINGSNAKES

(Class: Reptilia Order: Squamata)

There are seven species of kingsnake. They belong to the Colubridae family, which also contains garter snakes and grass snakes. They are found in the Americas from Canada to Equador, where they occupy a wide variety of terrestrial habitats. The colouration in kingsnakes is diverse. The common kingsnake (*Lampropeltis getulus*) is black with cream markings while the scarlet kingsnake (*Lampropeltis doliata*) mimics the bold markings of coral snakes. Kingsnakes hunt small mammals, amphibians and other snakes. They usually kill by constriction assisted by a potent bite. All kingsnakes are immune to the venom of other snakes, even that of pit vipers.

➠ *Coral Snakes, Snakes*

KIWIS

(Class: Aves Order: Apterygiformes)

Native to the New Zealand islands, these flightless birds are protected by law to prevent their numbers from falling. Kiwis are nocturnal animals, passing the day in burrows to avoid predators. They have poor eyesight but have a well-developed sense of smell. Their nostrils are placed at the tips of their bills so that they can smell their prey, such as earthworms. Kiwis lay enormous eggs in comparison with their body size. This gives their hatchlings a head start, being so large. There are three species of kiwi. It is likely that they were related to the extinct moas.

➠ *Birds, Moas*

KOALAS
(Class: Mammalia Order: Diprotodontia)

With a diet consisting largely of leaves from the eucalyptus or gum tree, the koala (*Phascolarctos cinereus*) is a specialised animal. It has become scarce over the past century, but not through a lack of habitat. It was hunted for its fur for many years and now its surviving populations are threatened by bush fires and vehicles, both taking their toll. Koalas are marsupial mammals like kangaroos and rear their offspring in pouches. They have a habit of eating soil which either aids digestion by helping to grind down eucalyptus leaves or supplements their diet with vital minerals, perhaps both.

➠ *Marsupial Mammals, Possums*

BELOW Koalas live on a diet of gum leaves and soil.

KOMODO DRAGONS

(Class: Reptilia Order: Squamata)

The Komodo dragon (*Varanus komodensis*) is a giant monitor lizard which inhabits the islands of Komodo, Flores, Pintja and Padar near Java. It has been driven close to extinction by hunters but is now a protected species. Tourism is helping to conserve it.

Komodo dragons share a number of characteristics with other monitor lizards. They have long necks with narrow heads and slender snouts. They have strong limbs and powerful tails. Their tongues are long and forked. While all monitor lizards are big, Komodo dragons are the largest of all terrestrial reptiles. They may grow to 3 m (10 ft) in length and attain a colossal weight of 135 kg (300 lb). They are extremely aggressive animals, preying on snakes, rodents, mammals and other lizards, including their own kind. Large adults may even attack pigs or humans. Komodo dragons also eat carrion and, thanks to their highly developed sense of smell, can detect carcasses several kilometres away. When defending themselves Komodo dragons may turn their backs to the aggressor and lash out with their tails. They also use their sharp claws and teeth to inflict wounds, which become infected.

Komodo dragons lead largely solitary lives, since they have cannibalistic tendencies. During the mating season males may congregate to fight for a female, wrestling with one another on hind legs. Females lay up to 25 eggs in a burrow but neither parent raises the young, which are born able to fend for themselves. Young Komodo dragons seek refuge in trees. They eventually descend to the ground in early adulthood.

❧ Komodo dragons can run short distances at 18 kph (11 mph).

❧ It has been known for Komodo dragons to reach 100 years of age in captivity.

❧ Their eggs are laid in burrows that may be 9 m (30 ft) deep.

➠ *Lizards, Monitors*

BELOW Komodo dragons are very aggressive and can be cannibalistic.
BELOW RIGHT Lampreys have round, sucking openings lined with teeth.

KRAITS

(Class: Reptilia Order: Squamata)

In the cobra family, there are 12 species of snake called kraits. They possess venom, although they are not all considered dangerous to humans. Kraits have shiny scales and are normally boldly patterned with black and white or black and yellow bands. They are nocturnal snakes and often hunt other snakes. The venom of the common krait (*Bungarus caereus*) is so venomous that it kills half of the people it bites, despite the administration of antivenin. The sea krait is a marine species that only comes on land to lay its eggs. It typically inhabits mangrove swamps and coral reefs.

➠ *Cobras, Snakes*

KRILL

(Subphylum: Crustacea Class: Malacostraca)

Krill are shrimp-like in form and live in the surface waters of oceans. They frequent the cooler waters nearer the poles, but require warmer spring waters to breed. As a result the predators of krill complete migrations north and south in search of their food. One species of krill from the southern hemisphere is *Euphausia superba*, which grows to about 25 mm (1 in). *Meganyctiphanes norvegica* is a species from the northern hemisphere. Krill multiply in such numbers that they form immense shoals which seem to tinge the water reddish. Krill consumers include the baleen whales and filter-feeding sharks.

➠ *Crustaceans, Shrimps*

LACEWINGS

(Class: Insecta Order: Neuroptera)

There are brown lacewings – *Hemerobiidae* – and green lacewings – *Chrysopidae*. Their larvae are all predators of aphids and as such are a useful natural means of controlling infestations on crops. The larvae of green lacewings often camouflage themselves with the desiccated bodies of their victims. They hatch from eggs which are held at the end of slender stalks, designed to prevent predators from reaching them during development. The adult insects have four large wings with a lace-like

BELOW Lacewings feed on aphids and can be seen in gardens and woodlands.

system of structural veins, hence their name. They frequent places where aphids flourish, such as woods and gardens. The adults also eat aphids.

➠ *Aphids, Insects*

LAMPER EELS

(Class: Amphibia Order: Caudata)

The lamper eel (*Amphiuma means*) is also known as the two-toed amphiuma. It is not an eel, but a large species of salamander that can reach 114 cm (45 in) in length. It can be recognized by a solitary gill opening on each side, with no external gills. Its four tiny legs are not used to support weight or move and each foot only has two toes. This is an aquatic salamander but it can be found on land during rainstorms or when conditions are very damp. It requires a muddy bottom with lots of debris where it can burrow.

➠ *Amphibians, Salamanders*

LAMPREYS

(Class: Agnatha Order: Petromyzontiformes)

Like their close relatives, the hagfish, lampreys belong to an ancient group of fish that first appeared 500 million years ago. Their cylindrical bodies lack scales and their skeletons are made of cartilage, not bone. They do not have jaws, but their mouths are round, sucking openings that are lined with horny teeth. Lampreys live in freshwater and coastal regions in temperate parts of the world. Larvae emerge from eggs and live in rivers for several years before migrating to the sea as adults. Lampreys use their sucking mouthparts to attach themselves, parasitically, to other fish and drink their blood.

➠ *Fish, Hagfish*

LANCETFISH

(Class: Osteichthyes Order: Aulopiformes)

Lancetfish are closely related to lanternfish, lizard fish and tripod fish, although they are dissimilar in appearance. Lancetfish are deepwater, marine fish that are widespread in temperate and tropical oceans and seas. Their bodies are long and very slender. Their large mouths contain many pointed teeth. They eat fish and crustaceans. Lancetfish have tall dorsal fins and, in some species, elongated dorsal rays. The longnose lancetfish reaches 2.7 m (9 ft) in length and has a huge dorsal fin that extends along most of the upper surface and is held upright and rigid. Its purpose may be a defence against predators.

➧ *Fish, Lanternfish*

LANTERNFISH

(Class: Osteichthyes Order: Aulopiformes)

Lanternfish are related to lancetfish, tripod fish and lizard fish. They are an important part of the marine ecosystem since they live in huge shoals, feeding on plankton, and are then eaten by many other fish further up the food chain. Lanternfish are small, elongated fish with bright, silvery scales. They possess numerous light-producing organs – photophores – on their heads, bellies and tails. These can emit blue, yellow or green light. There are over 150 species of lanternfish and their varying patterns of photophores are used to identify them. Lanternfish are found in both coastal and deeper ocean waters.

➧ *Fish, Lancetfish*

LARKS

(Class: Aves Order: Passeriformes)

There are about 80 species of these songbirds, predominantly in Europe, Asia and Africa. They are most commonly found in open areas such as grasslands, semi-deserts, coastal regions or mountains. Larks are ground nesters. They are protected from predators by cryptic plumage that camouflages them against their surroundings while incubating eggs. They eat seeds and insects. All larks are known for their tuneful song, especially the male skylark (*Alauda arvensis*). The skylark maintains its courtship song as it flies upwards into the sky. This species was introduced to Australia and New Zealand by British ex-patriots to remind them of home.

➧ *Pipits, Wagtails*

LEAF INSECTS

(Class: Insecta Order: Phasmida)

Leaf insects and stick insects are masters of disguise in every way. They mimic the parts of plants so accurately that it is often nigh on impossible to single them out from their habitat with the human eye. They even move in a jerky, swaying manner that imitates the way foliage moves in a breeze. In addition their eggs are designed to resemble seeds. Development is through a series of nymph stages. Many leaf insects and stick insects have the ability to multiply parthenogenetically, so there is no need for a male of the species. They also regenerate lost limbs.

➧ *Insects, Stick Insects*

LEATHERY TURTLES

(Class: Reptilia Order: Chelonia)

Most turtles are known for their hard carapaces, that protect their vulnerable bodies within. The outer layer of the carapace is made of plates, or scutes, and these contain pigment. Some species have developed carapaces without these horny plates and the surface of the shell is soft and leathery. The leatherback turtle (*Dermochelys coriacea*) and soft-shelled turtles are examples. Leatherback turtles are adept ocean swimmers and divers so it is possible that their light and smooth carapaces are adapted to their marine lifestyle. There are over 20 species of soft-shelled turtle and they are inhabitants of freshwater pools and rivers.

➧ *Terrapins, Turtles*

RIGHT The leatherback turtle is soft-shelled, which suits its marine lifestyle.
FAR RIGHT The migration of lemmings is linked to their population levels.

LEECHES

(Phylum: Annelida Class: Hirudinea)

These are segmented worms, typically adapted for feeding on the blood of vertebrates, although some are predators of invertebrates. Most leeches live in freshwater ponds and streams, but some species are terrestrial. Aquatic leeches swim by undulating their bodies at a vertical plane, rather like miniature eels. They can also walk among weeds by looping from head to tail with suckers. The medicinal leech (*Hirudo medicinalis*) was once used for bloodletting, a practice believed, erroneously, to purge the body of disease. However, they have found a new and genuine medical use – when applied to the finger of a badly-cut hand for example, the leech will draw blood through the area, ensuring a fresh flow of blood to the wound and improving circulation.

➠ *Annelid Worms, Invertebrates*

LEMMINGS

(Class: Mammalia Order: Rodentia)

The Norway or Norwegian lemming (*Lemmus lemmus*) is famed for its mass migrations, where individuals will stop at nothing to keep moving, even drowning themselves trying to cross lakes and rivers. These migrations are tied in with fluctuations in the availability of food and number of predators, so that every few years the lemming

population reaches exaggerated levels. This triggers a response in the lemmings to spread out and find new territory. The lemming population then falls as food runs low and predators flourish, thereby starting the cycle again. Lemmings are an important component in the diet of many predators.

➠ *Hamsters, Rodents*

BELOW The ring-tailed lemur is a rather cat-like species.

LEMURS

(Class: Mammalia Order: Primates)

True lemurs come from the island of Madagascar in the Indian Ocean. The island became isolated at a time before monkeys and apes had evolved from their lemur-like ancestors, so it is a time capsule in evolutionary terms. The name 'lemur' is strictly used scientifically to describe particular species on Madagascar, but it is also used more generally to include sifakas, indris, avahis, and the aye-aye, since they are closely related to the lemurs.

Lemurs are essentially forest creatures, but they are not all arboreal. The ring-tailed lemur (*Lemur catta*) as its scientific name suggests, is rather cat-like. It spends a great deal of time on the ground in thinly wooded areas, walking on all-fours with its stripy tail held aloft. Lemurs have an omnivorous diet. They will take invertebrates, other small animals and fruits.

- Some of the smaller mouse lemurs have the capacity to store food as fatty tissue in their tails, which they need to get them through the dry season until the rains bring a new flush of life.
- Lemurs are distantly related to humans. Their most telling characteristics are stereoscopic or binocular vision and hands and feet that display opposable thumbs and big toes respectively.

➠ *Monkeys*

LICE

(Class: Insecta Order: Siphunculata and Mallophaga)

Lice that fall into the order Mallophaga are biting lice. They are wingless insects that feed primarily on the hair and feathers of their hosts. The order Siphunculata contains the blood-sucking lice, including the Human Louse. It exists as two sub-species – the human head louse (*Pediculus humanus capitis*) and the human body louse (*Pediculus humanus humanus*).

➡ *Booklice, Insects*

LIVE-BEARING FISH

Most fish reproduce by laying eggs, either as strands that float in the water or protected in nests. This method of reproduction does not require

much input from either parent but it does result in a high mortality of eggs and larvae. Some fish have evolved more complex methods of reproduction that increase the likelihood of their offspring's survival. Two such methods are ovoviviparity and viviparity; both result in the birth of live young.

Ovoviviparous fish retain the eggs inside them while they mature. The eggs have abundant yolks that contain sufficient nutrition to feed the young, which hatch in the ovary. The guitarfish (*Rhinobatus lentiginosus*) is an ovoviviparous species. Viviparous fish also retain the eggs inside them while they mature but the growing embryos receive nutrients from the mother. The ovary develops a placenta-like structure through which these nutrients pass.

About 12 families of bony fish, some rays and skates and most sharks bear live young. Some cartilaginous fish

ABOVE The white-spotted guitarfish is an example of a ovoviviparous fish.
RIGHT Lizards bask in the sun to soak up its energy.

– sharks and so on – lay eggs in leathery cases, some are ovoviviparous and others are viviparous. Fertilization occurs internally in all cases. The young of most sharks are born with the egg sac still attached. This contains enough food to support them for their first few days of independent life.

❧ The eggs of female North Atlantic redfish are fertilized in February. Females shoal and swim to warmer regions while the eggs develop within their oviducts. When the larvae emerge into this less hostile environment they are very small.

❧ Only one foetus of the sandtiger shark survives until birth. It emerges from its own egg, inside the uterus, and then consumes all of its siblings.

❧ A viviparous cowshark was found to have 108 embryos developing within it.

❧ The spiny dogfish bears its live young nearly two years after having mated.

➡ *Fish, Sharks*

LIZARDS

(Class: Reptilia Order: Squamata)

Of all living reptiles the lizards are the largest group, with over 3,000 species. Most are found in tropical and sub-tropical regions although lizards are also found in temperate zones. None inhabit the cold polar regions. Habitats vary; some are arboreal while others live in dry and hot scrub.

Lizards differ from other reptiles; they have distinct heads and four well-developed limbs. Their long tails may

be modified, as in chameleons, to grasp onto branches. Some species are able to lose their tails if grabbed in attack. A new tail then grows, in a process known as regeneration. Unlike salamanders, lizards have dry, scaly skins, clawed toes and external ear openings. The lower jaw bones are fused in lizards but not in snakes. The skin is often camouflaged.

Most lizards are insectivorous, although some are herbivorous. Others, especially the large monitor lizards, hunt for prey such as small mammals or eat carrion. It is uncommon for lizards to display any parenting behaviour. Usually the female lays eggs that are left to hatch without any nurturing. Lizards are noted for their basking behaviour; they soak up the sun's energy to raise their body temperature high enough for activity.

A fossil ancestor of lizards, lived in the Permian Period, 250 million years ago. A true fossil lizard has been identified in the rocks of the Late Triassic (210 million years ago). Many fossil species dating from 30 million years ago are remarkably similar to living forms found today.

❖ Two species of lizard are venomous; the beaded lizard and the gila monster.

❖ The horned lizard defends itself by spraying blood, from the corners of its eyes, at an attacker.

❖ The marine iguana, of the Galapagos Islands, is the only lizard to spend part of its life in seawater.

➡ *Reptiles, Snakes*

LIZARDS, COMMON

(Class: Reptilia Order: Squamata)

The common lizard (*Lacerta vivipara*), also known as the viviparous lizard, occupies a similar range to the common frog. It lives in northern Europe and can even survive within the Arctic Circle. It achieves this by hibernating throughout the coldest months. Common lizards may hibernate for up to eight months at a time. Lizards, like all reptiles are cold-blooded (ectothermic); they are unable to generate their own body heat. They live in dense vegetation at ground level, seeking out small invertebrates such as insects and spiders. Unlike most lizards, common lizards do not lay eggs, bearing live young instead.

➡ *Lizards, Reptiles*

BELOW Llamas live in the mountains and cold deserts of South America.

LLAMAS

(Class: Mammalia Order: Artiodactyla)

Wild llamas are the camels of South America. There are two species: The vicuña (*Llama vicugna*) and the guanaco or huanaco (*Llama huanacos*). The latter is the ancestor of domesticated llamas, still used as beasts of burden. Both species are adapted for life in the cold deserts and mountainous slopes of the Andes, which is why they possess such fine wool, as insulation from sub-zero temperatures. They lack the humps of camels and are far smaller animals. Llamas live in herds comprising a dominant male, several females and their young. They graze and browse on a variety of vegetation.

➡ *Camels, Herbivores*

LOACHES

(Class: Osteichthyes Order: Cypriniformes)

Over 200 species of these small freshwater fish are recognized. Loaches are found in Europe, Africa and, most commonly, Asia. They are popular aquarium fish worldwide. Loaches are normally elongated and covered in little scales. Some loaches have movable spines in front of their eyes and most species have barbels around their mouths. These are used to locate prey, such as worms and larvae, on the river bottom, particularly at night when loaches are most active. In stagnant or shallow water the fish may come to the surface to gulp air. The oxygen is then extracted in the intestine.

➡ *Bony Fish, Fish*

LOBSTERS

(Subphylum: Crustacea Class: Malacostrata)

 Lobsters, like crabs, have five pairs of limbs with the first pair modified into pincers for seizing and

manipulating food, as well as defence. Their body shape is quite different however. They have an elongated design, with a barrel-shaped carapace followed by a muscular abdomen and tail fan. The group includes both marine and freshwater species, since crayfish are among their number. Saltwater lobsters are fairly long-lived animals, matching humans for longevity. *Nephrops norvegicus* is an interesting species, if only because it is widespread and known by various common names – Norway lobster, scampi, Dublin Bay prawn and langoustine.

➠ *Crabs, Crustaceans*

LOCUSTS

(Class: Insecta Order: Orthoptera)

These are the largest members of the grasshopper family. Locusts are well known for their ability to form huge migratory swarms which denude the landscape of its greenery, including crops. Most of the time locusts are in fact quite harmless in this respect, because they can appear in two very distinct phases. Their normal condition is described as the 'solitary phase', due to their habit of keeping themselves to themselves and behaving like any other grasshopper. Every now and then

LEFT The lobster is similar in design to the crab, but has an elongated body. BELOW Lorises move slowly and are very patient hunters.

however, conditions are right for the 'gregarious phase'. The locusts gather together in a frenzied and voraciously hungry, travelling mass.

➠ *Crickets, Grasshoppers*

LONG-NOSED TREE SNAKES

(Class: Reptilia Order: Squamata)

The Indian long-nosed tree snake (*Ahaetulla natsuta*) is a unique species of snake. It is the only snake with truly stereoscopic or binocular vision. The eyes are set wide apart and each one looks forward down a groove in the snake's skull so that the creature has a three-dimensional view of its environment. As a strictly arboreal species, this means that the snake can judge distances accurately, helping it climb through the branches of trees and strike its prey efficiently. It is also equipped with powerful venom, so thats its prey is paralysed before it has a chance to escape.

➠ *Reptiles, Snakes*

LORISES

(Class: Mammalia Order: Primates)

The animals in this family are nocturnal creatures, related to the lemurs. The slender loris (*Loris tardigradus*) and the slow loris (*Nycticebus coucang*) both inhabit Asia, while the potto (*Perodicticus potto*) and

angwantibo (*Arctocebus calabarensis*) come from Africa, as do the bush-babies or galagos. They are all insectivorous, stalking their prey with the utmost patience. They avoid predators by remaining high in the canopy at all times, hugging the branches and only daring to move under cover of darkness. Bush-babies are fairly agile creatures, able to jump from branch to branch, but the other species are characteristically slow moving.

➡ *Primates*

LUNGFISH

(Class: Osteichthyes Infraclass: Dipnoi)

Most fish rely on gills for respiration. The lungfish, however, are able to extract oxygen from the air using lungs. They are an unusual group of fish, having fins that are joined to the skeleton with muscles – only coelocanths shares this characteristic. There is some disagreement about the classification and evolution of these fish but there is some speculation that they belong to an ancient group that led to the first land-living vertebrates. Their fleshy fins are used for locomotion, rather like limbs. Some species are able to lie dormant during dry weather, encased in cocoons made of dried slime within the hardened mud of the river bed.

➡ *Amphibians, Coelocanths*

LYREBIRDS

(Class: Aves Order: Passeriformes)

There are two species of lyrebird – the superb lyrebird (*Menura novaehollandiae*) and Albert's lyrebird (*Menura alberti*). Both are native to southeastern Australia where they live on the ground in forest and scrub, feeding on insects. Their name comes from the tail of the male superb lyrebird, which resembles a lyre – a harp-like musical instrument. These birds are noted for their ability to mimic sounds as part of their courtship. As well as mimicking natural sounds they will even do a striking impression of a chainsaw or telephone. Lyrebirds are the size of roosters and lay the largest eggs of passerine birds. The bodies of male and female lyrebirds are similar; the superb lyrebird has grey plumage and the smaller Albert's lyrebird has chestnut brown plumage. Only the males, however, have the long and ornate tail feathers of different textures, shapes and colours. Male lyrebirds use

BELOW The tail of the superb lyre bird resembles a lyre, hence its name.

their tails as an important part of their courtship display. They stand on small mounds in forest clearings to show off their tails while running through a repertoire of calls to attract and impress females. Having mated, the males play no part in the rearing of offspring, perhaps because they might draw attention to the nest.

➡ *Birds, Passerines*

MACKEREL

(Class: Osteichthyes Order: Perciformes)

The term 'mackerel' is actually used to describe several species of fish from a number of different families. Perhaps the most familiar species is the Atlantic mackerel (*Scomber scombrus*), an abundant and widespread marine fish that is of considerable economic importance as a source of food and fish oil. The Atlantic mackerel is fusiform with a slender body that is patterned in cream and blue bands on its dorsal surface and flanks. The belly is smooth and silvery. Mackerel swim in large shoals, migrating towards the coasts to spawn in springtime. They prey on planktonic animals, crustaceans and smaller fish.

➡ *Bony Fish, Tuna*

MAMBAS

(Class: Reptilia Order: Squamata)

The mambas are highly venomous snakes and are related to cobras, coral snakes, sea snakes and kraits. They inhabit rainforests, woodlands and open grasslands in sub-Saharan Africa. Mambas are very agile snakes, creeping up on small mammals or birds, often in trees. They usually have large scales and long front teeth. Venom is produced in the upper jaw and pumped into the victim via hollow fangs.

There are several species of mamba, the most famous of which is the black mamba (*Dendroaspis polylepis*). Its notoriety comes, not just from its deadly venom, but from the speed with which it can attack. The black mamba can travel over the ground at speeds approaching 20 kph (12.5 mph). It rears up to attack, biting humans in the chest or head. Its bites are always fatal unless antivenin can be administered quickly. Despite their name these mambas are rarely black. They are more likely to be grey or dull green. They can reach 4.3 m (14 ft) in length.

❖ The Eastern green mamba (*Dendroaspis angusticeps*) is slender and can move quickly through trees, searching for prey.

❖ Although highly venomous this mamba avoids humans and is not considered as dangerous as the black mamba.

➠ *Cobras, Kraits*

MAMMALS

There are three sub-classes of mammal: monotreme mammals, marsupial mammals and placental mammals. All mammals are warm-blooded vertebrates, with hair or fur and an ability in the female to secrete milk for the nourishment of young. Monotreme mammals lay leathery eggs, from which slightly developed young hatch before entering the female pouch. Marsupial mammals give birth to slightly developed young which enter the female pouch. Placental mammals give birth to fully formed, but immature, young that live freely but feed from the female's mammary glands. The three types of mammal show a clear evolutionary progression.

RIGHT Male manakins are usually dark with splashes of bright colour and perform elaborate courtship rituals which involve dances and noises.

As demonstrated by the monotremes, the mammals evolved from reptilian ancestors. The advantage of evolving into mammals was that more investment was made in nurturing offspring. This meant that fewer offspring had to be produced per individual for a species to ensure its long-term survival. Becoming warm blooded also meant that more habitats could be exploited, although birds evolved the same ability, suggesting a common reptile ancestor.

❖ There are currently around 4,000 species of mammal. Fossils tell us that they first appeared on the planet about 200 million years ago, but their heyday only came with the extinction of the dinosaurs.

➠ *Marsupial Mammals, Monotreme Mammals, Placental Mammals*

MANAKINS

(Class: Aves Order: Passeriformes)

Manakins are native to the tropical rainforests of lowland Central and South America. There are 59 species of these birds, that range in size from 8.5–16 cm (3.5–6.5 in). They eat berries and insects. The plumage of male manakins is usually dark, with splashes of bright colour in some species. The females are commonly green or olive. Male manakins are renowned for their courtship behaviour. In many species, groups of males come

together in a communal display area, lek, to attract females. Males perform courtship dances and some use modified feathers to make rasping and snapping noises.

➠ *Birds, Passerines*

MANTA RAYS

(Class: Chondrichthyes Order: Myliobatiformes)

Manta rays are cartilaginous fish of warm coastal waters and are found throughout the world. They are also known as devil fish, devil rays and sea bats. There are several species of manta ray and they all have

BELOW The elongated pectoral fins of the manta ray resemble wings.

a distinctive flat and wide body shape. The pectoral fins are enlarged and appear as triangular 'wings'. In some species, such as the Atlantic manta (*Manta birostris*), there is a pair of forward-facing lobes on each side of the face that resemble 'devil horns'. The function of these lobes is to steer plankton, small crustaceans and small fish into the ray's mouth. As water passes through the gills the small particles of food are trapped in the gill rakers, which act like a sieve, and are then swallowed. The mantas propel themselves through the water by flapping their pectoral fins like wings.

❧ Manta rays can reach 7 m (23 ft) in width. They may be very large but they are harmless to humans, except when captured as their thrashing tails and fins may cause injury.

❧ Females bear only one to two live young every year. Mantas are ususally solitary fish but may sometimes travel in small shoals.

➠ *Rays, Sharks*

MANTIS SHRIMPS

(Subphylum: Crustacea Class: Malacostrata)

Mantis shrimps are crustaceans with a unique way of hunting their prey. They have acquired their name because their second pair of limbs bear a striking resemblance to the fore-limbs of mantids. However, their limbs are not solely used for seizing prey. Mantis shrimps effectively punch the life out of their prey. They live in burrows in marine environments patiently waiting for prey animals to pass closely by. When in range the mantis shrimps release their adapted limbs with enormous force towards the heads of their victims. In an instant the victims are rendered brain dead, since the usual outcome is severe head injury.

In the Caribbean region mantis shrimps are known locally as 'split-thumbs' or 'split-toes', such is their reputation for causing painful injuries when accidentally encountered. In laboratory conditions mantis shrimps have been observed shattering sheets of glass several millimetres thick with their clubbed limbs. The largest species is about 300 mm (12 in) long. They tend to live in warmer waters, although some species live in temperate areas.

❧ Around Europe there are several members of the mantis shrimp order that belong to the genus Squilla.

❧ The warm waters of the Mediterranean Sea are home to several mantis shrimp species.

➠ *Crustaceans, Shrimps*

metabolism and water balance. Marine iguanas have adapted to overcome this problem. They often appear to have white faces as they are caked in salt that has been expelled by their nasal glands. Marine iguanas are also adapted to survive cold ocean temperatures.

Marine iguanas are found only on the Galapagos Islands – home to a number of unusual species of animal. Large adults are able to dive to depths of 12 m (39 ft) in pursuit of food. They are able to stay underwater for up to an hour, foraging for algae upon which they graze. Smaller iguanas graze in shallower water where they can more easily control their body temperature by returning to the shore to bask. Males of the species are highly territorial and fight aggressively over females.

❧ An extinct family of marine lizards, called the Mososaurs, comprised species that reached a remarkable 10 m (33 ft) in length.

➡ *Goannas, Iguanas*

MARINE TURTLES
(Class: Reptilia Order: Chelonia)

'Land turtles' are tortoises and those from freshwater are referred to as turtles and terrapins. Marine, or sea, turtles live in the open sea or coastal waters. Their bodies are streamlined to suit this lifestyle and their limbs resemble flippers. Marine turtles are adept swimmers and rarely leave the water except to breed. Eggs are laid on sandy beaches. Once they have broken free of their eggs the hatchlings crawl to the sea. Many turtle breeding grounds have been destroyed and turtles and their eggs are sought by both humans and animal predators. Despite worldwide conservation efforts several species of marine turtle are nearing extinction.

The leatherback turtle (*Dermochelys coriacea*) is the largest of turtles, with an average length of 2.1 m (7 ft). The carapace, or shell, is covered with a leathery skin, rather than the horny plates seen in most species of turtle. Leatherback turtles inhabit tropical, sub-tropical and temperate waters around the world. The loggerhead turtle (*Caretta caretta*) is another endangered species of marine turtle.

MARINE IGUANAS
(Class: Reptilia Order: Squamata)

The marine iguana (*Amblyrhynchus cristatus*) is the only living lizard that is able to live and forage in the sea. It is unusual for a lizard to inhabit marine areas and enter the sea, because the high salt content of the water normally causes problems with the animal's

LEFT Marine iguanas often appear to have white faces due to encrusted salt.
RIGHT The marsupial cat has successfully evolved in isolated Australia.

❧ The smallest species of marine turtle is the Pacific ridley turtle (*Lepidochelys olivacea*). It is an inhabitant of tropical waters throughout the world. It migrates to breeding grounds in large numbers.
➥ *Pond Turtles, Tortoises*

MARLINS

(Class: Osteichthyes Order: Perciformes)

There are four species of these large marine fish. They have characteristically pointed snouts with long, spear-like upper jaws. Marlins' bodies are muscular and heavy. The black marlin has been known to reach 700 kg (1,500 lb) in weight. They are found throughout the oceans of the world, usually swimming near the surface in search of their diet of other fish. Their streamlined shape and powerful bodies enable marlins to achieve great spurts of speed. Marlins are a favourite catch of game fishermen but their continued existence is being put under a greater threat by the commercial fishing industry.
➥ *Swordfish, Tuna*

MARSH FROGS

(Class: Amphibia Order: Anura)

The marsh frog (*Rana ridibunda*) is closely related to the edible and common frogs. In Europe these frogs are all collectively known as the 'green frogs'. The marsh frog is found throughout Europe and western Asia where it lives an aquatic lifestyle. Its favoured habitats are marshes, slow flowing rivers and lakes. Marsh frogs are 90–130 mm (3.5–5 in) long with greenish skin. They may have black spots on their backs. Marsh frogs spend most of their time in water, even as adults. If they do wander onto land they never stray too far from their aquatic home.
➥ *Frogs, Toads*

MARSUPIAL MAMMALS

The mammals in this group represent the penultimate stage in the development of placental mammals. Marsupials are otherwise known as metatherians to distinguish

ABOVE Marsupial mammals develop in a pouch, a kind of external womb.

and eutherians (placental mammals). The foetus of a marsupial is attached to the wall of the uterus for only a short period before birth. It is not nourished via a placenta but exits the mother only slightly formed. From here it finds its way to the mother's pouch, where it latches onto a nipple and begins to feed on milk from the mammary glands. The pouch functions as an external womb for the growing offspring.

When the offspring reaches a certain stage in its development, equivalent to when a placental mammal would be born, it will begin to venture out of the pouch to explore its environment. It always has the safety of the pouch whenever danger threatens however. Indeed, it is not uncommon for the young of a previous season to still be making use of the pouch when the new season's young enter the pouch. Although the pouch seems to afford greater safety to the young marsupial than it would enjoy as a placental mammal, it is important to remember that carrying the extra weight of her young places the mother in greater danger of predation.

❧ Marsupial mammals comprise a wide variety of animal types. There are marsupial carnivores, marsupial herbivores, marsupial omnivores, marsupial insectivores.

❧ In fact the marsupials have filled all of the econiches that their placental counterparts have filled in other regions of the world. This is known as convergent evolution, a phenomenon often seen in nature.

❧ Were it not for the fact that Australasia became geographically isolated it is unlikely that many marsupial species would have competed effectively with the placental mammals.
➥ *Monotreme Mammals, Placental Mammals*

MAYFLIES

(Class: Insecta Order: Ephemeroptera)

 Fossil records show that mayflies are primitive insects. Their life cycle is unique, for they pass through a stage known as the subimago or dun, due to

their brownish colour. When the aquatic nymph is fully grown it floats to the water's surface where the dun emerges and flies to a perch. The sexually mature adult or imago then emerges from the dun. The adults cannot feed and their short lives – a day or two – are spent in pursuit of reproduction. It may be confusion with mayflies that has led to the urban myth that butterflies live for one day.

➠ *Caddis Flies, Stone Flies*

MEGAPODES

(Class: Aves Order: Craciformes)

There are 12 species of megapode, all of them native to Australasia and Southeast Asia. Megapodes are closely related to quails, grouse, partridges and other gamebirds. They are unique in that they do not directly incubate their eggs. Also known as mound-

builders or incubator birds, the megapodes use alternative sources of heat to keep the eggs warm while the chick develops within. All megapodes live in dense jungle areas, except for the mallee fowl (*Leipoa ocellata*), which lives in the hot and arid eucalyptus scrubland of central and southern Australia.

The maleo fowl (*Macrocephalon maleo*) of Sulawesi ventures onto beaches of dark volcanic sand in order to lay its eggs. It chooses a site exposed to sunlight, and therefore warm for incubation. It digs holes up to 1 m deep (36 in) and lays one egg in each hole. Some utilize underground steam on the sides of the volcanoes themselves.

The mallee fowl uses the heat from rotting vegetation to incubate its eggs. A depression is dug out and filled with foliage, in which the eggs are laid. A mound of sand is then built above to seal in the heat as the foliage begins to ferment. The parent bird keeps a check on the temperature with its bill, removing or adding sand as appropriate. The hatchlings emerge from the sand fully able to fend for themselves, and are even ready to fly within 24 hours.

❀ Scrub fowl (*Megapodius* spp.) and the brush turkey (*Alectura lathami*) build incubating mounds similar to those of mallee fowl. As the mounds take considerable work to create and suitable sites may be difficult to find, individuals compete for them and they are reused year after year.

❀ The name 'megapode' is derived from the Greek for 'large foot' since all species have relatively robust feet, adapted for digging.

➠ *Birds, Fowl*

ABOVE Adult mayflies live for only one or two days.
ABOVE RIGHT An Old World field mouse with its young.

MICE

(Class: Mammalia Order: Rodentia)

There are many species of true mouse. The term 'mouse' is used somewhat liberally to describe many small rodents or rodent-like animals with long tails. There are two groups of true mice: New World mice and Old World mice. The two groups have been isolated for millions of years, but have descended from the same stock and are more-or-less identical, although this is actually due to convergent evolution to suit similar econiches. All mice are essentially herbivorous, but many species supplement their diet with animal foodstuffs. The house mouse (*Mus musculus*) will eat a wide variety of processed human foods.

➡ *Rats, Rodents*

MILLIPEDES

(Phylum: Arthropoda Class: Diplopoda)

The millipedes differ from centipedes in that they have two pairs of legs on each body segment rather than one. They are also plant feeders, not predators. Millipedes browse on dead and living plant tissue and are common among leaf litter and vegetation. In cross-section millipedes are essentially circular, as it is a structurally sound design. This, coupled with their tough exoskeleton, provides the animals with a reasonable degree of protection from predators. Many species coil themselves to conceal their heads and limbs for additional protection. All species are relatively slow-moving, but they are strong for their size and good at burrowing.

➡ *Centipedes, Invertebrates*

MINNOWS

(Class: Osteichthyes Order: Cypriniformes)

The term 'minnow' is used throughout the world to refer to numerous species of small fish or the young of large fish. In Europe and Asia the term is applied mainly to a member of the carp family – *Phoxinus phoxinus*. This European minnow is a small, freshwater fish with shiny scales and a slender body. It reaches 75 mm (3 in) in length and ranges in colour from golden yellow to green. Males develop a red belly during the breeding season, which occurs in springtime. Minnows inhabit rivers and streams and are a source of food for other animals.

➡ *Fish, Sticklebacks*

MITES

(Class: Arachnida Order: Acari)

Of the arachnid species the mites and ticks – *acari* – are by far the most numerous. There are over 15,000 species recorded, but it is likely that twice as many exist, as they are easily overlooked. There are terrestrial and aquatic mites. Some mites are plant-feeders while others are predators, often preying on other mites. Plenty of mites are blood-suckers. They are frequently vectors of diseases in vertebrates, examples include mange, Texan fever, spotted fever, tularaemia and relapsing fever. Plant-feeding species can multiply to pest proportions, causing severe damage to fruit trees and crops, as well as disease.

➡ *Arachnids, Ticks*

BELOW Millipedes have two pairs of legs on each body segment.

MOAS

(Class: Aves Order: Dinornithiformes)

The moas were large, flightless birds that once inhabited New Zealand. It is thought that between 13 and 25 species once lived. The number is not exact because the fossil record is poor and most species died out too recently for their remains to have been preserved. It is likely that the larger species were gone by the seventeenth century and the smaller species went extinct by the

BELOW Now extinct, moas could reach up to 3 m (10 ft) in height.
BELOW RIGHT Moles use their hands as spades for burrowing.

❁ The lack of a good fossil record for the moas means that it has not been possible to determine their evolutionary path or their relationship with other flightless birds, but it seems likely that the kiwis were relations.

➠ *Elephant Birds, Kiwis*

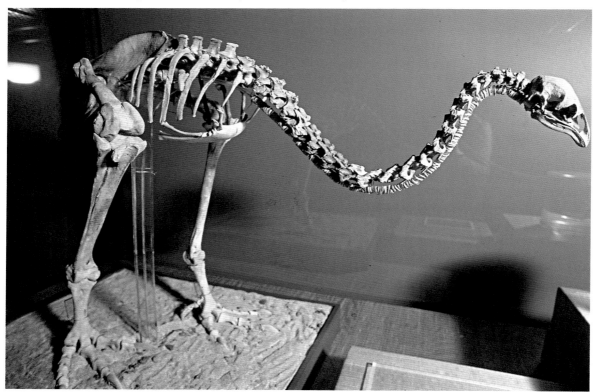

beginning of the nineteenth century. The Maori settlers seem to have hunted the birds for food and used their bones for weapons and jewellery. The word 'moa' is Polynesian for 'fowl'.

Moas ranged in size from that of a turkey to 3 m (10 ft) in height. It is believed that moas were grazing birds that ate seeds, fruit and leaves. Like many other flightless birds, moas had robust legs for running at speed and for defence against predators. Single eggs, 18 cm (7 in) in diameter were laid in holes in the ground.

MOCKINGBIRDS

(Class: Aves Order: Passeriformes)

Mockingbirds, like other members of the family Mimidae, are skilful songsters and mimics. There are 30 species of mockingbird, most of which live in North, South and Central America. They frequent a variety of habitats including mountain, desert, tropical rainforest and urban. Most are ground-dwelling birds that forage for insects and fruit. The common mockingbird (*Mimus polyglottos*) typically sings at dusk. It has been known to copy and sing the songs of up to 20 other birds in less than 10 minutes. Mockingbirds are also known as fierce defenders of their nests, attacking potential predators, including people, who threaten them.

➥ *Birds, Passerines*

MOLE-RATS
(Class: Mammalia Order: Rodentia)

Mole-rats are exactly what they seem – rats that have evolved to live underground like moles, although they are herbivorous. There are several species from different sub-families. Most species have little or no tail, with downy fur covering their bodies. Their incisor teeth are greatly enlarged to assist the front claws with excavating tunnels. The most interesting species is the naked mole-rat (*Heterocephalus glaber*) from Kenya and Somaliland. As well as being almost totally lacking in fur the animal has evolved a colonial life history very similar to social insects, such as ants and termites, with sexually inert females called workers.

➥ *Rats, Rodents*

MOLES
(Class: Mammalia Order: Insectivora)

The forelimbs of moles are very well adapted for excavating tunnels. The five digits on each hand are aligned together and equipped with robust claws so that each limb acts like a spade to dig and push the soil aside. Moles have very sensitive noses for detecting their

food, which comprises subterranean invertebrates, such as earthworms and insect grubs, found as they tunnel. They have eyes, but they are vestigial because the moles have no real use for them. The fur of moles has a soft velvety texture which produces a self-cleansing effect so that the animals remain clean.

➥ *Desmans, Insectivores*

MOLLUSCS
(Phylum: Mollusca)

The molluscs are all soft-bodied animals, many of which have developed an ability to produce calcareous shells, externally or internally. The only other hard part of the animal may be its mouthparts, depending on its method of feeding. Molluscs include slugs, snails, bivalves, monovalves, cuttlefish, octopuses and squid. There are molluscs in marine, freshwater and terrestrial environments, numbering over 80,000 species. Some species are plant-feeders, many are filter-feeders, others are scavengers and plenty are predators.

Land-living molluscs travel by means of a muscular foot, as do their counterparts in aquatic habitats. Other aquatic methods of locomotion are water jetting and the undulation of fins or vanes. The majority of mollusc species have separate sexes, but bivalves and gastropods are often hermaphrodite. The bivalves are the only molluscs to typically lack eyes. When mollusc shells are external they are primarily a means of protection from predators, but when internal they perform the same function as skeletons in bony animals.

❖ Most aquatic molluscs have a swimming, larval stage before miniature adults appear, while in terrestrial species the larval stage is completed within the egg.

❖ The giant clam (*Tridacna gigas*) is the largest bivalve at 120 cm (48 in) wide.

➥ *Bivalves, Cephalopods*

ABOVE Some molluscs, like the spider conch, have developed shells.

MONGOOSES
(Class: Mammalia Order: Carnivora)

The word 'ichneumon' is derived from Greek for 'tracker'. It is used as the name for a species of wasp – ichneumon flies – because they track down the larvae of other insects. It is also used for a species of mongoose which was used to keep houses free of pests in ancient Egypt. The ichneumon or Egyptian mongoose (*Herpestes icheumon*) lives over most of Africa. The Indian grey mongoose (*Herpestes edwardsi*) is famed for its fearless confrontations with cobras. It actually has an evolved immunity to the venom of cobras and gets good-sized meals once it has dispatched its poisonous victims.

➡ *Carnivores, Indian Cobra*

MONITOR LIZARDS
(Class: Reptilia Order: Squamata)

Monitor lizards belong to the same family of reptiles as the venomous gila monster and beaded lizard. Monitors are characterised by elongated heads and necks, muscular limbs and powerful tails. They have large teeth, strong jaws and pointed snouts. Monitors are predators but their diets are determined by their habitats. The Nile monitor (*Varanus niloticus*), for example, feeds on crabs and molluscs. Monitors have an excellent sense of smell that can lead them to carrion. They are found in tropical regions of the Old World. There are about 30 species of monitor lizard and the largest is the Komodo dragon.

➡ *Komodo Dragons, Lizards*

ABOVE The ring-tailed mongoose comes from Madagascar
ABOVE RIGHT This New World woolly monkey is barely two weeks old.

MONKEYS – NEW WORLD
(Class: Mammalia Order: Primates)

The monkeys from the New World – the Americas – differ from other monkeys because they have been geographically isolated for millions of years. Of

course, they are identical to the untrained eye, but there are some determining characteristics. Most New World monkeys have prehensile tails, which means they use them as a fifth limb. This enables them to hang from branches with both forelimbs free to collect food, which is usually foliage and fruits. Most species have atrophied or vestigial thumbs, as they have no need for the 'opposable grip' seen in other monkeys and apes. They also tend to have nostrils that are widely spaced and are generally less intelligent than their Old World cousins.

New World monkeys include howler monkeys, spider monkeys, squirrel monkeys, capuchins, dourocoulis, woolly monkeys, titis, sakis and uakaris. The howler monkeys have booming voices that carry through the forest canopy. Their voice boxes are especially adapted for this purpose, as it is the only way for them to communicate effectively in their habitat. All New World monkeys live in the tropical zone of the Americas – from northern South America up to Meso-America.

❧ Black spider monkeys (*Ateles paniscus*) make popular pets because they are very affectionate animals.

➡ *Apes, Primates*

MONKEYS – OLD WORLD

(Class: Mammalia Order: Primates)

The Old World monkeys are a more varied group than the New World monkeys and many have adopted lifestyles that are both arboreal and terrestrial. Unlike their American counterparts, Old World monkeys do not have prehensile tails, but they do have opposable thumbs and big toes, making their limbs more versatile. In fact, their tails are often reduced to nothing more than stumps, since they proved only a disadvantage in the past by helping predators to catch them. The Old World monkeys include macaques, baboons, mangabeys, langurs, colobuses, guenons, patas monkeys and mandrills.

Many Old World monkeys live in organized groups, where strict hierarchies are adhered to. They have complex relationships with one another that demonstrate to anthropologists how human behaviour first evolved. Such behaviour is designed to increase the survival of the strongest genetic traits, so that individuals will often appear to display altruistic tendencies, especially to other closely related monkeys. Team work also helps to improve the chances of survival for all members of a troop.

❧ Although the Old World includes all of Africa, Europe and Asia, few monkeys live in temperate areas.

❧ The Japanese macaque (*Macaco fuscata*) is the most northerly of all monkeys.

➠ *Apes, Primates*

Old World monkeys form a varied group, which includes mandrills (BELOW) and pangurs (BOTTOM).

MONOTREME MAMMALS

 Monotremes are mammals that lay eggs, indicating that they are only one step away from their reptilian ancestors. They are otherwise known as prototherians ('first-mammals'); therians being both marsupial and placental mammals. The eggs are leathery, like those of reptiles, and the young hatch only partly developed. They then spend a pseudo-gestation period, blind and helpless, when they are nourished by milk from the mother's mammary glands, until ready to face the world alone.

There are three species of monotreme and they fall into two families. The first family is Tachyglossidae. It contains the two species of echidnas or spiny anteaters, as they are sometimes called. *Tachyglossus aculeatus* is found in Australia and New Guinea; *Zaglossus bruijni* in New Guinea only. Echidnas are terrestrial, burrowing animals that resemble hedgehogs. They have no teeth and have specialised in eating ants and termites, which they lap up with their sticky tongues. The second family – Ornithorhynchidae – contains just one species: The platypus or duck-billed platypus (*Ornithorhynchus anatinus*). Platypuses are quite different from echidnas. They are aquatic animals that look something like a cross between a duck and a beaver. Their soft beak-like mouths are very touch sensitive and are used for searching out aquatic invertebrates on which they feed.

Despite their differences, platypuses and echidnas have similarities other than the fact that they both lay eggs. The males have spurs on their ankles that are used in defence against predators. The spurs are not only sharp but they are equipped with poison glands. The venom runs along a groove in the spur, by capillary action. Adult platypuses also lack teeth.

❖ Platypuses mate in water. The female then lays two eggs in a special burrow at the side of the watercourse.

❖ Echidnas lay just one egg, which is kept in a pouch.

➠ *Echidnas, Platypuses*

MONOVALVES

(Phylum: Mollusca Class: Gastropoda)

The term 'monovalve' is a non-specific one used generically in describing certain marine and freshwater molluscs which possess a single shell rather than two halves, as in the bivalves. They include limpets, topshells, periwinkles, slipper limpets, whelks, conches and oysterdrills. The most primitive are the limpets and topshells. They typically comprise a conical-shaped shell with the animal living within its concave depression beneath. They browse plants from the surfaces of rocks which need to have been worn smooth by the action of waves so that the limpets can adhere themselves in the face of danger. Providing they get a good seal, limpets and topshells can be extremely difficult to dislodge.

Other monovalves are typically snail-like in form, although slipper limpets represent an intermediate form. These species often possess a flat disc at the rear of their muscular foot which is used to protectively seal the

LEFT The baby short-nosed echidna continues to develop after it hatches.
RIGHT Although fierce in appearance, the mountain devil is quite placid.

entrance to their shells when the animals are retracted inside. There are plant-feeding species, carnivorous species and those that are essentially opportunist omnivores.

* On European shores one of the most numerous and widespread limpets is the common limpet – scientific name *Patella vulgaris*, which translates as 'common kneecap' due to the shape of its shell.
→ *Bivalves, Molluscs*

MOTHS

(Class: Insecta Order: Lepidoptera)

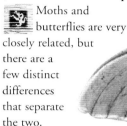 Moths and butterflies are very closely related, but there are a few distinct differences that separate the two. Perhaps the most obvious difference is that most moths rest with their wings flat against their body, whilst butterflies hold them up together so that the undersides are visible. This explains why the colouration and patterning on the wings of moths are often cryptic on the upper side of the fore wings, as they are used as camouflage. If a moth has any bright colours they are usually found on the upper side of the hindwings and used to surprise predators as a means of escape.

The antennae of moths are always a give away that they are not butterflies, as they never end with an abrupt club-like tip. In many moth species there is sexual dimorphism, or difference between the sexes, displayed in their antennae. The females' tend to be wire-like, whilst the males' are feather-like and designed to sense the perfume emitted by the females.

* There are day-flying moths which confuse things because they possess bright, contrasting colours and look very much like butterflies.
* Their colours are a warning to predators that eating them would leave a bad taste in the mouth.
→ *Butterflies, Insects*

BELOW Most moths, such as the luna moth, rest with their wings flat.

MOUNTAIN BEAVERS

(Class: Mammalia Order: Rodentia)

Although rodents, these animals are not closely related to true beavers. It is true that they often frequent places near to water, but they are adapted for burrowing, not swimming. There is only one species, the sewellel (*Aplodontia rufa*) and its range is confined to the southern Pacific coast of North America. Sewellels are about the size of rabbits and have only vestigial tails. They live in mountainous terrain, where they dig extensive tunnel systems in soft, valley soils. They are herbivorous and are known to store vegetable matter in underground chambers from which to feed during the winter months.
→ *Beavers, Rodents*

MOUNTAIN DEVILS

(Class: Reptilia Order: Squamata)

The spiny lizard or mountain devil (*Moloch horridis*) is an extraordinary reptile of the Australian deserts. It is a placid insectivore, yet it looks ferocious for it is covered in sharp spines as a protection from predators. Ants form the greater part of its diet, but offer little by way of moisture, so the lizard has evolved a unique way of drinking in the absence of standing water. Mountain devils possess special grooves on their undersides that lead to their mouths. When the creatures lie upon damp sand, following rainfall, the water is channelled to the mouth using capillary action.
→ *Gila Monsters, Horned Toads*

MOUNTAIN LIFE

For any animal to thrive in mountainous terrain it has to cope with three key problems. Firstly, living at high altitudes requires breathing 'thin' air. This means it is less dense than air at sea level, for example, so the amount of available oxygen is lower. The animals need to have relatively large lungs and blood with a high percentage of red blood cells to be able to breathe effectively enough to search for food and escape dangers.

High altitudes also mean low temperatures and less availability of water, which is frozen into ice and snow. Some animals, particularly the smaller species, tend to live in burrows, where they can escape the cold and access melt water. The larger animals opt for seasonal migration up and down the mountain sides. Summers are spent above the tree line in the alpine zone, and winters are spent below in the sub-alpine zone.

RIGHT The condor is the world's largest bird of prey.
FAR RIGHT Vizcachas live in the mountains of South America.
ABOVE RIGHT The snow leopard is an endangered species.
MAIN Ibex live below the permanent snowline of mountain regions.

MOUNTAINOUS REGIONS

Rocky Mountains

ARCTIC

Alps

NORTH
AMERICA

EUROPE

Himalayas

Tropic of Cancer

ASIA

AFRICA

Equator

SOUTH
AMERICA

Tropic of Capricorn

AUSTRALIA

The Andes

Major mountain ranges

ANTARCTICA

MUDPUPPIES

(Class: Amphibia Order: Caudata)

Mudpuppies are related to newts and salamanders, but they are more closely related to olms. They have external gills, long, pigmented bodies and four digits on each of their four small limbs. They are grey, black or brown in colour but may have black spots. They inhabit lakes and streams where they are active at night. Mudpuppies feed on small invertebrates that live in their aquatic habitat. They lay their eggs in burrows or beneath rocks. Mudpuppies cope with stagnant water by developing enlarged gills to increase their intake of oxygen but they cannot thrive in polluted or silted water.

➡ *Newts, Owls*

MUDSKIPPERS

(Class: Osteichthyes Order: Perciformes)

Mudskippers look unlike most other fish, but they are related to the large family of gobies. There are six species of mudskipper and they all share an unusual ability to move around out of water. They reach lengths of 30 cm (12 in) and have tapering bodies with large, blunt heads. Their eyes are very prominent and placed at the top and front of the heads. The pectoral fins of mudskippers are particularly strong and manoeuvrable and are used by the fish to climb out of water. They breathe air when out of water and eat crustaceans, insects and larvae.

➡ *Amphibians, Lungfish*

MULLETS

(Class: Osteichthyes Order: Mugiliformes)

Mullets are abundant marine fish of economic significance as a food source. There are about 100 species and they are all similar in appearance, with stocky, silvery-grey bodies with few or no distinctive markings. The upper lip is often thickened, the tail is forked and there are two distinct dorsal fins. They inhabit coastal, brackish or estuarine water in tropical and temperate areas and consume small plants and animals that they find in the mud. The common or striped mullet (*Mugil cephalus*) is farmed commercially. The red mullet (*Mullus surmuletus*) is actually a goatfish, not a true mullet.

➡ *Fish, Goatfish*

ABOVE Mudskippers live in humid forests and can survive out of water.
RIGHT The red mullet is not in fact a true mullet, but a type of goatfish.

NATTERJACK TOADS

(Class: Amphibia Order: Anura)

The natterjack toad (*Bufo calamita*) is one of two species of toad found in Britain – mainly in the northeast and Scotland. It is identifiable by three characteristics with which it differs from the common toad (*Bufo bufo*). It has a thin yellow stripe on the centre of its back, runs rather than walks and has a very loud call that can be heard over a considerable distance. The males congregate in shallow ponds at mating time and compete vocally for females. Natterjack toads inhabit dry lowland heath and coastal dune systems. They hunt for invertebrates at night.

➡ *Frogs, Toads*

NAUTILUSES

(Phylum: Mollusca Class: Cephalododa)

In prehistoric times the oceans were filled with animals called ammonites and belemnites, the ancestors of modern cephalopods. They had shells, used both for protection and floats for swimming. The ammonites had snail-like, coiled shells while the belemnites had slender, pointed shells. There are still some species – the nautiluses – that retain shells. There are three species of nautilus, all of which are predators. They use their shells to achieve neutral buoyancy, enabling them to move efficiently in three dimensions. A fourth species – the paper nautilus or argonaut – is an octopus which creates a delicate, coiled shell for holding its eggs.

➡ *Cephalopods, Molluscs*

NEMATODE WORMS

(Phylum: Nematoda)

Nematode worms or nematodes are also known as roundworms due to their circular shape in cross-section. They are an extremely successful class of animals, able to thrive in just about every environment where life is possible. The majority of nematodes are scavenging species which are largely responsible for the breakdown of organic matter, in soil on land or in the mud at the bottom of rivers, ponds, lakes and oceans. There are also some fearsome parasitic nematodes, which infest the bodies of vertebrates, including humans. The guinea worm (*Dracunculus medinensis*) can grow to 1 m (3 ft) inside human blood vessels.

➡ *Annelid Worms, Tapeworms*

ABOVE Nautiluses share the ancestors of cephalopods, but have kept their shells. TOP The male natterjack toad uses its loud call to compete for a mate.

NEWTS

(Class: Amphibia Order: Caudata)

There is no obvious scientific distinction between newts and salamanders. Generally salamanders spend their whole lives in water while newts tend to live terrestrial lives except during the larval and breeding stages of their lifecycle. However, this is a behavioural distinction, not a physical one, and there are many exceptions.

Newts and salamanders have long, slender bodies and long tails. They have four legs of equal length and size. They are found only in moist habitats and are mostly confined to the northern hemisphere. Unlike other amphibians, fertilization of eggs is internal. Newts lay their eggs in water during spring. The eggs hatch into the larval stage. The larvae are carnivorous. In late summer/early autumn the larvae metamorphose into adult newts which then leave the water and lead a terrestrial life. They return to the water several years later to mate.

❖ Newts may be camouflaged to prevent predation. Others exhibit garish colours to warn predators that they contain toxins in their skin. Some species are able to shed their tails if attacked.

❖ Common prey for newts are small aquatic invertebrates. Newts are able to store fat in their bodies so they can survive periods when food is not readily available to them.

➡ *Efts, Salamanders*

ABOVE The skin of the rough-skinned newt contains deadly toxins.
RIGHT Numbats have more teeth than any other terrestrial mammal.

NIGHTJARS

(Class: Aves Order: Caprimulgiformes)

This order includes nightjars, potoos, frogmouths and oil birds or guacharos (*Steatornis caripensis*) which are the only nocturnal plant-feeding birds. Living in South America, oil birds roost in caves by day, venturing out at dusk to feed on palm fruits. The other members of the order are typically insectivorous with gaping mouths designed to capture flying insects at night. By day they rely on cryptic colouration and their shape to conceal their whereabouts from predators as they perch. Most species have distinctive calls, which they use to communicate with one another in the darkness.

➠ *Bats, Swifts*

NUMBATS

(Class: Mammalia Order: Dasyuromorphia)

Numbats are rat-sized marsupials from Australia. They are otherwise known as banded anteaters, but they are not related to true anteaters. There are two species; the numbat (*Myrmecobius fasciatus*) and the rusty numbat (*Myrmecobius rufus*). They have the distinction of possessing more teeth than any other terrestrial mammal – 50. Like all animals that have specialised in feeding on ants and termites numbats have heavily clawed front limbs for excavating the nests of the insects. They also have the characteristic, long sticky tongue for lapping their food. This is an excellent example of convergent evolution between marsupial and placental mammals.

➠ *Anteaters, Marsupial Mammals*

BELOW *Nuthatches work their way down tree trunks in search of food.*

NUTHATCHES

(Class: Aves Order: Passeriformes)

These birds characteristically search the bark of trees for insects and other invertebrates by working their way downwards. The tree creepers avoid direct competition with them by working *their* way upwards.

Nuthatches also eat seeds and nuts, which they store for winter consumption. There are over 20 species of nuthatch found in Europe, Asia, Africa and North and Central America. They generally live in woodland regions. Plumage varies, but they typically have a dark back with a pale belly and a black head cap. Nuthatches are social birds, often seen roaming for food in the company of finches and tits.

➠ *Treecreepers, Woodpeckers*

OCEANIC LIFE

The oceans of the world provide a multitude of habitats for animals to exploit – they comprise over 90 per cent of the available living space on earth. Oceans at their deepest measure several kilometres and they are all hundreds of kilometres across, from continent to continent. As such, oceans need to be regarded as collections of environments, such as deep sea, open water and coastline. Furthermore, these environments alter with latitude, from the equator towards both poles, and are subject to seasonal currents and surface weather conditions.

Nevertheless, every ocean habitat is home to one animal or another, more usually hundreds or thousands. There are only a few classes of animal that have failed to evolve species adapted for marine environments – insects for example. Some classes – the birds and mammals in particular – have been very successful at returning to the oceans from terrestrial ancestry.

RIGHT The sea dragon lives in the waters around Australia.
FAR RIGHT The parrot fish's fused teeth form a beak-like mouth.
ABOVE RIGHT The grey whale filter-feeds on krill and small fish.

OCEANIC LIFE

ARCTIC

Arctic
Ocean

NORTH
AMERICA

EUROPE

Tropic of Cancer

Atlantic
Ocean

ASIA

Red Sea

AFRICA

Great Barrier Reef

Equator

SOUTH
AMERICA

Tropic of Capricorn

Indian
Ocean

AUSTRALIA

Pacific
Ocean

Southern
Ocean

Major coral reefs

ANTARCTICA

OCTOPUSES

(Phylum: Mollusca Class: Cephalopoda)

Of all the millions of invertebrate species, the octopuses are the most intelligent. They are capable of solving fairly complex problems in order to gain food. In addition, their soft bodies enable them to negotiate surprisingly awkward passages by contortion. Octopuses are hunters, preying primarily on crustaceans and fish by stalking and ambushing them, hence their evolved talents. Despite their being so advanced for invertebrates they do remain quite primitive in many respects. Having reached sexual maturity, adult octopuses put all of their energy into reproduction. The result is that they die soon afterwards, allowing new generations to take their place.

➧ *Cephalopods, Squid*

ABOVE The rings of the blue-ringed octopus glow when it is angry.
RIGHT Orioles are shy birds and tend to stay in the treetops.

OLMS

(Class: Amphibia Order: Caudata)

Olms are related to newts and salamanders but are most closely related to mudpuppies. They live in caves within the Carpathian Mountain range of south-eastern Europe. Their whole lives are spent in water, where they feed on aquatic invertebrates. Olms are virtually blind. Their eyes are sensitive to light but are covered in skin. Their bodies are long, slender and white or pink due to their skin lacking any pigment. Olms' heads are narrow with a blunt snout. There are two digits on each hind limb and three on each forelimb. The external gills of olms are red and feathery.

➧ *Mudpuppies, Salamanders*

OMNIVORES

Any animal that eats both plant matter and other animals can be described as an omnivore. More generally such animals are also described as opportunists, because they will feed on a wide variety of foodstuffs as and when the opportunity arises. Being an omnivore affords certain advantages as it means that the animal can be resourceful when its preferred foods are in short supply. It is therefore more likely to survive than an animal that can only eat particular foods. That is unless there are lots of other omnivores about, in which case more specialised animals might end up with more food to themselves while the omnivores compete over the same food.

Good examples of omnivores are bears, badgers, pigs, foxes, pandas and racoons. All of them are essentially carnivorous, yet they take all manner of vegetable matter when times are hard. On the other hand, rats and mice are essentially herbivorous, but will take flesh when push comes to shove. Many birds are omnivores too.

❧ Adapting to an omnivorous diet also means that different, seasonal food sources can be exploited at certain times of year, meaning the animal avoids any need to migrate in search of food.

➧ *Carnivores, Herbivores*

OPOSSUMS

(Class: Mammlia Order: Didelphimorphia)

 Strictly speaking the appelation 'opossums' describes American marsupials, as opposed to their Australian counterparts, called 'possums', but the two terms do get misused. There are around 70 species of opossum. They are all confined to South and Central America except one species, the Virginia opossum (*Didelphis virginiana*), which ranges into the southern states of the USA. The Virginia opossum has the characteristic marsupial brood pouch, but in many species it is reduced or absent altogether, so that the young are required to hang on to their mother's fur. They are arboreal and most have bare, prehensile tails to assist climbing.

➠ *Marsupials, Possums*

ORIOLES

(Class: Aves Order: Passeriformes)

When Europeans arrived in the Americas they saw birds resembling the orioles that lived in Europe and so they named them orioles too. In fact the two types of bird belong in different families. The Old World orioles are placed in the family Oriolidae while the New World orioles are in the family Icteridae. They are all shy, but noisy, birds that live in the treetops in warm regions. They are mainly insect eaters, with some species eating fruits too. Orioles are characterised by having bold, two-tone plumage – yellow and black, red and black and orange and black.

➠ *Passerines, Rollers*

OSTRICHES

(Class: Aves Order: Struthioniformes)

The ostrich (*Struthio camelus*) is the largest living bird, at 2.8 cm (9.3 ft). It lives on savannah in eastern and southern Africa. Ostriches are flightless but are equipped with powerful, naked legs that enable them to achieve speeds of 65 kph (40 mph) when pursued. Their unique, two-toed feet resemble hooves and can be used to deliver deadly kicks if the birds are threatened. Ostrich males – cocks – are black with white feathers on tails and wings. Females – hens – are mostly brown. Male ostriches mate with several hens, which then lay 15–60 eggs in a communal nest.

➠ *Emus, Rheas*

OTTERS

(Class: Mammalia Order: Carnivora)

Otters are adapted for semi-aquatic lifestyles. They have streamlined bodies and webbed feet to optimize their locomotion underwater. Most species frequent freshwater habitats, but the sea otter (*Enhydra lutris*) lives around the coast of the North Pacific. It is a large animal – 1.5 m (5 ft) – so that it can cope with the cold temperatures and the waves. Otters have dense fur to provide insulation and this has put them high on fur trappers' wanted lists. The common otter (*Lutra lutra*) is found along watercourses over the whole of Europe, where it hunts for fish, invertebrates, small mammals and birds.

➠ *Beavers, Rodents*

ABOVE To survive in cold water, the sea otter is fairly large and has dense fur.

OVENBIRDS

(Class: Aves Order: Passeriformes)

 This large group of songbirds, with over 220 species, is confined to Central and South America.

 The members of this group vary greatly in size, lifestyle and habitat. Most have brown or reddish brown plumage on their backs, and paler plumage on their fronts. They vary in size from 15–20 cm (6–8 in). The group gets its name from some of its members' nesting habits. They build domed, oven-like nests from mud in the branches of trees. A small hole marks the entrance to the chamber. Many species, however, build nests in natural cavities or excavated holes.

➡ **Birds, Weaver Birds**

OVIPAROUS REPTILES

As one might expect in such a large and diverse group of animals as the reptiles, there are various methods of reproduction. Most reptiles are oviparous – they lay eggs outside their bodies which, after a period of time, hatch into young. It is rare for reptiles to nurture their eggs once they have been laid. An exception is the crocodilians who may care for their offspring for up to two years after they have emerged from their nests. Skinks, a family of lizards, also show greater parental care than most other reptiles. Females may protect their eggs after laying them by lying on them as they incubate and even moving them if threatened by predators.

Turtles and tortoises lay their eggs on land. Clutches of 1–100 eggs may be laid at various times depending upon the species. Some female turtles are able to store sperm in their bodies, enabling them to lay several clutches of eggs over the year without having to find a new mate.

Young snakes are often equipped with a sharp, but temporary, egg-tooth that is used to break the leathery shell from within. Other snakes, notably the pythons, incubate and protect their eggs. Females coil themselves around their clutches of eggs to keep them warm. Some species are able to generate heat in their own bodies to keep the eggs at a constant temperature – an exceptional feat in creatures that are generally considered 'cold-blooded'.

❧ Some reptiles are ovoviviparous. This means that the eggs are retained within the body while the embryos develop. The female then gives birth to live young, rather than eggs.

❧ Several species of lizard and one species of snake display parthenogenesis. This is a process by which a female can reproduce without the fertilization of the eggs by a male.

➡ **Reptiles, Viviparous Reptiles**

ABOVE The ovenbird's name is derived from its dome-shaped nest.
RIGHT Parson's chameleons are oviparous and their young hatch from eggs.

OWLS

(Class: Aves Order: Strigiformes)

Owls are divided into two families. Strigidae are the 'typical owls', comprising most species, and Tytonidae comprising 'barn owls', of which there is one species – *Tyto alba* – although it has 30 sub-species worldwide. Owls are usually nocturnal hunters. Their eyes are placed at the front of their heads, providing them with stereoscopic or binocular vision. They are also relatively large to enable the birds to optimize available light. The ears of owls – not the tufts on their heads – are placed asymmetrically on the sides of their skulls so that the birds can assess direction three dimensionally, thereby enabling them to strike accurately at their prey in the half-light.

BELOW Owls can turn their heads almost all the way round.

Owls feed on a variety of prey animals, depending on the size of the birds and any specialization they may have. Prey includes small mammals, invertebrates, reptiles and fish. Pell's fishing owl (*Scotopelia peli*) has a relatively long bill and talons for dealing with fish, therefore looking more like a hawk than an owl.

❧ Owls have adapted neck vertebrae that allow them to rotate their heads as much as 270 degrees in one direction. This allows them to search for prey while perched, without having to move and risk making any noise.

➧ *Birds, Birds of Prey*

PACIFIC GIANT SALAMANDERS

(Class: Amphibia Order: Caudata)

This large salamander – *Dicampodon ensatus* – reaches a length of 30 cm (14 in) from nose to tail tip. It is found in warm, coastal areas of the Pacific. It burrows amongst damp mosses and fallen trees in woodlands and is nocturnal. These salamanders have smooth marbled skin, often black marbling on a grey or brown background, and as they age their colour pales. When frightened the Pacific giant salamander makes a barking noise – the only salamander to have a voice. Females protect their eggs from predators. The larvae live under water, feeding on invertebrates such as mayfly larvae.

➧ *Newts, Salamanders*

PADDLEFISH

(Class: Osteichthyes Order: Acipenseridae)

These unusual fish belong to a primitive group of bony fish and are probably related to sturgeons, gars, bichirs and the Bowfin. They all show a partial loss of bony skeleton which has been replaced by cartilage. The cranium of paddlefish, for example, is almost entirely made of cartilage.

There are two species of paddlefish – the American or Mississippi paddlefish (*Polyodon spathula*) and the Chinese paddlefish (*Psephurus gladius*). Both are freshwater fish that feed on plankton. The American paddlefish reaches 1.8 m (6 ft) in length and the Chinese paddlefish is slightly larger. Both have fusiform bodies with well-developed fins. Their snouts are made of cartilage and are elongated into paddle-shapes. American paddlefish are exploited as a food source and they provide a variety of caviar. They breed when seven or eight years old and spawn during spring floods.

❧ The study of paddlefish has given some insight into a large group of extinct but similar fish forms that first appeared 375 million years ago and were most numerous in the Carboniferous Period (362–290 million years ago).

❧ The ancestors of paddlefish emerged 100–65 million years ago and the fossil record suggests that the group specialised early and changed little subsequently.

➧ *Gars, Sturgeons*

PAINTED FROGS

(Class: Amphibia Order: Anura)

The term 'painted frog' has been applied to a number of frog species because of the blotchy appearance of their skin. The Spanish painted frog (*Discoglossus pictus*) is an inhabitant of small ponds and rivers. It has a pointed nose and a greenish-brown colour to its smooth skin, with pale yellow lines and spots crossing its back. The painted frog of South Africa has brown or olive blotches on a yellow or grey base colour. Often there is a pale yellow stripe running down its back. It lives in woodland and burrows into the humus during summer to aestivate.

➠ *Frogs, Toads*

PANDAS

(Class: Mammalia Order: Carnivora)

Although both bear-like, the red panda (*Ailurus fulgens*) is more closely allied with the racoon family, while the giant panda (*Ailuropoda melanoleuca*) is usually included in the bear family. Both species are fundamentally vegetarian, but will take small mammals, birds, invertebrates and eggs as dietary supplements. The red panda is an arboreal animal of Asian forests. The giant panda is terrestrial, due to its size, and lives in remote bamboo forests of western China. It is adapted to eating vast amounts of nutritious bamboo shoots and leaves. It has a marsupial-like life history, where the young are born partially developed, naked and blind.

➠ *Bears, Raccoons*

ABOVE The giant panda eats vast amounts of bamboo shoots and leaves.
ABOVE RIGHT The pangolin's armoured body recalls that of the armadillo.

PANGOLINS

(Class: Mammalia Order: Pholidota)

Pangolins might be described as Old World equivalents to the armadillos of the New World. They have evolved a similar form of armoured protection, although in the pangolins it comprises hairs that are

modified into overlapping scales, rather than the bony plates seen in armadillos. Pangolins also possess heavily clawed forelimbs for excavating tunnels and finding food. They specialise in eating ants and termites, using a protractible sticky tongue for the job. There are seven species, found over Africa and southern Asia. Tree pangolins (*Manis tricuspis*) have long prehensile tails which they use to grip onto branches while feeding.

➠ *Anteaters, Armadillos*

PARROT FISH

(Class: Osteichthyes Order: Perciformes)

These attractive tropical fish are inhabitants of coral reefs. They have deep bodies, covered with large scales, and blunt heads. Their teeth are fused to form a solid row, giving the appearance of a beak, hence the name 'parrot fish'. The scales of parrot fish are commonly brightly coloured and patterned. The male rivulated parrot fish, of the Indo-Pacific, for example, is green and orange while the female is blue and yellow. The rainbow parrot fish of the Atlantic is orange and green with a blue beak.parrot fish may reach 1.2 m (4 ft) in length and may weigh up to 20 kg (45 lb). Parrot fish are placed in the order Perciformes and are related to wrasses.

❖ Parrot fish scrape algae off the surfaces of corals by pecking with their bill-like teeth. They also specialise in eating the polyps within the coral structures. Pieces of coral are removed with the algae and consumed by the fish.

❖ The coral is broken down by rows of teeth in the fish's throat and ground into sand, which is then removed by defecation. This erosive method of eating leaves scarring on the coral and causes the deposition of sand sediment on reefs.

➥ *Bony Fish, Wrasses*

PARROTS

(Class: Aves Order: Passeriformes)

 The parrot family is broadly divided into different groups according to characteristics in shape and size. The macaws are the largest parrots. They have very bright colouring and long tapering tails. The parrots are medium to large birds with rounded-off or square tails. They are typically colourful too, although the African grey parrot (*Psittacus erithecus*) is grey all over apart from its red tail. Cockatoos are like parrots, except that they have erectile crests. Parakeets, lorikeets and conures all have the tapering tails of macaws, but they are smaller species. Other members of the parrot family include lovebirds, lories, amazons, and the budgerigar (*Melopsittacus undulatus*).

Many parrot species are popular as pets, because they are social and intelligent birds, able to mimic the human voice. Of late though it has been made illegal in many countries to deal with wild specimens in an effort to preserve wild populations.

Most of the 300 parrot species are found in Central and South America and Australasia. New Zealand has three species of parrot, each quite unusual. The arrival of rats and cats to New Zealand has threatened the survival of the flightless kakapo or owl parrot (*Strigops habroptilus*). The inquisitive kea (*Nestor notabilis*) is noted for acquiring its carnivorous habit of feeding on the kidney fat of domestic sheep, killing if necessary to obtain it, which has resulted in its persecution by farmers. The kaka (*Nestor meridionalis*) has developed the habit of digging insect grubs from rotting wood in the same manner as a woodpecker.

❖ Although domestic budgerigars come in a wide variety of colour combinations, wild budgerigars are usually green, with a yellow face and blue tail.

❖ Lovebirds are famous for the close mating bonds that they form. If one partner disappears its mate may die, apparently from loneliness.

➥ *Birds, Toucans*

PASSERINES

(Class: Aves Order: Passeriformes)

The passerines form the dominant group of all birds. Of the 8,600 species of bird, 5,100 are passerines, and 4,000 of those are songbirds. They are also known as 'perching birds'. Their feet have four toes in an arrangement ideal for providing a secure attachment onto branches – three toes face forwards and one backwards. Passerines occupy a variety of terrestrial habitats around the world, everywhere except Antarctica and some oceanic islands. The largest passerine by weight is the common raven (*Corvus corax*), while the longest is the male superb lyrebird (*Menura novaehollandiae*) at 97 cm (38 in) including its tail.

➥ *Birds, Songbirds*

ABOVE The hyacinth macaw is native to the South American rainforests.

PEA CRABS

(Subphylum: Crustacea Class: Malacostraca)

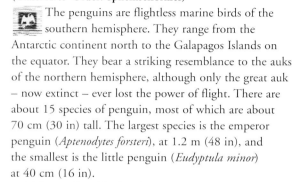 Pea crabs typically measure a few millimetres across. Some pea crabs are somewhat larger than peas, but the reason why they are so small is that they live in association with other animals. Many live within the shells of living bivalves, but they cause no harm. Over 200 species are known. European mussels often contain the pea crab *Pinnotheres pisum*. It scavenges fragments of food from its host but may also serve to keep the mussel clean, thereby having a symbiotic – mutually beneficial – relationship with the shellfish. Another species – *Pinnotheres ostreum* – lives in the mantle cavities of oysters.

➥ ***Crabs, Crustaceans***

PELICANS

(Class: Aves Order: Pelecaniformes)

The six species of pelican are among the largest birds. They can reach 1.8 m (70 in) in length, have wingspans of 3 m (10 ft) and weigh up to 13 kg (30 lb). Like their relatives, the cormorants, darters, frigate birds and gannets, pelicans have webbing between all four toes. They are aquatic birds that frequent saltwater and freshwater habitats. Fish make up the greater part of the pelican diet. They fish communally, corralling shoals by forming circular barrages and then lunging into the water in synchronized fashion. They possess elastic throat pouches for holding large numbers of fish.

➥ ***Comorants, Gannets***

ABOVE Pelicans can hold plenty of fish in their throat pouches.
ABOVE RIGHT Penguins are clumsy walkers, but very graceful in the water.

PENGUINS

(Class: Aves Order: Sphenisciformes)

The penguins are flightless marine birds of the southern hemisphere. They range from the Antarctic continent north to the Galapagos Islands on the equator. They bear a striking resemblance to the auks of the northern hemisphere, although only the great auk – now extinct – ever lost the power of flight. There are about 15 species of penguin, most of which are about 70 cm (30 in) tall. The largest species is the emperor penguin (*Aptenodytes forsteri*), at 1.2 m (48 in), and the smallest is the little penguin (*Eudyptula minor*) at 40 cm (16 in).

Fish, squid and krill make up the diet of all penguin species. In exchange for their loss of flight, penguins have become superbly adapted for swimming. They have streamlined bodies with their feet set at the back to reduce drag. Their wings have become flippers, ideally suited to propelling the birds through the water in a similar manner to flight. Penguins are typically rather awkward on land as a result, so they generally stay fairly near to the water.

❖ Penguins' single eggs are incubated in colonies called rookeries.

❖ The chicks huddle together in crèches while the parents hunt for food and they are fed on partially digested seafood.

➥ ***Auks, Birds***

PERCH

(Class: Osteichthyes Order: Perciformes)

Two species of perch are recognized – the common perch (*Perca fluviatilis*) and the yellow perch (*Perca flavescens*) – although the name is widely given to a number of unrelated fish species. The true perches inhabit still ponds and lakes. The common perch is native to Europe and northern Asia while the yellow perch is native to North America. Young fish tend to live in groups, feeding on tiny plant and animal organisms. The mature fish live solitary lives and feed on insects, crustaceans and small fish. They are popular as a food fish, being caught commercially and for sport.

➠ *Bony Fish, Carp*

PHALANGERS

(Class: Mammalia Order: Diprotodontia)

Phalangers are squirrel-like or lemur-like marsupials from Australasia. They are also known variously as possums, cuscus and gliders. Many species have prehensile tails to assist with climbing. Others are adapted for gliding from tree to tree, like flying

squirrels and flying lemurs. The sugar glider (*Petaurus breviceps*) is one such species. Its range extends from Australia to New Guinea, where it makes a living by feeding from the sap of gum and wattle trees. The striped phalanger (*Dactylopsila picata*) has an elongated finger on each forelimb especially adapted for hooking out wood-boring insect larvae, in the same way as the aye-aye of Madagascar.

➠ *Possums, Opussums*

PHALAROPES

(Class: Aves Order: Charadriiformes)

This family of birds is related to sandpipers, gulls, terns and auks. Their name is derived from the Greek for 'coot-foot', as phalaropes have long, coot-like toes and are excellent swimmers. They feed on small aquatic animals. Phalaropes are remarkable because they exhibit a highly unusual behaviour – gender role reversal. The females are larger than the males and are the more brightly coloured. They fight with one another for mating territories and they court the males, who take over all nesting duties. The males even take the young on their first migration southwards in autumn.

➠ *Gulls, Waders*

PIGEONS

(Class: Aves Order: Columbiformes)

There is no real difference between pigeons and doves. Smaller species tend to be called doves but there are exceptions. For example, feral or town pigeons are descended from the rock dove (*Columba livia*). Of the 250 species, two thirds of them live in southeast Asia and Australasia. Pigeons and doves are either fruit-eaters or seed-eaters. Many species have brightly coloured plumage, especially those from tropical regions. Pigeons and doves feed their young – squabs – on a secretion from the throat which is called 'crop-milk'.

The passenger pigeon (*Ectopistes migratorius*) was once one of the most numerous birds in North America. However, a government-sponsored culling programme led to its eventual extinction with perhaps 100 million specimens shot dead. The dodos and solitaires – Raphidae family – were relatives of the pigeons that used to frequent the islands of Mauritius, Rodriguez and Reunion. They were flightless and tame birds that were all extinct by 1800 due to the introduction of rats and cats and being hunted for food.

♣ The pink pigeon, from Mauritius, is one of the world's rarest creatures. At one time only 20 birds survived in the wild but breeding programmes have resulted in a gradual increase in its population.

➠ *Birds, Passerines*

ABOVE The sugar glider can 'fly' between trees in order to find food.

PIGS

(Class: Mammalia Order: Artiodactyla)

 The wild boar (*Sus scrofa*) is the ancestral species of domesticated pigs. It still roams most of Europe in its wild form. Other wild pigs include the wart hog (*Phacochoerus aethiopicus*) and bush pig (*Potamochoerus porcus*) from Africa. In Central and South America the wild pigs are known as peccaries. One of the oddest

looking pigs is the Babirusa (*Babirousa babyrussa*) which frequents the Celebes and Moluccas Islands of the East Indies. It has tusks that emerge through the muzzle and look similar to the antlers of small deer. All pigs are omnivores and use their keen sense of smell to root out food.

➠ *Mammals, Omnivores*

ABOVE The babirusa is an odd-looking pig with tusks on its muzzle.
ABOVE RIGHT Pikes lie in wait before suprising unsuspecting prey.

PIKAS

(Class: Mammalia Order: Lagomorpha)

Pikas are otherwise known as rock rabbits or mouse-hares, because they are members of the order Lagomorpha. Unlike their cousins, they have short ears and no tail. They can hop, but are nowhere near as fast on their feet. Their typical habitat is mountainous, rocky slopes with plenty of crevices for hiding from predators. During late summer, pikas harvest plants and dry them in the sun. Once dry the plants are stored in crevices as a supply of hay over the bleak winter months. Pikas are also known as calling hares, because they communicate to one another with bleating calls.

➠ *Hares, Rabbits*

PIKE

(Class: Osteichthyes Order: Esociformes)

Pike are related to the salmon and, like them, are freshwater predators. They are found throughout the northern hemisphere. Their camouflaged bodies are long and covered with small scales. Their heads are long and their large mouths are filled with strong teeth. The northern pike (*Esox lucius*) of Europe, reaches 1.4 m (4.5 ft) in length. Pike lie in wait amongst the vegetation of a river or pond and spring out at unsuspecting prey, such as small fish, invertebrates, amphibians and even small birds. Pike are hunted for sport but are also caught for the commercial market, being edible fish.

➠ *Bony Fish, Salmon*

PIPEFISH

(Class: Osteichthyes Order: Gasterosteiformes)

Pipefish and seahorses belong to the same family and share a number of physical and behavioural characteristics. Pipefish are covered in rings of bony armour, have long slender snouts and small mouths. Their bodies are long and slender and equipped with a single dorsal fin and a small tail fin. They, like seahorses, are weak swimmers, living amongst seaweed and other vegetation, where they can hide from predators. Male pipefish protect the fertilized eggs by carrying them in a brood pouch or keeping them stuck to their bodies. Pipefish typically live in warm marine habitats, though some venture into freshwater.

➠ *Fish, Seahorses*

PIPITS

(Class: Aves Order: Passeriformes)

These small brown insectivorous birds are related to wagtails and are placed in the same family. They are both ground-dwelling birds but pipits have a much larger distribution, being found worldwide. Wagtails are often brightly coloured but since pipits nest at ground level they have developed cryptic plumage as camouflage. Males and females have similar plumage. Between two and seven eggs are laid in one clutch and incubated by the female. Young pipits may leave the nest after only two weeks, often before they can fly. Like wagtails, pipits have long legs and feet. Pipits are often migratory.

➠ *Larks, Wagtails*

PIRANHAS

(Class: Osteichthyes Order: Characiformes)

Piranhas are fish notorious for their ability to attack and consume large animals in minutes, reducing them to bare bones. Most species, however, are plant-eaters and only four species are considered dangerous. Piranhas are inhabitants of freshwater in central and eastern parts of South America. They have deep bodies, blunt heads and powerful jaws. In carnivorous species these are lined with razor-sharp triangular teeth. When the jaws are closed the teeth can shear flesh like a pair of pinking shears. Piranhas are variable in length and colour. Some are silver with bright orange bellies, others are completely black. The red piranha (*Serrasalmus nattereri*) is silvery-grey on its back and sides but has a red belly. It reaches 30 cm (12 in). Carnivorous piranhas feed mostly on other fish, small

birds and aquatic invertebrates. However they can detect traces of blood in water and shoal in response.

❧ A large shoal of piranhas attacks in a rapid and frenzied manner and large mammals and even humans have been killed and eaten in this manner.

❧ Piranhas are egg-laying fish. The eggs are laid in long strands and attached to the roots of trees and both parents guard the eggs until they hatch.

➠ *Bony Fish, Fish*

PIT VIPERS

(Class: Reptilia Order: Squamata)

Pit vipers belong to the viper family but they have an unusual adaptation that warrants them being placed in a separate sub-family – Crotalinae. This adaptation is the presence of two sensory pits on the snakes' heads, enabling them to detect and accurately attack warm-blooded animals nearby. Pit vipers are found principally in the Americas in a wide range of habitats. They inhabit both desert and rainforest and may be aquatic, terrestrial or arboreal. They are all venomous. Some are egg-laying while others bear live young. The rattlesnakes, the copperhead (*Ancistrodon contortix*) and the fer-de-lance (*Bothrops atrox*) are all pit vipers.

➠ *Snakes, Vipers*

ABOVE The jaws of a piranha are lined with razor-sharp teeth.

PLACENTAL MAMMALS

Placental mammals represent the most advanced stage in mammalian development. The evolution of the placenta or afterbirth meant that the mammalian foetus could remain inside the uterus or womb until the young was in an advanced stage of development. A placental mammal is therefore born to the world at a point where it is far more likely to survive infancy, because it is essentially a free living animal. It is true, though, that some placental mammals are born more independent than others. The offspring of herbivores are able to walk within minutes of birth, so that they can evade predators. Yet carnivores give birth to young that require nurturing for some time before they can walk.

Eutheria is another name for the placental mammals, which includes humans. In many species the placenta is eaten by the mother following birth, because it comprises valuable nutrients that would otherwise go to waste. It is likely that humans continued doing the same until they reached a point where the nutritional loss was not significant enough to bother with. The placenta is a temporary organ which develops between the foetus and the mother. It is made of vascular tissue, looking somewhat like a liver. Its purpose is to supply oxygen and nutrients to the foetus from the mother's own blood. It also removes waste products from the foetus's metabolism so that they can be expelled in the mother's urine.

* Placental mammals have largely replaced marsupial mammals (metatheria) because they are better able to compete for habitat and resources. A few marsupials survive in the Americas, but their only real stronghold is Australasia because the region became geographically isolated before placental mammals had evolved.
* Giving birth to more advanced young meant that placental mammals were able to colonize areas with cold climates, and the oceans.

➡ *Marsupial Mammals, Monotreme Mammals*

ABOVE The platypus looks like a hybrid of a beaver and a duck.
RIGHT A snapping turtle defends its nest.

PLATYPUSES
(Class: Mammalia Order: Monotremata)

Along with echidnas, the platypus is the only egg-laying mammal. Known collectively as monotremes or prototheria, they demonstrate a link between reptiles and mammals. There is only one species, the platypus (*Ornithorhynchus anatinus*). It is sometimes called the duck-billed platypus, even though it is the only one. The platypus is very well adapted for an aquatic lifestyle. It has the body of a beaver and the feet and bill of a duck, resulting in a curious looking animal. However, it moves efficiently underwater and is adept at searching out invertebrates from mud and under stones using its sensitive mouth.

➡ *Echidnas, Monotreme Mammals*

POLLOCK
(Class: Osteichthyes Order: Gadiformes)

Pollock are marine fish of northern waters and are members of the codfish family. They are of commercial significance since they are valued as a food fish, often known as saithe or coley. Pollocks have streamlined bodies, three dorsal fins and a broad tail fin. They are greenish-brown or black on the dorsal surface and white underneath. Young fish remain in coastal waters and are commonly sighted in harbours. Older fish form large shoals that undertake long migrations to deeper waters where they feed almost exclusively on other fish. They can be distinguished from cod by their slightly forked tails.

➡ *Cod, Haddock*

POLYZOANS
(Phylum: Entoprocta and Ectoprocta)

These creatures are similar to corals in that they often live in colonies, enabling them to join forces in building large encrustations. They are variously known as polyzoans, bryozoans, ectoprocts and moss animals. The last name is probably the most useful in common language because the structures they make do indeed look rather like clumps of moss. Each living animal inhabits a narrow tube or test made from chitinous material at the outermost part of the structure. They use outstretched tentacles to catch particles of food in the surrounding water. There are species that live in marine and freshwater habitats.

➥ *Corals, Invertebrates*

POND TURTLES

(Class: Reptilia Order: Chelonia)

The order Chelonia includes tortoises, which are terrestrial, and turtles, which are aquatic. At one time the term 'turtle' was confined to describing those chelonians that are marine, but it is now applied to some of those that inhabit freshwater too – which were all previously named 'terrapins'.

Pond turtles live in freshwater, such as ponds, lakes and streams. Two species are well known – the snapping turtle (*Macrochelys temmincki*) and the European pond turtle (*Emys orbicularis*). The snapping turtle is so called because it is equipped with beak-like jaws which it uses to secure its prey. It ambushes animals from below, such as small aquatic rodents and birds, which it drags below the surface to drown. It waits for the carcasses to decompose before being able to bite off morsels to swallow. Other food includes aquatic invertebrates.

BELOW When threatened, porcupinefish inflate their bodies.

- Pond turtles have colouration of browns and greens so that they are camouflaged against the background of their habitat.
- They are also equipped with eyes and nostrils placed at the uppermost point of the skull so that they can breathe and keep an eye on the water's surface without being seen.
- This is an example of convergent evolution with the crocodile family.

➥ *Marine Turtles, Terrapins*

PORCUPINEFISH

(Class: Osteichthyes Order: Tetradontiformes)

Like their relatives, the puffers, these marine fish are able to inflate their bodies when attacked. Their scales are modified to carry long spines so when the fish are startled they inflate themselves and the spines become erect. In some species the spines are permanently erect, in others they can lie flat against the body when not required. Porcupine fish inhabit shallow water, and some species, such as the common porcupine-fish (*Diodon hystrix*) are found throughout the tropical oceans of the world. They are broad-bodied fish with relatively large eyes. They reach a maximum length of 90 cm (3 ft).

➥ *Cowfish, Puffers*

PORCUPINES

(Class: Mammalia Order: Rodentia)

Like hedgehogs and echidnas, porcupines have evolved sharp spines as a defence against predators. All three are unrelated though. The spines or quills are modified hairs and cause painful infections when they detach themselves into the flesh of predators. The animal

raises its spines and reverses into its adversary. The crested porcupine (*Hystrix cristata*) is a terrestrial species that lives communally in burrows and feeds on all manner of vegetable matter. The coendou (*Coendou prehensilis*) is an arboreal species with a prehensile tail to assist climbing. It has shorter spines to avoid getting caught up in the foliage of trees.

➧ *Hedgehogs, Rodents*

PORPOISES

(Class: Mammalia Order: Cetacea)

Porpoises differ from dolphins by having smaller, rounded dorsal fins and rounded snouts. They are stockier in shape and smaller, although there are exceptions that prove the rule on all counts. Porpoises are difficult to identify, but they have specific ranges, so a process of elimination can be used. Dall's porpoise (*Phocoenoides dalli*) is only found in the northern hemisphere, while Burmeister's porpoise (*Phocoena spinipinnis*) only frequents the southern hemisphere. Porpoises are shy creatures that live alone or in family

pods. There are six species altogether, including the smallest cetacean, the vaquita (*Phocoena sinus*), from the Sea of Cortez, West of Mexico.

➧ *Dolphins, Whales*

POSSUMS

(Class: Mammalia Order: Diprotodontia)

The name 'possum' is used to describe most of the arboreal marsupials in Australasia, as opposed to the 'opossums' of the Americas. More specifically it covers various members of the phalanger family. One of the most ubiquitous species is the brush-tailed or vulpine possum (*Trichosurus vulpecula*) which emanates from Tasmania as well as the mainland. It is hunted for its fur. ring-tailed possums (*Pseudochirus* sp.) are noted for their habit of making squirrel-like nests or drays in the forest canopy. They are the only possum to do this. Although

ABOVE LEFT The porcupine's quills cause infections in its predators' flesh.
ABOVE Ring-tailed possums make their nests in the forest canopy.

primarily herbivores, possums will also take insects, eggs and hatchlings when found.

➡ *Marsupials, Opossums*

PRAIRIE DOGS

(Class: Mammalia Order: Rodentia)

Despite its name, the prairie dog (*Cynomys ludovicianus*) is a rodent – a North American ground squirrel to be exact. Prairie dogs are communal animals, living in intricate burrow networks. Each individual has its own quarters and there are often so many animals that the burrows are described as 'towns'. When European settlers first arrived there were towns that extended for tens of kilometres. The animals became known as 'dogs' because they have a dog-like bark which they use to warn one another of danger. They take it in turns to stand on sentry duty while others forage nearby for food.

➡ *Rodents, Squirrels*

PRAYING MANTIDS

(Class: Insecta Order: Dictyoptera)

These insects are so called because they adopt a posture reminiscent of a person praying. Their forelegs are especially adapted for seizing prey animals at speed so that they have no opportunity to escape. Mantids hunt with a great deal of patience. They wait for another insect to come close and then stalk it using slow movements and acute eyesight. When they are close enough they strike with precision and immediately devour the head of the victim. They will take on any insect, provided it is small enough and will not sting, but their favourites are grasshoppers and crickets.

Praying mantid females are typically larger than the males, who need to approach with caution before mating to avoid being eaten. It is not unusual though for the

BELOW Mantids stalk their victims slowly and then eat their heads.
BELOW LEFT The prairie dog is a North American ground squirrel.

male to lose his life in the process of mating. This makes evolutionary sense as he is effectively providing nutrition for the development of his own offspring, and he would otherwise eventually die anyway.

❧ To help with their hunting technique, mantids are usually cryptically coloured, and can even adopt a suitable colour for their surroundings.

❧ Some mantids have eye-markings on their hindwings, which they use to scare away predators.

➡ *Cockroaches, Insects*

PRIMATES

(Class: Mammalia)

Humans (*Homo sapiens*) are included in the Primates order. The other primates are the apes, monkeys and strepsirhines. There are certain characteristics that define primates, but the order covers a range of species, so considerable variation is seen. Strepsirhines have a moist, dog-like snout. The strepsirhines are the lemurs, lorises, bush-babies, sifakas, indris, avahis, and aye-ayes. They all show the early stages of primate evolutionary adaptation, leading towards monkeys. Namely, the development of stereoscopic or binocular vision, increased brain size (relative to body size), and opposable thumbs and big toes.

In the monkeys there is a marked trend towards terrestrial habits, combined with the development of complex social behaviour. In the apes the tail is lost in favour of brachial locomotion (swinging from arm to arm) and the elongated foot and improved intelligence are seen, marking the final stages towards the earliest human design.

- There are many 'missing links' between the living apes and humans, but fossils have given physical anthropologists a good idea of how people evolved from ancestral apes.
- The first free-standing apes have been given the name 'australopithecines' which translates as 'southern-apes' as their fossils were first found in southern Africa.

➡ *Apes, Monkeys*

PRONGHORNS

(Class: Mammalia Order: Artiodactyla)

As its family (Antilocapridae) name indicates, the pronghorn (*Antilocapra americana*) seems to share affinities with both antelopes and goats, so it is classified on its own. All hollow-horned ungulates have unbranched horns except for the pronghorn, which has horns that are roughly 'y' shaped. Both sexes have horns. Pronghorns are herd animals that graze and forage on the plains of Canada, USA and Mexico. A herd comprises a dominant buck, a harem of does and their offspring. They are effective at evading predators by running at great speed. They can also swim across watercourses if the need arises.

➡ *Antelopes, Goats*

LEFT The northern-dwelling Japanese snow monkey, with young.
ABOVE Pronghorns live in herds on the Central and South American plains.

PROTOZOANS

(Kingdom: Protista)

 Protozoans include a vast assemblage of animal-like single-celled organisms that were once classified as animals but are now included in the kingdom Protista with algae and other unicellular organisms. As life-forms they have an obvious problem – they have to fit everything they need for survival into one cell. The most basic functions required for any protozoan species to survive are acquiring food, metabolism and reproduction. Then there is locomotion to find food and to evade predators. To do these the protozoa also need some rudimentary senses. And yet, they have managed all of these for nearly 2,000 million years.

➡ *Invertebrates*

PSEUDOSCORPIONS

(Class: Arachnida Order: Pseudoscorpiones)

These diminutive creatures are not directly related to the scorpions, although they do belong to the same class of animals. Their pedipalps (appendages in front of the first pair of legs) have been adapted into pincers for seizing and manipulating prey just like scorpions, but they lack the arching tail. There are over 1,500 species known so far, but there are likely to be many more as they are so small. Most are less than 8 mm (0.25 in) in length. Pseudoscorpions live in nooks and crannies – under bark and stones and so on. Some species inhabit dwellings where they prey on booklice, which they kill with poison pincers.

➡ *Arachnids, Scorpions*

PUFF ADDERS

(Class: Reptilia Order: Squamata)

Puff adders are closely related to rattlesnakes, pit vipers and copperheads. They all belong to the family Viperidae and are venomous. The puff adder (*Bitis arietans*) inhabits terrestrial Africa, mostly south of the Sahara. This snake is large, heavy and extremely aggressive. When confronted it rarely shies away but rather holds its ground and attacks. The venom is injected via the large fangs at the front of its mouth and is frequently lethal to humans. The puff adder gets its name from its habit of inflating its body and hissing in a threatening gesture. It has a colouration of grey-brown with cream chevrons.

➡ *Adders, Snakes*

PUFFERS

(Class: Osteichthyes Order: Tetradontiformes)

A number of fish have developed the ability to inflate their bodies with air or water when

BELOW Puffers enlarge themselves in the face of danger, to frighten predators.

threatened. Their enlarged bodies appear almost spherical in shape and this change in size and shape often scares off potential predators. Ninety species of fish capable of this temporary metamorphosis belong in the puffer family. Puffers typically inhabit warm and temperate marine waters around the world. Many species of puffer also contain a poisonous substance in their bodies as an added disincentive to potential predators. This poison is highly concentrated within the fish's body and can cause death to humans who consume it.

➡ *Fish, Porcupinefish*

PYTHONS
(Class: Reptilia Order: Squamata)

In the snake family Boidea there are many species of python and boa. Both types of snake kill by constriction. Pythons are found in tropical and sub-tropical regions from Africa eastwards to Australasia. Most are slow-moving and relatively inactive. They are normally found close to water and are adept swimmers. Reticulated pythons (*Python reticulatus*) are the longest snakes in the world, reaching 10 m (33 ft) from snout to tail-tip. They are able to kill and consume entire goats or pigs. While not normally considered dangerous to humans they have been known, though very rarely, to kill children.

➡ **Boas, Snakes**

RABBITS
(Class: Mammalia Order: Lagomorpha)

Domesticated varieties of rabbit are all descended from the wild rabbit (*Oryctolagus cuniculus*) which has been introduced to many parts of the world by humans.

ABOVE Rabbits live in a warren – a complex of underground passages.
RIGHT The rattlesnake adds a segment to its rattle each time it sheds its skin.

Its original range extended over the greater part of southern Europe. They live in burrow complexes called warrens and are gregarious. There are many other wild rabbit species. They are all more-or-less monotone in colour from black, through greys to white, except for the Sumatran short-eared rabbit (*Nesolagus netscheri*) which has a striped coat. It is adapted for a forest life and the colouration mimics the dappled light on the forest floor as a camouflage.

➡ **Hares, Pikas**

RACOONS
(Class: Mammalia Order: Carnivora)

The racoon (*Procyon lotor*) is the most familiar member of the family Procyonidae. In North America it has become a ubiquitous inhabitant of urban environments, being very well suited to living alongside humans. It has very catholic tastes in food, taking just about anything edible from garbage – plant or animal, natural or processed. Other members of the racoon family are far less comfortable in human company, preferring to remain in the forests of Central and South America. The coati or coatimundi (*Nasua nasua*) lives as far north as Arizona. It is a fox-like animal, although its tail is long and striped.

➡ **Carnivores, Pandas**

RAILS
(Class: Aves Order: Gruiformes)

The rails (family Rallidae) form the largest family in this order that also includes bustards, trumpeters and sun-bitterns. All the birds in this order lack a crop – an enlargement of the bird's gullet that can store food. There are over 100 species of rail. They are found worldwide in aquatic habitats such as marshlands and lakes. Rails tend to be plump birds of various sizes. They have short wings and tails but long legs and toes. They are poor fliers, preferring to run through the dense vegetation of their waterside habitats. The plumage of rails is often cryptically camouflaged. Short-billed species of rail are sometimes known as 'crakes'.

Gallinules form a group within the family. The purple gallinule (*Porphyrula martinica*) is one species and the common moorhen (*Gallinula chloropus*) is another. The coots are more aquatic than most rails. As a result

they sit in water with a duck-like posture, but they still possess the slender bill. Coots are also uncharacteristically aggressive birds, always ready to fight over territory.

They will even see-off much larger birds, such as geese and swans, by splashing the water and voicing harsh calls, especially if they wander too close to a nest.

➠ *Bustards, Sun Bitterns*

RATS

(Class: Mammalia Order: Rodentia)

The name 'rat' is one of those words used generically in zoology, but here we are discussing true rats. The most famous, if not infamous, species has to be the black rat (*Rattus rattus*). It was responsible for harbouring the bacterium (*Yersinia pestis*) that caused outbreaks of bubonic plague across Europe in the middle and late Medieval periods, when fleas transmitted it to humans. Both the black rat and the brown rat (*Rattus norvegicus*) originated from Asia, but extended their range by associating themselves with humans. Rats are opportunist feeders and pests, taking all manner of discarded and stored foodstuffs.

➠ *Mice, Rodents*

LEFT Rails, like the moorhen, are plump birds with long legs and slender bills.

RATTLESNAKES

(Class: Reptilia Order: Squamata)

Thirty species of these highly venomous snakes are found in the New World, from Canada down to South America. Rattlesnakes are most commonly found in hot and arid regions. If conditions become too hot, rattlesnakes rest during the day and become active at night. They may hibernate during winter. Most rattlesnakes have patterns of diamonds or hexagons on their backs. No rattlesnakes lay eggs – the females give birth to live young instead.

Rattlesnakes are pit vipers. This means that they possess heat-sensitive pits between each eye and each nostril. These pits are able to detect the warmth from the snakes' mammal and bird prey, as well as their distance and approximate size. If the rattlesnake wishes to deter another animal, or a human, from coming closer it may employ its rattle. This 'early warning system' is unique to this group of animals. The rattle is made of six to ten segments of dried skin. Each time a rattlesnake sheds its skin another rattle segment is added.

❧ Rattlesnakes ambush their prey when they are hunting. The lethal venom is injected into the prey with a quick strike.

❧ The two diamondback rattlesnakes (*Crotalus* spp.) of the USA are particularly dangerous to humans.

➠ *Pit Vipers, Snakes*

RAYS

(Class: Chondrichthyes Superorder: Batoidea)

Like their close relatives, the sharks and skates, rays have skeletons made of cartilage, not bone. Their bodies, like those of skates, are flattened and plate-like, with mouths placed on the under surface. The pectoral

fins of rays are greatly enlarged and appear continuous with the body. They are used to help propel the fish through water. The fish has spiracles, or holes on the upper surface of its head through which water is drawn and then passed to the gills. Fertilisation of eggs is internal and rays bear live young. They inhabit warm marine waters, particularly in the tropics.

➨ *Rays, Sharks*

REMORAS

(Class: Osteichthyes Order: Perciformes)

Also known as the sharksucker, the remora (*Echenis naucrates*) is a marine fish, found worldwide. Remoras have an unusual adaptation of the first dorsal fin, which is transformed into a sucker. The rays of the fin are adapted to produce many folds in a disc. As the folds are raised and moved the water between them is pushed out and a vacuum created. The suction is sufficient to enable a remora to attach itself firmly to another fish's side, such as a shark or barracuda, so that it can hitch a ride and benefit from eating its meal leftovers.

➨ *Sharks, Wrasses*

ABOVE The eastern fiddler ray has a flat body with enlarged pectoral fins.
ABOVE Monitor lizards are cold-blooded and live in tropical environments.

REPTILES

(Class: Reptilia)

Reptiles are vertebrates that typically possess scaly skin, are cold-blooded and lay eggs on land. They usually have two sets of limbs, although these may be vestigial, atrophied or entirely absent in some species. They are a successful group of animals that first appeared about 340 million years ago but were particularly prevalent in the Mesozoic Period (245–65 million years ago) – also known as the 'Age of the Reptiles', when the dinosaurs flourished. Reptiles are able to survive in hot and dry conditions, unlike moisture-loving amphibians. The possession of a scaly skin and shelled eggs means that many species are able to live completely terrestrially, because they avoid desiccation. They remain largely confined to tropical and temperate climates however, because they are cold-blooded – ectothermic. This means that they are unable to regulate their own body temperature, and rely on their environment for warmth.

Reptiles bask in sunshine to raise their core temperature, or move into shade to lower it. Some species hibernate to avoid the potential problems of surviving a cold winter. Others become dormant – aestivate – during extremely hot periods. Reptilian reproduction occurs by internal fertilization. Although some species do produce live young (viviparity), most lay eggs (oviparity), and parental care is unusual.

✤ There are four orders of extant or living reptile: Squamata (lizards and snakes), Chelonia (tortoises, turtles and terrapins), Crocodilia (crocodiles, alligators, caimans and allies), and Rhynchocephalia (the two species of tuatara – genus Sphenodon).

i There are six extinct orders of reptile: Ichthyosauria, Sauropterygia, Saurischia, Ornithiscia, Pterosauria, and Therapsida. They comprised a wide variety of species that colonized the land, air, oceans and rivers in the earth's prehistory. We know of them from fossil evidence.

i The order Therapsida contained reptiles that are the possible ancestors of mammals.

➨ *Oviparous Reptiles, Viviparous Reptiles*

RHEAS

(Class: Aves Order: Struthioniformes)

These flightless birds of South America are related to the ostrich and emu. Two species are recognized – the common rhea (*Rhea americana*) and Darwin's rhea (*Pterocnemia pennata*). Rheas are smaller than ostriches and emus, and have three toes on each foot instead of two. The common rhea is found from Brazil to Argentina. It is 1.2 m (4 ft) tall. Darwin's rhea is found from Peru to Patagonia. Male rheas mate with several females and make communal nests for all their hens. The males also incubate the eggs and take care of the hatchlings.

➥ *Emus, Ostriches*

RHINOCEROSES

(Class: Mammalia Order: Perissodactyla)

Rhinoceroses, or rhinos, as they are often known, are mammals, although they do bear a superficial resemblance to some of the dinosaurs, such as triceratops. This is because they happen to have evolved a similar form of defence from predators, with very thick skin and one or two horns on their heads.

In Africa there are two species of rhino – the black rhino (*Diceros bicornis*) and the white rhino (*Diceros simus*). They got their names because the white rhino has a wide lip which sounds like 'white lip' in Afrikaans, so the other species became the black rhino to distinguish it. The black rhino is also known as the hook-lipped rhino. They possess different shaped lips because the white rhino is a grazing, herd animal, whilst the black rhino is a solitary animal which forages from bushes and trees.

The Asian rhinoceroses are the Indian rhino (*Rhinoceros unicornis*) which has one horn, the Sumatran rhino (*Dicerorhinus sumatrensis*) which has two and the javan rhino (*Rhinoceros sondaicus*), which is also known as the lesser rhino. The Indian rhino is a grazing species. It has very thick, armour-like plates of skin and a sharp, two foot horn for fending off attacks from tigers. The other two species are smaller creatures of dense forest. All rhinos are now rare due to a combination of hunting and habitat destruction.

BELOW The northern white is the world's rarest species of rhino.

❖ The white rhino is the largest terrestrial mammal after elephants and giraffes. It holds the record for longest horn at 1.6 m (5 ft 2 in).

❖ White rhinos weigh between three and four tons as adults.

❖ All rhinos have relatively small brains, but plenty of brawn.

❖ Rhinos have tridactyl feet – meaning they each have three hooves.

❖ Rhinoceroses are herbivores, eating a variety of plant material.

❖ The horns of rhinoceroses are made from modified clumps of hair.

➥ *Elephants, Herbivores*

RODENTS

The order Rodentia includes mice, rats, hamsters, mole-rats, porcupines, cavies, agoutis, chinchillas, pacas, squirrels, beavers, gophers, voles, dormice, jerboas,

lemmings and muskrats. Clearly they are a successful group of mammals in both the Old and New Worlds. They also vary considerably in shape and size, but the one consistent and easily discernible characteristic is their dentition. They all have prominent chisel-like incisors, which they use for gnawing at their food. These teeth have enamel only on their outer surface and are forever growing so that the animal has no concern about excessive wear.

However, domesticated rodents may suffer from insufficient tooth wear, leading to the incisors growing far too long for use. Behind the incisors are grinding teeth, for breaking down foodstuffs, which can often be very tough plant matter. Rodents lack canine teeth and often have only molars, with no premolars. Although rodents are essentially herbivorous, many species will take an omnivorous diet.

ABOVE The mammalian order Rodentia includes the coendon.
RIGHT The lilac-breasted roller is related to kingfishers and bee-eaters.

Most rodents are medium- or small-sized animals, but a few are large. Capybaras, along with the porcupines and beavers, are the biggest rodents. Harvest mice are among the smallest. Rodents are famed for their ability to multiply rapidly, given the right conditions. This characteristic is so pronounced in some species that it causes fluctuations in the numbers of predators that feed on them. Voles and lemmings are good examples. Rodents are usually terrestrial, subterranean or arboreal in habit, but many can swim and some have taken to a semi-aquatic lifestyle, such as capybaras and beavers.

❧ No rodents can truly fly, but flying squirrels have evolved an ability to glide from tree to tree.

❧ There are rodents that live in desert, polar, mountainous, tropical, temperate, and marine habitats.

❧ Rodentia is the largest mammalian order, with nearly 2,000 species.

➽ *Beavers, Rats*

ROLLERS

(Class: Aves Order: Coraciiformes)

Rollers are related to kingfishers, bee-eaters and hornbills. There are 17 species of roller, found in warm regions of Eurasia, Africa and Australia. The name 'roller' comes from the extraordinary aeronautic displays that the birds conduct as part of their courtship rituals,

in which they somersault, swoop and dive to impress. Rollers are stocky in build with short legs. Their bills are fairly robust and equipped with a slight hook for tearing flesh. They are pigeon-sized birds, with bright plumage in blues, violets and greens, that congregate in noisy flocks. Rollers eat ants, lizards, locusts and small mammals.

➠ *Bee-eaters, Kingfishers*

ROUNDWORMS

(Phylum: Nemotoda)

The term 'roundworm' is usually used to refer to nematodes, although it is sometimes loosely used to describe other groups. They are not segmented and possess a fully developed digestive tract with a mouth and anus at either end. One interesting detail is that they all display a phenomenon known as 'cell constancy'. This means that after hatching from their eggs they always comprise the same number of cells even though they may grow considerably larger. Over 12,000 species are recorded, of which the nematodes make up the vast majority. Many are serious parasitic pests of humans and their livestock.

➠ *Annelid Worms, Nematode Worms*

RUDD

(Class: Osteichthyes Order: Cypriniformes)

The rudd (*Scardinius erythrophthalmus*) is a member of the carp family and is found naturally in Europe and Asia, but has recently been introduced to North America. It is an edible, freshwater fish that is caught commercially and for sport. The rudd has a heavy, medium-length body that is golden in colour. Its eyes are yellow and its fins are red. It is very similar in appearance to the roach, but its dorsal fin is set farther back. The rudd lives in heavily vegetated and still water where it eats plant and animal matter. It lives in small shoals.

➠ *Carp, Goldfish*

BELOW Rudd are edible and fished both commercially and for sport.

SALAMANDERS

(Class: Amphibia Order: Caudata)

 Salamanders and newts are very similar physically but differ in their behaviour. Since there is no clear or obvious physical difference between newts and salamanders they are not given different scientific classifications. Some salamanders spend their whole lives in water and others tend to live terrestrial lives, even during the larval and breeding stages of their lifecycle.

Salamanders have slender bodies, long tails and four legs of equal length. They absorb oxygen through their skins, and are found only in moist habitats, mostly confined to the temperate regions of the northern hemisphere. Unlike other amphibians, fertilization of eggs is internal. The lifecycle is complex and, like that of other amphibians, has a larval stage which may last months or years. The larvae have external gills, teeth in both jaws and no eyelids. These features may continue into adulthood – a phenomenon known as neoteny and exemplified by the axolotl. Some species of salamander require a moist habitat but shun the aquatic habitat, even being able to breed on land.

❧ Salamanders are often boldly coloured and brightly patterned.

❧ They are normally 100–150 mm (4–6 in) in length although the largest salamander, the Chinese salamander, is 1.5 m (5 ft) long.

➥ *Axolotls, Newts*

Similar to newts, salamanders are often brightly coloured. Shown here are Pyrenean fire (ABOVE) and cave (TOP) salamanders.

SALMON
(Class: Osteichthyes Order: Salmoniformes)

The term 'salmon' applies both to the species *Salmo salar*, or Atlantic salmon, and to all fish of the family Salmonidae. These fish characteristically have elongated, fusiform bodies that are covered with small and rounded scales. They have an extra fin between the dorsal fin and the tail. They are normally carnivorous, eating crustaceans, insects and small fish. Salmon are found in both marine and freshwater regions of the northern hemisphere. They are inhabitants of cold and temperate areas.

❖ Although many salmon are still fished in the open sea they are increasingly being produced intensively on commercial farms.

➥ *Char, Trout*

SAND LIZARDS
(Class: Reptilia Order: Squamata)

The sand lizard (*Lacerta agilis*) belongs to the same family as the skinks, wall lizards, tegu lizards and girdled lizards. Together they form the largest group of lizards with over 1,800 species worldwide. The sand lizard inhabits scrubby, heathland areas from the British

Members of the salmon family tend to be dull in colour when not breeding. As the breeding season approaches the males usually turn red, developing a hooked snout and a humped back. Most species return to fresh water to breed, locating the same spawning grounds from which they themselves emerged. Spawning normally occurs in free-running and clean water. The king salmon and chum salmon, of North America, swim over 3,200 km (2,000 miles) from the ocean to the headwaters of the River Yukon, in order to spawn.

❖ Pacific salmon and Atlantic salmon are two of the most commercially important species of salmon.

Isles across Europe and into Central Asia. It is variable in colour although it is commonly a greenish brown. The male has brighter colouring during the mating season. This lizard eats small invertebrates such as spiders and insects. If attacked it can drop its tail. This defence mechanism, called autotomy, leaves the lizard free to escape.

➥ *Lizards, Skinks*

ABOVE The chinook salmon takes its name from tribes living along the banks of the Columbia river.

SAVANNAH LIFE

Savannahs are typically flat plains covered by grasses, with the occasional tree. They present particular problems for predator and prey animals alike, because visibility is high in such open places. Many animals have evolved colours and patterns that help to conceal their whereabouts or blur the outlines of their bodies against the background. Most animals on the savannah lack colour vision, so colours and patterns that seem garish to the human eye work very effectively in the eyes of their adversaries.

Prey animals often gather in herds so that they can work as a team. There is always at least one pair of eyes on the lookout for danger and stampeding helps to confuse predators during the chase. Predators therefore have to approach with stealth and hope to single out vulnerable members of a herd so that they stand a better chance of making a kill.

RIGHT Oxpecker birds eat ticks and insects from this warthog's skin.
FAR RIGHT Giraffes are able to reach leaves on high branches.
ABOVE RIGHT Lions are the only cats to live in large family groups
MAIN African elephants inhabit the Savannah plains.

SAVANNAH REGIONS

ARCTIC

NORTH
AMERICA

EUROPE

Tropic of Cancer

ASIA

AFRICA

Equator

SOUTH
AMERICA

Tropic of Capricorn

AUSTRALIA

African Savannah

South American Pampas

Savannah regions

ANTARCTICA

SAWFISH

(Class: Chondrichthyes Superorder: Batoidea)

Sawfish are fish with skeletons made of cartilage, not bone. They are types of ray, belonging to the family Pristidae and are closely related to sharks and skates. They inhabit shallow coastal water in tropical and sub-tropical areas where they dwell on the seabed, rooting out small animals to eat with their long saw-like snouts, that give them their name. Their snouts have strong teeth on either side which are thrashed through the water to disable prey. Although primarily marine fish, sawfish do swim in estuaries and have been known to swim upriver and breed in freshwater lakes.

➡ *Rays, Sharks*

SAWFLIES

(Class: Insecta Order: Hymenoptera)

These insects are appropriately named as females often possess an ovipositor with a saw-like edge which is used to cut into plant stems. Unlike their relatives – ants, bees and wasps – sawflies do not have a distinct waist between their thorax and abdomen. Sawflies are solitary insects, although their larvae are often found living in close-knit groups, and can sometimes infest plants in great numbers. Their larvae are always vegetarian, either feeding on foliage or wood. The larvae that feed on leaves are like the caterpillars of butterflies and moths, while those that feed on wood are more like the grubs of ants and bees.

➡ *Bees, Wasps*

SCORPIONFISH

(Class: Osteichthyes Order: Scorpaeniformes)

This family of marine fish is characterised by the possession of bodies that are covered in armoured scales, well-developed spines on the head and robust rays in the fins. They are related to gurnards or sea robins. The scorpionfish (*Scorpaena porcus*) is an inhabitant of the North Atlantic and the Mediterranean Sea. It hides from predators on the seabed, amongst seaweed. If attacked its spines administer doses of poison into the predator's skin.

ABOVE Scorpions have been in existence for as long as 400 million years.
TOP Scorpionfish have poisonous spines and protective armoured scales.

Its mottled brown body is well camouflaged amongst the vegetation and this also helps it to catch its unsuspecting prey of invertebrates and smaller fish.

➡ *Bony Fish, Gurnards*

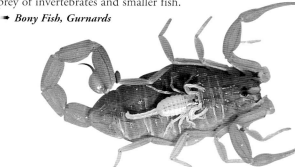

SCORPIONS

(Class: Arachnida Order: Scorpiones)

With their fearsome-looking pincers and sting-laden tails, scorpions are impressive creatures. They are the most ancient of the terrestrial arthropods and obviously very well designed. 400 million-year-old fossil scorpions have been found. Scorpions range in size from 12 mm (0.5 in) to 180 mm (7 in) and some 700 species are known. Most are harmful only to their prey but a few are dangerous to humans. The poison in their sting is made from chemicals called neurotoxins, which attack the nervous system. Paralysis of vital muscles, used in circulation and breathing, is what kills the victim.

➡ *Pseudoscorpions, Sunspiders*

SCREAMERS

(Class: Aves Order: Anseriformes)

There are only three species in this South American family of waterfowl. Like their relatives, the ducks, geese and swans, screamers live on estuaries, rivers and lakes. They congregate in large numbers at the water's edge, eat marsh plants and make their reed nests. Screamers are big, turkey-like birds, reaching 75 cm (30 in) in length. They have plump bodies on long legs with wide, webbed feet. They are competent fliers and can soar at great heights. The species are the horned screamer (*Anhinga cornuta*), the crested screamer (*Chauna torquata*) and the black-necked screamer (*Chauna chavaria*).

➡ *Waders, Waterfowl*

SEA COWS

(Class: Mammalia Order: Sirenia)

There are four species in this order; three manatees and the dugong (*Dugong dugon*). Sea cows are not related to terrestrial cows, but are plant feeders that graze water plants like cows. The dugong frequents the Indian Ocean rim, from the eastern coast of Africa to the northern coast of Australia. Of the manatees, one is marine, like the dugong, and lives in tropical, Atlantic waters. The other two inhabit rivers of west Africa and the Amazon Basin. Sea cows offer some idea about the evolution of whales and dolphins from terrestrial ancestors, although they are descended from herbivores, not carnivores.

➡ *Seals, Whales*

SEA CUCUMBERS

**(Phylum: Echinodermata
Class: Holothuroidea)**

Despite their name these organisms are animals and not plants. They are, though, cucumber-like in shape, being cylindrical with a rosette of tentacles at one end. They have a skeletal framework of microscopic spicules – needle-like calcareous structures – within their skins. Sea-cucumbers feed by filtering mud from the ocean floor. Organic matter is digested and indigestible material is expelled

BELOW Cone shells are tropical sea snails which use venom to deter predators.

from the body. The mouth is at one end, surrounded by the tentacles. The animals travel by walking on tube feet or by contractions of the body. They eject their innards through their anus as a decoy defence against predators.

➡ *Sea Urchins, Starfish*

SEA SLUGS

(Phylum: Mollusca Class: Gastropoda)

These are a solely marine group of gastropods. Those that still possess a shell have it reduced to a vestige which is external or internal. Having no protective shells has led to some interesting forms of defence. Sea slugs come in a wide variety of shapes and colours. Some are designed to be camouflaged against their habitats while others are designed to deliberately stand out to warn predators that they are poisonous. Similarly, sea slugs have adopted various forms of locomotion and feeding preferences. Some are plant eaters while others are carnivores, even preying on other sea slugs.

➡ *Molluscs, Sea Snails*

SEA SNAILS

(Phylum: Mollusca Class: Gastropoda)

Sea snails are broadly divided into three groups. There are 'archeogastropods' (old gastropods), 'mesogastropods' (intermediate gastropods) and 'neogastropods' (new gastropods). These classifications reflect their order of evolutionary development. Archeogastropods have simple domed shells, such as the limpets. Mesogastropods and neogastropods have spiral shells and are equipped with more advanced muscular feet for locomotion. Those which frequent the muddy ocean floors often possess a siphonal tube with which they can draw in clean water to their gills, rather like a snorkel. Most species from the lower groups are plant feeders, but the neogastropods are all carnivorous snails, with a specialised proboscis.

➡ *Molluscs, Sea Slugs*

SEA SNAKES

(Class: Reptilia Order: Squamata)

 Snakes are normally considered terrestrial animals, with a few species being able to live in freshwater. The marine sea snakes are an extraordinary exception. There are at least 50 species of these venomous creatures that inhabit the tropical western Pacific and Indian Oceans. Their bodies are specifically adapted for dealing with reproduction and locomotion in the marine environment.

They swim with an eel-like undulation. The tails and bodies of sea snakes are compressed laterally into large, paddle-shaped structures and their nostrils have valves to prevent water flooding in. The bias of weight is towards the trunk of the body; the head and neck are small and lightweight. This enables the snake to strike forward to catch prey without producing a significant backward thrust.

❧ Sea snakes are usually 1–1.2 m (3–4 ft) long. They live on a diet of fish and, while some species lay eggs on land, most give birth to live young while at sea – a process called viviparity.

❧ Some sea snakes are so well-adapted to a marine life that they are virtually helpless on land. Sea snakes are, like the elapids – cobras and vipers – a highly venomous group.

❧ They are reluctant to attack humans but their venom can be lethal.

➠ *Coral Snakes, Snakes*

SEA SPIDERS

(Subphylum: Chelicerata Class: Pycnogonida)

The taxonomy of these creatures is a matter of contention, because they are somewhat bizarre in form. Their bodies are very small relative to their legs, giving them a rather skeletal appearance. In fact, the legs have evolved to contain the ovaries, such is the lack of room. Although described as 'spiders'

ABOVE Seahorses anchor themselves to seaweed with their tails.

they are not related and any resemblance is only in passing since they often have five or six pairs of legs. Sea spiders feed on sedentary, soft-bodied, marine organisms such as sea anemones. They insert a massive tubular proboscis and slowly suck out the victims' bodily fluids.

➠ *Arachnids, Crustaceans*

SEAHORSES

(Class: Osteichthyes Order: Gasterosteiformes)

Seahorses are all members of the genus Hippocampus and they are closely related to the pipefish. The unusual appearance of seahorses makes them popular aquarium fish. They are inhabitants of shallow, coastal waters in tropical and temperate areas.

They live amongst the seaweed where they hunt food. They eat small marine organisms that cannot escape easily, for they are not adept swimmers. They move forwards and backwards with use of their lateral fins while vertical movements are controlled by their swim bladders.

Seahorses have an upright posture that they maintain even when swimming. Their slender bodies terminate in long curved tails that are prehensile. This adaptation enables the fish to clasp on to seaweed. The heads of seahorses are similar to those of horses, hence their common name. The integument, or outer layer of the body, is covered in large, rectangular bony plates. They often have plant-like projections and spines that help camouflage the fish among strands of seaweed.

❧ Seahorses are egg-laying fish but they have an unusual method of nurturing the developing embryos. The female puts her fertilized eggs into the abdominal brood pouch of the male. He carries the eggs until they hatch. The hatchlings are then expelled.

➠ *Fish, Pipefish*

SEALS

(Class: Mammalia Order: Carnivora)

The seals and walruses make up this group of aquatic mammals – the pinnipeds. They are all marine species except for the Baikal seal (*Pusa caspica*) of Lake Baikal, southern Siberia. All species are carnivorous, taking a variety of foods, including fish, crustaceans, cephalopods, seabirds and shellfish, depending on the species. Pinnipeds typically have a layer of subcutaneous blubber and a layer of dense fur for insulation. They range from the coldest polar waters to the Galapagos Islands at the Equator.

Seals are divided into two families; earless seals (*Phocidae*) and eared seals (*Otariidae*). The eared seals comprise sea lions and sea bears or fur seals. All other seals are earless, or rather they lack outer ear flaps. Eared seals are less aquatic than earless seals, with strong limbs with which they can walk on land quite effectively. Earless seals struggle to move on land and are therefore far more vulnerable to predators when out of water. Walruses are classified in a third family of their own – *Odobenidae*. There is one species (*Odobenus rosmarus*). Walruses have enormously enlarged upper canine teeth or tusks, which they use to prize animals from the ocean bed, and crushing molars to grind them into a paste.

There is usually marked sexual dimorphism in pinniped species. The larger bulls compete for cows by duelling with one another. Calves are born on land and suckled by their mothers on rich milk. As the calves begin to mature they enter crèches so that they remain safe while their mothers are out at sea feeding.

BELOW Leopard seals are fierce predators, feeding on small seals and penguins.

❧ The leopard seal (*Hydrurga leptonyx*) of the Southern Ocean is a fearsome predator of other smaller seals and penguins.

❧ Seals will haul themselves from the water for three reasons – to rest, to breed and to moult, usually on safe, inaccessible beaches or rocky outcrops.

➠ *Dolphins, Manatees*

SEED SHRIMPS

(Subphylum: Crustacea Class: Ostracoda)

These animals are unique among crustaceans in having evolved a bivalved carapace just like the bivalve shellfish. They have adapted to marine and freshwater environments and are all small species, the largest being no more than 18 mm (0.75 in) in length. A few have become terrestrial. Many are free swimming, but others scuttle about on the floor of their habitat. When danger threatens they withdraw their limbs and other appendages enabling them to close the two halves of their shell together. Most species consume organic debris and algae or are filter-feeders. Some larger species predate other smaller organisms.

➠ *Crustaceans, Shrimps*

SHARKS

(Class: Chondrichthyes Sub-Class: Elasmobranchi)

 Sharks, skates, rays and chimaeras are all cartilaginous fish that are believed to have evolved from a common ancestor. There are approximately 340 species of

shark and they represent a very successful group of animal that has changed relatively little in the last 100 million years. They are predominantly marine fish of tropical and temperate waters.

These large fish are commonly grey in colour with a leathery skin that is covered in tooth-like scales. Their skeletons are made of cartilage, not bone. Shark teeth are normally arranged in rows and are replaced when lost. They have five to seven gill slits on either side of their heads. Unlike most bony fish, sharks do not have swim bladders and this means they typically need to keep moving in order to ensure a continual flow of water through their gills. Some sharks have oil-filled livers that aid buoyancy.

Fertilization is internal in all species of shark, although there are considerable variations in other aspects of reproduction. Some species lay eggs in leathery pouches, others are live-bearing.

Most sharks are efficient predators, although a few are plankton-eaters. Acute senses of hearing and smell

ABOVE The whale shark is the largest fish and can grow up to 15 m (49 ft).
RIGHT Shrimps and prawns eat whatever scraps of food they can find.

contribute to the shark's ability to hunt. They are also able to detect weak electrical stimuli caused by muscle contractions in other fish. Sharks may attack in groups or singly, often attracted by trace amounts of blood in the water. Attacks on humans are rare but only two-thirds of people attacked by sharks are likely to survive.

❖ The largest fish is the whale shark (*Rhincodon typus*) which can reach lengths of 15 m (49 ft). It is a plankton feeder, like the baleen whales.

❖ The cookie-cutter shark reaches only 50 cm (19 in).

❖ Sharks often fast during the breeding season but utilize lipid – oil – reserves in their livers to maintain them.

➡ ***Cartilaginous Fish, Fish***

SHEATHBILLS

(Class: Aves Order: Charadriiformes)

This family of birds is unusual in that it is the only group of birds that is found exclusively in the Antarctic region. There are only two species of sheathbill – the snowy sheathbill (*Chionis alba*), which measures 40 cm (16 in) and has a yellow bill and the lesser sheathbill (*Chionis minor*), which is slightly smaller and has a black bill. They are related to gulls, terns and auks. Sheathbills have short, blue-grey legs and eyes that are rimmed with pink. Generally sheathbills are found at the shoreline, where they live in groups and nest in rocky crevices. They are primarily scavenging birds.

➡ ***Gulls, Skuas***

SHEEP

(Class: Mammalia Order: Artiodactyla)

Goats and sheep are very similar, but there are a few subtle differences. Sheep have relatively long, drooping tails and no bearded chin in the male. Sheep's horns also tend to be placed wider apart and grow more-or-less sideways, rather than backwards. In terms of lifestyle, sheep are better adapted for easier terrain, not being equipped for climbing rocky mountainsides, but preferring pastured valleys. The many varieties of the domestic sheep (*Ovis aries*) are descended from the mouflon (*Ovis musimon*), a European wild sheep that still frequents remote areas in Corsica and Sardinia. There are reintroduced flocks in mainland Europe.

➡ ***Cattle, Goats***

SHREWS

(Class: Mammalia Order: Insectivora)

Being so small, shrews have a very high surface area to volume ratio, which means that they have a job maintaining their homeostasis – stabilizing body temperature. They lose body heat easily and their invertebrate diet has little to offer in terms of carbohydrate (energy) value. Consequently, shrews have an interesting strategy for survival. They live by a cycle, throughout the night and day, of three hours feeding then three hours resting and so on, continually throughout their lives. They also have to eat relatively large amounts of prey – something like their own weight in food every 24 hours. They taste unpleasant to predators.

➡ *Desmans, Hedgehogs*

SHRIKES

(Class: Aves Order: Passeriformes)

This family contains the true shrikes and the bush shrikes. There is another family –Vangidae – which contains the vanga-shrikes of Madagascar. Shrikes are typically solitary birds found in scrubland and open woodland. They are usually two-tone in colour – dark above, pale below – and make harsh calls. Shrikes have slightly hooked bills which they use to kill their prey such as insects, lizards, mice and small birds. They are known to impale their prey on thorns, giving rise to their nickname 'butcherbirds'. They do this to store food at times of plenty so it remains out of reach from scavengers.

➡ *Flycatchers, Rollers*

SHRIMPS

(Subphylum: Crustacea Order: Malacostraca)

Shrimps and prawns must be among the most familiar crustaceans, being important food animals for humans around the world. Like lobsters and crabs, they are decapods – having 10 limbs. There are many thousands of species of

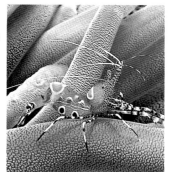

shrimp and prawn. Most are opportunistic feeders, taking whatever scraps of food they can find. This can include eggs, plankton and the remains of dead animals. The two most familiar species served on European tables are the common brown shrimp (*Crangon vulgaris*) and the common prawn (*Palaemon serratus*). Both are coastal species that feed in shoals during incoming and outgoing tides over sandy beaches.

➡ *Crabs, Crustaceans*

BELOW The sidewinder propels itself across the sand, leaving distinctive tracks.

SIDEWINDERS

(Class: Reptilia Order: Squamata)

The sidewinder rattlesnake (*Crotalus cerastes*), from North America, gets its common name from its unusual method of locomotion. Instead of slithering forwards with its body in contact with the ground, the sidewinder propels its body over loose sand diagonally, leaving a characteristic series of j-like marks. This method of locomotion is also used by the horned viper (*Cerastes cerastes*), from Africa, as it happens to be the most efficient mode of travel over sand for a snake. The sidewinder has a body coloured pale tan, pink or grey. It has a pale pattern of spots on its back and sides.

➡ *Horned Vipers, Snakes*

SILVERFISH

(Class: Insecta Order: Thysanura)

These are small, primitive insects that lack wings and display only very slight metamorphosis as they grow. Silverfish are fish-like in appearance, being shuttle-shaped and covered by silvery scales. They are otherwise known as bristletails because they possess three tail-like appendages which are covered by tiny bristles. In homes silverfish often thrive by feeding on detritus beneath cupboards and the like, but most species live in wild habitats; under tree bark for example. They have catholic tastes in food, taking all kinds of organic debris, especially starchy substances.

➡ *Insects, Invertebrates*

SKATES

(Class: Chondrichthyes Superorder: Batoidea)

Skates are closely related to sharks and placed in the same group as rays. Their bodies are flat and contain skeletons made of cartilage, not bone. A skate's pectoral fins are greatly enlarged to form wing-like structures that extend from the snout to the beginning of a slender tail and are used for swimming. Unlike other rays, which bear live young, skates lay eggs. These are protected in leathery cases which have curly tendrils at each corner and are known as 'mermaid's purses'. Skates live in most parts of the world dwelling on the sea-floor in shallow or deeper waters.

➡ *Rays, Sharks*

SKIMMERS

(Class: Aves Order: Charadriiformes)

Skimmers are related to the gulls, turns and skuas. They live in estuaries and wide rivers in warm climates. There are three species of skimmer – the black skimmer (*Rynchops nigra*), the African skimmer (*Rynchops flavirostris*) and the Indian skimmer (*Rynchops albicollis*). All possess the characteristic blade-like bill, but only as adults. The lower half of the bill extends beyond the upper half as an adaptation for catching fish. The birds fly low over water with the lower mandible cutting through

the water – skimming the water. When the birds strike fish their bills close on them with a reflex action.

➡ *Gulls, Skuas*

SKINKS

(Class: Reptilia Order: Squamata)

There are over 1,200 members of the lizard family Scincidae and they are collectively known as skinks. Skinks are typically found in tropical regions throughout the world, particularly in Asia. Their bodies are long and cylindrical with shiny scales – an adaptation that suits their burrowing way of life. Most skinks are under 20 cm (8 in) in length but some reach 66 cm (26 in). Many skinks have reduced or absent limbs. The majority of skinks are ground-dwelling, but some species are arboreal and others are aquatic. Skinks are closely related to girdled lizards, whiptails, wall lizards and tegus.

➡ *Lizards, Reptiles*

SKUAS

(Class: Aves Order: Charadriiformes)

Like their relatives, the gulls and terns, skuas are predatory seabirds. The great skua or bronxie (*Catharacta skua*) is the only bird to breed in both the Arctic and Antarctic. It can reach 60 cm (24 in) in length and is an efficient scavenger as well as predator. It harasses other seabirds into dropping their catches of fish. In the USA the smaller, Arctic-breeding skuas are known as 'jaegers'. Skuas nest close to colonies of other seabirds, such as auks and penguins. Although they raid nests for eggs and chicks, they also remove carcasses and single out the genetically weak.

➡ *Auks, Gulls*

ABOVE Most skinks are ground-dwelling and their shiny scales aid burrowing. RIGHT Sloths are so-called because they can only move very slowly.

SKUNKS

(Class: Mammalia Order: Carnivora)

Skunks are renowned for their smell. It is a defence mechanism that works so well that they scarcely bother to evade predators. If its warning colouration of black and white markings fails to register with a predator the skunk turns around so that its rear end is facing the adversary. It is then able to squirt the foul smelling fluid from its musk glands, right into the enemy's face. There is no predator that will persist once dealt with in this way, since the odour is strong enough to halt breathing for an effective period, while the skunk slips away.

➠ *Badgers, Weasels*

SLATERS

(Class: Crustacea Order: Isopoda)

Slaters are essentially woodlice adapted for aquatic and semi-aquatic environments. They are isopods. Marine species tend to be known as sea slaters, while freshwater species are called water slaters. They have other colloquial names such as hoglice and sowbugs. Most species are quite small, but some sea slaters reach 25 mm (1 in) or more. Slaters generally prefer to feed under cover of darkness, so they are typically found hiding during daylight hours, in weed or under stones. They feed on organic detritus, helping to keep the habitat clean. They often have their front legs modified for holding food.

➠ *Crustaceans, Woodlice*

SLOTHS

(Class: Mammalia Order: Xenarthra)

There are five species of sloth, divided into two families – three species of three-toed sloth (*Bradypus* spp.) and two species of two-toed sloth (*Choloepus* spp.). The first family have three toes on each limb, while the second family have three toes on their

LEFT Skunks have a very effective form of defence – a foul smell.

hindlimbs but just two toes on their forelimbs. They also have differences internally, such as their number of ribs. They all live in South American tropical forests. Sloths are folivores, meaning they eat leaves and buds from trees, especially Cecropia trees. They acquired the name 'sloths' because they are able to move only very slowly.

Their slow movement is an adaptation designed to save energy, because their food is low in carbohydrates. Also, hanging from branches takes very little effort because their claws are hook-like. The only trouble is that they cannot escape predators very easily as a result. Consequently they always remain high in the canopy, out of easy reach. Additionally, algae grows on their fur, providing them with a green colour a functions as camouflage.

❧ Despite their awkwardness on the ground, sloths can swim across rivers quite easily when required. Their strongest motive for doing so is to meet mates from different forest areas.

➠ *Herbivores, Mammals*

SLOW-WORMS

(Class: Reptilia Order: Squamata)

 Regardless of their name and snake-like appearance these animals are actually limbless lizards. Also, they are only slow when cold. They can be identified as lizards by their eyelids that can be closed and their ability to shed their tails – autotomy – when captured by predators. Regeneration of tails can be slow. Common throughout Britain and most of Europe, slow-worms are absent from Ireland. They live in hedgerows, grassland, heathland and woodland borders, where they prey on soft invertebrates such as earthworms and slugs. Slow-worms are usually a shiny golden brown colour although in some regions they have bluish spots.

➨ *Glass Lizards, Lizards*

SLUGS

(Class: Mollusca Order: Gastropoda)

Slugs are really snails without shells. In fact, some slugs do have vestigial shells. Because they lack shells, slugs are more vulnerable to desiccation than snails. As a result they tend to frequent places that are damper and cooler. Their slime is more viscous too. Slugs are also more vulnerable to predation, so they prefer to hide away during daylight hours. Their skins are tougher than snails for this reason and they often have a distasteful flavour, coupled with bright colouration, to deter predators. The advantage of having no shell is being able to squeeze through tiny gaps or holes.

➨ *Molluscs, Snails*

SMELTS

(Class: Osteichthyes Order: Osmeriformes)

The term 'smelt' is applied to various unrelated species of fish, but is used more specifically to refer to relatives of salmon and trout, particularly the rainbow or European smelt (Osmerus eperlanus). Smelts have slender, rounded bodies that are slightly flattened on the flanks. Like trout they possess an adipose fin, which is used to store fat. Their jaws are long and extend beyond the eyes. They have teeth in both jaws, on the tongue and on the roof of the mouth. Smelts reach 30 cm (12 in) in length. They are fished and farmed in Europe and North America.

➨ *Salmon, Trout*

SMOOTH NEWTS

(Class: Amphibia Order: Caudata)

The smooth newt (*Triturus vulgaris*) is widespread and common throughout Britain. It is the only

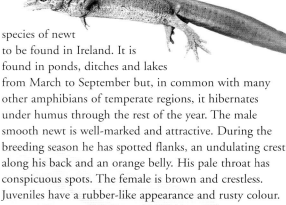

species of newt to be found in Ireland. It is found in ponds, ditches and lakes from March to September but, in common with many other amphibians of temperate regions, it hibernates under humus through the rest of the year. The male smooth newt is well-marked and attractive. During the breeding season he has spotted flanks, an undulating crest along his back and an orange belly. His pale throat has conspicuous spots. The female is brown and crestless. Juveniles have a rubber-like appearance and rusty colour.

➨ *Efts, Newts*

SMOOTH SNAKES

(Class: Reptilia Order: Squamata)

The term 'smooth snake' has been used colloquially to describe many different species of snake around the world. In Britain the smooth snake (*Coronella austriaca*) is a rare and endangered species. It is an inhabitant of dry, sandy heaths in the lowlands of southern England. The smooth snake feeds on slow-worms, sand lizards, nestlings and insects. It subdues and kills its prey by constriction, lacking a venomous bite. The smooth snake is similar in appearance to the adder or viper (*Vipera berus*) but is more slender and has a dark pattern on its back. It hibernates from October until April.

➨ *Reptiles, Snakes*

SNAILS

(Class: Mollusca Order: Gastropoda)

Snails are very successful animals considering that they are soft-bodied, moist creatures. This is wholly due to their shells which serve as protection from predators and desiccation. They can survive in much drier

ABOVE The female smooth newt lacks the crest and bright colours of the male.

places than slugs, and when things get too dry they are able to aestivate, which is a summer hibernation. To do so they seal the opening of the shell against a flat, non-porous surface with their glue-like slime and remain dormant until rain arrives. Snails and slugs are hermaphrodite. This means each individual is both male and female, but still needs to mate with another individual.

➠ *Molluscs, Slugs*

SNAKES

(Class: Reptilia Order: Squamata)

Snakes are closely related to lizards (from which they evolved) and the worm-like amphisbaenians. They form a hugely successful group of predators that have established themselves on all the continents of the world except Antarctica. The greatest diversity of snake species is found in tropical regions, although snakes can be found in many varied habitats – the sea-snakes, for example, have adopted a marine lifestyle.

Snakes are characterised by their long, limbless bodies. They do not possess eyelids and they have one lung either reduced or absent altogether. Their internal organs are, of necessity, elongated. Snakes have scaled skin, which may be brightly coloured and boldly patterned or cryptically camouflaged to offer protection and cover. Their skins may be rough or smooth, not wet. Some snakes are able to produce venom that is injected into prey or predators alike. Others attack by constriction.

❧ The long, slender bodies of snakes enable them to seek prey in the nooks and crannies between rocks, or among foliage.

❧ Snakes are most limited by their cold-bloodedness or ectothermy.

❧ Since they are unable to control their own body temperatures, snakes, like other reptiles, must seek sunshine or shade to regulate their core temperature.

➠ *Reptiles, Lizards*

ABOVE Young emerald tree boas are a brownish colour, becoming green by the time they are nine months old. As they age, the green becomes darker.

SNAPPERS

(Class: Osteichthyes Order: Perciformes)

About 250 species of snapper are recognized. These are tropical, marine fish that are plentiful in number and variety. They have large, elongated bodies, up to 90 cm (3 ft) in length. Snappers have large mouths and sharp teeth. They feed on other marine animals such as fish and crustaceans. They often swim and feed in groups. Snappers are a valuable food source though some species, such as the dog snapper, are poisonous. The red snapper (*Chrysophrys auratus*) is common in deep Atlantic waters and is a popular food fish. It's family – Sparidae – is commonly known as the porgy family.

➠ *Bony Fish, Fish*

SNIPEFISH

(Class: Osteichthyes Order: Gasterosteiformes)

There are 12 species of snipefish and they share a number of characteristics with their relatives, the seahorses and pipefish, such as tube-like snouts and a partial armour of bony scales. These fish are mainly tropical and sub-tropical. They inhabit shallow marine waters although some species can be found in deep water. The dorsal fin is covered in spines, including one very long one. Their deep bodies reach up to 30 cm (12 in) in length and can be pink, red or silver in colour. Like their relatives they have very small mouths, so they specialise in eating planktonic animals.

➠ *Pipefish, Seahorses*

SONG BIRDS

(Class: Aves Order: Passeriformes)

Nearly half of the world's birds are songbirds. They are all members of the perching bird order Passeriformes. Songbirds are terrestrial and show a wide range of habitat preferences and diversity in lifestyle. The ability of songbirds to sing comes from the development of their windpipes into a specialised vocal organ, the syrinx. The syrinx is located at the base of the windpipe and it consists of a bony framework that is covered in finely-stretched membranes. As air passes over these

ABOVE The chaffinch is a common British songbird and can be found in a variety of habitats, including woodland, gardens, parks and orchards.

membranes they vibrate, creating sound. Local muscles adjust the tension and position of the membranes, varying the notes and loudness to create song.

Some birds are born with an innate ability to sing the song of their species, but it is more common for birds to learn their song from their parents. There may be considerable local variations in these songs. Other birds – mimics – retain the ability to learn new songs throughout their lives.

❖ Singing is most common in male birds and is used frequently as part of courtship displays and mating rituals.

❖ Not all songbirds produce attractive sounds – the crows for example.

❖ The nightingales, mockingbirds, larks and thrushes are all noted for their beautiful song.

➠ *Birds, Passerines*

SPADEFOOT TOADS

(Class: Amphibia Order: Anura)

There are a number of species of spadefoot toad, all belonging to the family Pelobatidae. They share a common characteristic that gives them their name – horny 'spades' projecting from each hind foot. These spades enable the toads to dig backwards into soil. Spadefoot toads are found in Europe, western Asia and

North and Central America. They are normally nocturnal and reside in burrows underground. They return to water in the mating season. The European spadefoot (*Pelobates fuscus*) emits a foul smell to deter predators such as snakes and puffs up its body to appear larger when threatened.

➠ *Frogs, Toads*

SPARROWS
(Class: Aves Order: Passeriformes)

The term 'sparrow' has been applied to several groups of birds. They are generally all seed-eating birds with conical bills that are ideally suited to opening hard seeds. The house sparrow (*Passer domesticus*) is related to the weavers in the family Ploceidae. It originated from Eurasia and was introduced to North America in 1852. In a hundred years it had spread across the entire continent. The American tree sparrow (*Spizella arborea*) belongs to the family Fringillidae. Sparrows are typically small birds with cryptic plumage. There is usually some difference between the plumage of male and female sparrows, although it is not always obvious.

➠ *Buntings, Weaverbirds*

SPIDERS
(Phylum: Arthropoda Class: Arachnida)

Although somewhat insect-like in form, spiders differ from insects in a number of ways. The most noticeable differences are that spiders have four pairs of legs rather than three pairs and two body sections instead of three. There are no spiders with wings either. All-in-all spiders are more primitive than insects, but no less successful. They are present in most terrestrial environments, providing the climate is warm enough to breed for at least part of the year, although some species live in association with human habitations.

All spiders are carnivorous, preying on a variety of animals depending on the species. They lack chewing mouthparts, however, and instead use hollow fangs to suck up the body fluids of their prey. They acquire their prey in a variety of ways. Many species construct webs to catch their food. Others use mobile webs which they carry with their legs and drop on their prey like a basket to net their victims, while some actively stalk their prey. Most species carry venom which is injected with the

fangs. It serves to kill or immobilize the prey and dissolve the body so that the fluids flow more readily.

Spiders have very good eyesight and are very sensitive to vibrations, making them extremely effective predators. They are themselves preyed upon by other animals, particularly birds. Most spiders are very small and cryptically coloured, making identification of different species difficult. In tropical regions spiders tend to be larger, with some species growing to proportions that have given them an unfounded reputation as dangerous creatures.

❧ The largest spiders are called birdeaters because they do occasionally prey on nestling birds, which they find by climbing up trees.

❧ The name 'tarantula' alludes to Taranto in Italy. In the late Medieval period people from the town suffered from a mysterious disease that was attributed to the bite of the spider *Lycosa tarentula*.

➠ *Arachnids, Insects*

BELOW The red-footed bird spider lives in the forests of South America.

SPONGES
(Phylum: Porifera)

These are very primitive animals that are the sole members of the parazoa sub-kingdom. They are unique among animals in being multicellular, but without tissue differentiation. They grow into masses supported by frameworks of spicules that can be glassy, fibrous or calcareous. To feed they rely on particles of organic matter in water, which are extracted, along with oxygen, as the water passes through their porous bodies. Sponges cannot move and tend to grow secured to rocks and other stationary objects. Most sponges are marine, but a few are found in freshwater. Not all sponges are soft to the touch.

➡ *Corals, Invertebrates*

SPOONBILLS
(Class: Aves Order: Ciconiiformes)

There are six species of spoonbill. They are all long-legged wading birds that live in estuaries and lakes. They build their nests from sticks in bushes and trees. Three to five eggs are laid in one clutch. Most spoonbills are predominantly white, but the roseate spoonbill (*Ajaia ajaja*) has a bubblegum-pink body and wings, with white neck and back. These birds get their name from their spoon-like bills designed for filtering animals from water. The birds stand in the shallows, sweeping their bills from side to side, catching crustaceans and small fish as they are caught up in the eddies.

SQUID
(Phylum: Mollusca Class: Cephalopoda)

Squid include the fastest marine invertebrates. Many are designed with torpedo-shaped bodies for hunting the surface waters of oceans, where they prey on fish and

BELOW LEFT Sponges extract food and oxygen from the surrounding water.
BELOW Chipmunks are adapted to both arboreal and terrestrial life.

other animals, such as crustaceans. They swim by undulating vanes or fins that run along the sides of their bodies. They can move backwards or forwards in this manner. Enormous shoals of squid prowl the surface, usually at night when they are protected from predators by the cover of darkness. Many species of seabird, fish and sea mammals feed on squid. The species of squid that live at greater depths tend to have more rounded bodies, for they swim less rapidly. Among them is the giant squid (*Architeuthis* sp).

Like all cephalopods, squid have a definite life span. That is because they put all of their energy into reproduction and die shortly afterwards, leaving their spawn to produce the next generation. Spawning grounds are found at the bottom of oceans, where squid congregate in vast shoals prior to breeding. The result is a mass of gelatinous eggs, many of which are lost to predators and scavengers. Many squid have an internal structure called a quill. It is a glassy, bone-like support for the soft body.

➡ *Cephalopods, Octopuses*

SQUIRRELFISH
(Class: Osteichthyes Order: Beryciformes)

Squirrelfish are also known as soldierfish. The pectoral, dorsal and anal fins all have spines and the skin is covered in rough, prickly scales. There are about 70 species of squirrelfish and they all inhabit tropical reefs. They are very colourful fish with large eyes suitable for hunting prey, such as smaller fish and invertebrates, amidst a coral reef. Squirrelfish are most active at night and hide in the reef by day. They are edible fish that reach 60 cm (24 in) in length. The pink squirrelfish (*Holocentrus ascensionis*) frequents the waters surrounding Ascension Island, South Atlantic.

➥ *Bony Fish, Fish*

SQUIRRELS

(Class: Mammalia Order: Rodentia)

Among the many squirrels are ground (terrestrial) squirrels, arboreal squirrels, woodchucks, flying squirrels, chipmunks, marmots and prairie dogs. They are all small-to-medium sized animals and there is little real difference between species despite their adaptations to different habitats and modes of locomotion. Arboreal species have long, bushy tails that are used as counterbalances and stabilizers while climbing and jumping through the branches of trees. Terrestrial species tend to have reduced tails because they are largely redundant. Species that conduct both arboreal and terrestrial lives, such as chipmunks, have medium-sized tails. All squirrels feed on plant matter.

➥ *Prarie Dogs, Rodents*

STARFISH

(Phylum: Echinodermata)

Starfish typically have five arms, with each arm connected to a central disc. Some starfish have up to fifty arms. They used to be classed as members of the 'radiata' along with jellyfish and anemones, due to their lack of bilateral symmetry, but that group no longer exists now that the taxonomy of animals is better understood.

Beneath each arm of a starfish is a groove which terminates at

BELOW The starfish eats using grooves that run along its arms to its mouth.

the mouth at the centre of the disc. Each groove is used to convey particles of food to the mouth. This is done with hundreds of finger-like projections called tube feet which cover the underside of each arm. The tube feet are also used for locomotion; they suck onto objects and move the starfish along in a slow gliding motion. The animal's upper surface is covered by calcareous plates that offer protection from predators. Starfish are themselves predators and scavengers. Being slow-moving they can only prey on other slow moving or sedentary animals. Favourite prey are bivalves, such as scallops and oysters.

❖ Starfish wrap themselves around bivalves and pull against the shell from both sides until the bivalve eventually tires. The starfish's stomach then enters the shell to digest the victim.

➥ *Sea Cucumbers, Sea Urchins*

STARLINGS

(Class: Aves Order: Passeriformes)

 There are over 100 members of the family Sturnidae, which includes the mynahs and oxpeckers. Starlings are found worldwide, often congregating in huge flocks. Typically they have sharp bills that are slightly downcurved, pointed wings and strong legs. Plumage is often dark but with a metallic sheen. Starlings tend to chatter continuously, both in flight and while roosting. The common starling (*Sturnus vulgaris*) can congregate in huge flocks that cause a nuisance in urban areas, both in terms of noise and pollution from droppings. They get their name because of the star-like markings on their breeding plumage.

➡ *Passerines, Thrushes*

STICK INSECTS

(Class: Insecta Order: Phasmida)

Stick insects use their resemblance to twigs as a camouflage to protect them from predators. Their

colouration, form and movements all complete the deception. As stick insects have long and narrow bodies they have been able to grow quite large without hindering the process by which insects breathe – through spiracles along the sides of the abdomen. The Australian giant spiny stick insects (*Palophus titan*) grows to 25 cm (10 in). Most species are somewhat smaller. Stick insects

ABOVE The stick insect is a master of disguise.
ABOVE RIGHT The stingray's poison can be fatal to humans.

are predominantly tropical creatures, but a few live in temperate regions, such as the laboratory or Indian stick insect (*Carausius morosus*).

➡ *Insects, Leaf Insects*

STICKLEBACKS

(Class: Osteichthyes Order: Gasterosteiformes)

These little fish, native to the northern hemisphere, are characterised by a row of spines on their dorsal surfaces, in front of the dorsal fin. There are about 12 species of stickleback and they are all freshwater fish of temperate regions. Some species are able to live in salt and freshwater, for example the three-spined stickleback (*Gasterosteus aculeatus*). When it is spawning season male sticklebacks develop a red colouring and they build nests from vegetation and mucous. After courtship they drive the females towards their nests and fertilize the eggs. The males bear the responsibility of guarding the eggs and young.

➡ *Fish, Minnows*

STINGRAYS

(Class: Chondrichthyes Superorder: Batoidea)

Like other rays, stingrays are cartilaginous fish that are closely related to sharks. They have flattened bodies and extended pectoral fins that are used for swimming. Their mouths are on the underside of the body. Stingrays characteristically have sharp spines on their tails. They live in temperate and tropical marine waters, sometimes in very large numbers. They lie on the seabed, hidden by a light coating of sand or shingle. They prey upon worms, molluscs and other small creatures. They use their spiny tails like whips when threatened. The wounds inflicted by their poisonous spines can be fatal to humans.

➡ *Rays, Skates*

STONE FLIES

(Class: Insecta Order: Plecoptera)

These insects are similar to mayflies. There are more than 3,000 species known, yet they are all inconspicuous, dull-coloured insects. They can be distinguished from mayflies by the pattern of veins –

venation – on their wings. The forewings each have a double row of cross-veins looking something like a pair of ladders. The larvae of stone flies are aquatic. Most are vegetarian, although a few prey on other insect larvae. The adults, which emerge after three or four years, do not usually feed at all, but some nibble at algae or pollen. Their prime concern is to reproduce as quickly as possible.

➠ *Insects, Mayflies*

STORKS

(Class: Aves Order: Ciconiiformes)

Storks are large wading birds, related to herons, flamingos and ibises. Most of the 17 species live in Africa, Asia or Europe. The black-necked stork or Australian jabiru (*Xenorhynchus asiaticus*), lives in southern Asia. Storks can be 1.5 m (5 ft) in length. Plumage is typically a combination of black and white. Storks do not have a syrinx – voice box – so they communicate by clapping their bills. Storks stand in the shallows hunting their diet of small animals. The marabou stork (*Leptoptilos crumeniferus*)

has a bare neck and head to avoid clogging its feathers while eating carrion.

➠ *Herons, Ibises*

STURGEONS

(Class: Osteichthyes Order: Acipenseriformes)

Sturgeons belong to an ancient group of fish, called the chondrosteans, which first appeared 375 million years ago. Sturgeons, like paddlefish, bowfins and gars, have skeletons that are partly bone and partly cartilage. They live in saltwater and freshwater areas of the northern hemisphere and migrate upriver at spawning time. They are bottom-dwellers, feeding on small invertebrates and fish that they locate using their barbels. It is believed that sturgeons can reach a great age; some reports suggest that individuals have lived for between 200 and 300 years. Sturgeons are the fish from which caviar – their roe – is obtained.

➠ *Gars, Paddlefish*

ABOVE The black-necked stork is a wading bird from southern Asia.

SUCKERS

(Class: Osteichthyes Order: Cypriniformes)

These freshwater fish are closely related to carp and minnows. They have protruding, fleshy lips and no teeth. They also lack adipose fins and barbels. The majority of the 100 or so species of sucker live in North America, although a few species inhabit Asia. They live at the bottom of lakes and ponds where they feed on invertebrates that they suck into their mouths. They are fished for sport and food but they are not of any real economic significance. The Chinese sucker reaches 60 cm (24 in) in length and is orange in colour, with broad black bands.

➠ *Carp, Minnows*

SUN SPIDERS

(Class: Arachnida Order: Solifugae or Solpugida)

Sun spiders are also known as camel spiders or wind spiders. All three names allude to their semi-desert habitat. Also, they are often called scorpions rather than spiders, because they are something in between. Sun spiders are formidable-looking creatures, but they lack venom. Their large size and massive fangs compensate for this by allowing them to run down prey at speed and hold down their struggling victims while they feed on the internal fluids. About 900 species are known. They are absent from Australia and south-east Spain is their only European home. Offspring are initially fed by the female.

➠ *Scorpions, Spiders*

SUNBIRDS

(Class: Aves Order: Passeriformes)

This group of nectar-feeding birds is noted for the bright plumage seen in the males during the breeding season. Their plumage is usually iridescent with splashes of strong colour, but becomes green after the breeding season. The females are usually a dull green all year round. The sunbirds feed on nectar using their tubular tongues and long, curved bills. While the hummingbirds hover to reach nectar, the sunbirds perch on the flower stalk instead. Sunbirds are found throughout Asia and Australia but are most common in Africa. A similar group of birds, called the spiderbirds, is found in southeast Asia.

➠ *Honeyeaters, Hummingbirds*

ABOVE Male sunbirds have colourful plumage during the mating season.
RIGHT The sunbittern shades the water with its wings to catch its prey.

SUNBITTERNS

(Class: Aves
Order: Gruiformes)

The sunbittern (*Eurypyga helias*) is a ground-dwelling relative of the cranes, rails, bustards and trumpeters. It lives in the American tropics near streams and rivers. Both sexes possess similar plumage in cryptic browns, providing camouflage amongst the vegetation. The tail is long and similarly coloured. The male has patterned wings that are used in courtship displays. The long, pointed bill is used to spear fish, insects and crustaceans in the water. The bird hunts by shadowing the water with its wings, umbrella-fashion. Water animals instinctively head for the shade created by its wings and become sitting targets for feasting on.

➠ *Cranes, Rails*

SUNFISH

(Class: Osteichthyes Order: Perciformes)

Sunfish are popular food and game fish in North America and they are related to perch. They are characterised by a single continuous dorsal fin that has a spiny-rayed and soft-rayed portion. Their bodies are small, usually under 20 cm (8 in) in length, but relatively deep. Sunfish are brightly coloured, particularly during the breeding season when the males display their nests to the females. The males are responsible for guarding eggs and the newly-hatched young. The ocean sunfish (*Mola mola*) belongs to a different family – Molidae – which contains three species.

➠ *Carp, Perch*

SWALLOWS

(Class: Aves Order: Passeriformes)

The swallows include the birds called martins, which typically have less strongly forked tails. Swallows and martins are small birds that are extremely agile, elegant fliers. They have narrow, pointed wings for the purpose. Plumage is similar in both sexes – usually dark above and pale beneath as a counter-shading against falcons. The short bill has a surprisingly wide gape for catching airborne insects. Swallows may build nests in natural tree cavities, burrows in cliffs or use mud to build cup-shaped nests under the eves of buildings. Being insectivorous, many swallows and martins complete seasonal migrations to find food.

➠ *Nightjar, Swifts*

SWIFTS

(Class: Aves Order: Apodiformes)

Swifts are related to hummingbirds and they too are agile fliers. This is because they have a specialised wing structure. The wings are attached to the body at a narrow point and the humerus bones are very short to provide universal joints. Swifts can achieve speeds of 110 kph (70 mph) and are so adept at life in the air that they bathe in rain showers, mate and even sleep on the wing. Swifts are found worldwide providing there are flying insects to eat. They are usually dark brown with occasional white markings. Their tails are typically short but forked.

➠ *Hummingbirds, Swallows*

ABOVE Swallows have narrow wings and are very elegant fliers.

SWORDFISH

(Class: Osteichthyes Order: Perciformes)

There is one species of swordfish – *Xiphias gladius.* This long fish – 4.5 m (15 ft) from snout to tail – is a popular food and sport fish that inhabits tropical and temperate oceans worldwide. The swordfish is a ferocious predator and powerful swimmer. It attacks fish and squid, impaling them with its long sword-like snout. It then slashes at its prey, cutting it into manageable pieces. Swordfish can even attack and sink small boats. These fish are purplish-blue on their upper surfaces, white or silver underneath. They have neither pelvic fins nor teeth and their skins lack scales.

➠ *Marlins, Tuna*

TANAGERS

(Class: Aves Order: Passeriformes)

There are over 200 species of these mainly tropical American birds. Tanagers are arboreal birds that primarily eat fruit, although some species eat insects too. Tanagers range in size from 10–20 cm (4–8 in). The males are often resplendent in bright plumage of reds, yellows, greens, blues or black, and they may be boldly patterned. In some species the females are also brightly coloured, in others they are plain.

The paradise tanager (*Tangara chilensis*) is the size of a sparrow but painted in gaudy colours. Others are named because of their colour – scarlet, blue-grey and silver-beaked for example.

➠ *Finches, Sparrows*

TAPEWORMS

**(Phylum: Platyhelminthes
Class: Cestoda)**

Tapeworms are endoparasites – living within the digestive tracts of other animals, especially mammals, birds, fish, and reptiles. They lack an alimentary system of their own and instead absorb nutrients from predigested food through their cuticle or skin. The worms comprise segments called proglottids which break away when mature and carry eggs out of the body. Tapeworms vary a great deal in length within species and between species. The human tapeworm (*Diphyllobothrium latum*) can have as many as 4,000 segments and measure an incredible 18 m (58 ft). Tapeworms that large can lead to serious malnutrition or even death in the host.

➠ *Annelid Worms, Nematode Worms*

TAPIRS

(Class: Mammalia Order: Perissodactyla)

Of the five species of tapir the Malayan tapir (*Tapirus indicus*) is the only one that does not come from Central or South America. It is an increasingly rare creature due to the destruction of tropical forest in southeast Asia where it lives. The American species are the Brazilian tapir (*Tapirus terrestris*), Baird's tapir (*Tapirus bairdi*), mountain tapir (*Tapirus roulini*) and Dow's tapir (*Tapirus dowi*). All five tapirs have offspring that are covered in whitish stripes and spots. This colouration mimics the dappled light on the forest floor and so acts as camouflage to conceal the calves' whereabouts from predators.

➠ *Horses, Rhinoceroses*

RIGHT Baird's tapir can be found in Central America.
FAR RIGHT The Tasmanian devil is not as fierce as its appearance suggests.

TARSIERS

**(Class: Mammalia
Order: Primates)**

Tarsiers have the distinction of possessing the largest eyes in relation to their body size of any mammal. Their enormous eyes are used at night to locate prey animals among the branches of the tropical forests in the Philippines and Indonesia in which they live. The western tarsier (*Tarsius bancanus*), one of four species, is little bigger than a human fist yet it can leap 4.5 m (15 ft) from one branch to another. Tarsiers have stereoscopic or binocular vision, giving them a three-dimensional view of their world and extremely accurate judgement of distance when pouncing on insects.

➠ *Primates*

TASMANIAN DEVILS

(Class: Mammalia Order: Dasyuridae)

This is one of the carnivorous marsupials from Australasia. It looks something like a cross between a bear and a cat. Once persecuted for fear of its reputation as a sheep worrier, the Tasmanian devil (*Sarcophilus harrisii*) has recovered its numbers fairly well. It is now recognized that the creature evolved as a scavenger rather than hunter, living largely on the remains of kills left by the thylacine – now extinct. It now relies on catching small prey animals and scrounging whatever it can. The Tasmanian devil is famed for its temper, but 'its bark is far worse than its bite'.

➠ *Marsupials Mammals, Thylacine*

TEGU LIZARDS

(Class: Reptilia Order: Squamata)

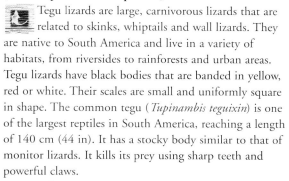

Tegu lizards are large, carnivorous lizards that are related to skinks, whiptails and wall lizards. They are native to South America and live in a variety of habitats, from riversides to rainforests and urban areas. Tegu lizards have black bodies that are banded in yellow, red or white. Their scales are small and uniformly square in shape. The common tegu (*Tupinambis teguixin*) is one of the largest reptiles in South America, reaching a length of 140 cm (44 in). It has a stocky body similar to that of monitor lizards. It kills its prey using sharp teeth and powerful claws.

➠ *Lizards, Reptiles*

LEFT Of all mammals, tarsiers have the largest eyes in relation to their bodies.

TENCH

(Class: Osteichthyes Order: Cypriniformes)

Tench belong to the same family as carp – Cyprinidae. The single species – *Tinca tinca* – inhabits European freshwater environments. The tench is particularly resilient to the effects of low oxygen levels in water and is found living in highly vegetated and muddy pools, lakes and ponds. Tench are omnivorous, eating both plant and animal matter. They are popular sport fish in Europe and are edible. Tench have small scales and slimy skins. They are normally greenish-brown in colour and have barbels on the corners of their mouths. Tench have been introduced as coarse fish elsewhere in the world.

➟ *Carp, Minnows*

TENRECS

(Class: Mammalia Order: Insectivora)

Tenrecs belong somewhere between the hedgehogs and shrews. They mainly live on the island of Madagascar in the Indian Ocean, but some species live on the Comoro Islands and in West Africa. They are a weird and wonderful group of creatures. Some look distinctly like shrews, others like hedgehogs and others like strange concoctions of the two. Those from Africa look like otters and so are called otter shrews. Some species retain the reptilian cloaca, which is a shared pouch for the urinary tract, genitals and anus. They are insectivores, taking invertebrates, fish and small mammals, depending on the species.

➟ *Hedgehogs, Shrews*

TERMITES

(Class: Insecta Order: Isoptera)

Although termites are often described as 'white ants' they are not closely related to true ants. They are very similar in appearance and behaviour though. This is due to a phenomenon known as convergent evolution, where both orders of insect have evolved in a similar way. Termites live in social colonies with different forms adapted for particular roles within the nest. There are four types of termite – primary reproductives, supplementary reproductives, workers and soldiers. The latter two are wholly responsible for the upkeep and defence of the nest

RIGHT The diamondback terrapin lives in estuaries and is eaten as a delicacy.

while the former two are concerned with populating the nest with new termites.

There are nearly 2,000 species of termite, comprising six families. Most are tropical but some species can tolerate temperate climates. The principal food of most species is dead wood or vegetable matter. This includes the structural timbers and floorboards of buildings, making termites serious pests in some parts of the world. They are able to digest the cellulose in wood and absorb the simpler compounds that result. Many species have a symbiotic protozoan in their gut which produces the enzymes needed for the task.

Termite nests are often extremely complex structures made from particles of soil shaped into galleries, with ventilation shafts for controlling the temperature and humidity. Nests can last for decades and grow to house millions of termites. The queen termite resides in a special chamber where she is tended by workers. They bring food, keep her clean and remove eggs which she lays continually for many years.

❧ In Northern Australia there is a species called the magnetic termite (*Amitermes meridionalis*). It is so called because nest mounds are always angled along the north-south axis. The reason for this is that the mounds maximize absorption of solar radiation in the morning and evening, and minimize it at midday.

➟ *Ants, Insects*

TERRAPINS

(Class: Reptilia Order: Chelonia)

The term 'terrapin' is fairly ambiguous. It can be used to describe any freshwater turtle. Or it may be used more specifically for a member of the family

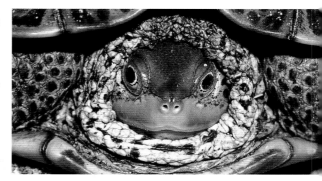

Emydidae, which is the largest group of turtles, comprising about half of all species. The diamondback terrapin (*Malaclemys terrapin*) of North America is unusual in being a species adapted for brackish water – which is the half freshwater and half seawater found in estuaries. It is eaten as a delicacy. The red-eared terrapin (*Pseudemys scripta*) is the species often kept as a pet in aquariums. It grows far larger, given its natural habitat.

⇒ *Marine Turtles, Pond Turtles*

TETRAS
(Class: Osteichthyes Order: Characiformes)

Tetras are small, attractive aquarium fish of the characin family. They are indigenous to Africa and South America where they inhabit freshwater habitats. There are numerous species of tetra of differing appearance.

The splash tetra of South America is also known as the jumping characin because of its unusual reproductive behaviour. The female carefully lays her eggs on the underside of leaves. As the water level drops and the

leaves become exposed the male splashes water on them to keep them wet. When the eggs hatch the young fall into the water. Splash tetras eat larvae, crustaceans and small insects.

❧ The neon tetra (*Pracheirodon innesi*) is a popular aquarium fish; it has bright red hindparts and blue-green stripes on its sides.

❧ The black tetra, also known as the petticoat fish, reaches a maximum length of 75 mm (3 in). Its black hindparts and dorsal and anal fins lighten to grey as it matures.

❧ The Mexican tetra (*Astanax mexicanus*) has two variant forms. One lives in sunlight and is brightly coloured. The other is a cave-dweller, has reduced

colouring and is blind. It relies on sensory organs contained in its lateral line and an acute sense of smell to locate food.

⇒ *Characins, Fish*

TEXAS BLIND SALAMANDERS
(Class: Amphibia Order: Caudata)

The Texas blind salamander (*Typhlomolge rathbuni*) is a wholly aquatic, cave-dwelling salamander, that has pinkish, translucent skin. Its inner organs and blood are visible through the skin, hence its colour. It has blood-red external gills and two dark spots where the vestigial eyes are located. This species is presently found only in the San Marcos Pool of the Edwards Aquifer in Hays County, Texas. There are no estimates of population size but it is considered an endangered species. The Texas blind salamander eats invertebrates including snails, shrimps and insect larvae. These salamanders are particularly vulnerable to deterioration in water quality.

⇒ *Axolotls, Salamanders*

THRUSHES
(Class: Aves Order: Passeriformes)

These songbirds have representatives in most regions of the world, except Antarctica and New Zealand. They are slender-billed, often with rather dull plumage but occasionally decorated with splashes of colour, especially the males. Those that live in the cooler northern regions, such as the Scandinavian redwing (*Turdus iliacus*), tend to be migratory birds. Most thrushes eat insects and fruit although some prefer snails and earthworms. Redstarts and the nightingale (*Luscinia megarhynchos*) are small thrushes, as is the European robin (*Erithacus rudecula*). The American robin (*Turdus migratorius*) is a large thrush however, in the same genus as the blackbird (*Turdus merula*).

⇒ *Passerines, Song Birds*

ABOVE LEFT The neon tetra is attractive and a popular aquarium fish.
ABOVE A song thrush braves the winter weather.

THYLACINES
(Class: Mammalia Order: Dasyuridae)

Otherwise known as the Tasmanian wolf, the thylacine (*Thylacinus cynocephalus*) was once a common Australasian marsupial predator. Unfortunately the animal had a liking for domestic sheep and was persecuted to extinction by European settlers. The last confirmed sighting came in the first half of the twentieth century. With likely advancements in genetic engineering scientists have predicted that the thylacine may one day be resurrected along with the dodo and other extinct species.

The thylacine looked something like a cross between a wolf and a tiger, having stripes across its back and tail. It was able to open its jaws very wide in relation to placental predators. This was probably an adaptation to ensure that it suffocated its prey quickly, since it lacked the claws of a cat and seems not to have hunted in packs like wolves.

Like all typical marsupials the thylacine had a pouch in which to nurture its young and this would have hindered hunting success in the female, so it may be that the male thylacine was an attentive partner.

* The thylacine, like other marsupials that walk on all fours, had a backward opening pouch. This ensured that obstacles didn't get caught on the pouch entrance.

➡ *Marsupial Mammals, Tasmanian Devils*

TICKS
(Class: Arachnida Order: Acari)

Ticks are ectoparasites – feeding on the blood of terrestrial vertebrates by piercing their skin. The larvae, which have just three pairs of legs instead of four, wait on plants until a host brushes past. They then lower themselves on silken threads and latch on. Having shed their skins several times they become adults, with eight legs. They then distend their abdomens with blood from the host until they look like swollen balloons. Mating takes place on the host before both males and females drop off. They can then last for many months without feeding again. Females lay thousands of eggs.

➡ *Arachnids, Mites*

TITS
(Class: Aves Order: Passeriformes)

The tit family (Paridae) contains about 60 species of small birds. Tits are woodland and garden birds found across the Palaearctic. In the USA they are known as titmice or chickadees. Tits are versatile feeders, eating insects, nuts and seeds. They will nest in tree holes or nest-boxes. The great tit (*Parus major*) is a common bird in Europe, often seen in mixed flocks foraging for food in winter. The blue tit (*Parus caeruleus*) is a frequent visitor to garden bird tables. The bearded tit (*Panurus biarmicus*), which frequents scattered reed marshes over Eurasia, belongs to a different bird family – the Timaliidae.

➡ *Birds, Wrens*

TOADS
(Class: Amphibia Order: Anura)

Toads, like frogs, are squat tail-less amphibians of the order Anura. There is no clear distinction between toads and frogs although it is broadly agreed that toads have a warty skin, a terrestrial lifestyle and a crawling, rather than jumping motion. Members of the family Bufonidae are known as toads, but those of the genus Bufo are known as the 'true toads'. Like frogs, toads have a complex lifecycle. Eggs are laid in freshwater and externally fertilized. The larvae are known as tadpoles and maintain an aquatic existence until metamorphosis occurs, seeing them develop into miniature copies of the adults.

➡ *Amphibians, Frogs*

ABOVE Now extinct, the thylacine was once a common marsupial predator.
RIGHT Toucans live in rainforests and are known for their large, bright bills.

TOADS, COMMON

(Class: Amphibia Order: Anura)

The common toad (*Bufo bufo*) is one of northern Europe's most common and widespread amphibians. Like most toads the common toad has warty skin and has a crawling, rather than leaping, mode of locomotion. Skin colour varies from muddy brown to olive green or dull red. Common toads tend to lead terrestrial lives in moist habitats near water or in woodlands and grasslands, returning to water only in the spring for the breeding season. Eggs are laid in still, freshwater and these hatch into tadpoles that eventually metamorphose into the adult form. Adults eat small invertebrates such as slugs and insects.

➡ *Frogs, Common, Toads*

TORRENTFISH

(Class: Osteichthyes
Order: Cypriniformes)

Torrentfish belong in the same order of fish as carp and catfish. They possess only one row of teeth and their air bladders are simple and divided into two halves. The pelvic and pectoral fins are enlarged relative to their bodies. Torrentfish are found in fast-flowing streams and rivers in southeast Asia. The fish use their over-large pectoral and pelvic fins to anchor themselves onto the river bed. With their bellies lying on the bottom they are able to create a partial vacuum. This gives them some suction and enables them to resist the current in fast-moving bodies of water.

➡ *Carp, Catfish*

TORTOISES

(Class: Reptilia Order: Chelonia)

Tortoises offer a glimpse into the evolutionary past of living reptiles. They first appeared over 200 million years ago and have changed remarkably little since then. Unlike turtles, tortoises live wholly terrestrial lives.

Their shells, or carapaces, are high and domed to offer maximum protection from predators. Turtle shells, by comparison, are more streamlined and suited to swimming. Tortoises lack teeth and chew with their hard jaws. Their limbs are hard and scaly. Tortoises belong to the family Testudinidae. There are about 40 tortoise species in both tropical and temperate regions, but the majority are found in Africa and Madagascar.

➡ *Pond Turtles, Terrapins*

TOUCANS

(Class: Aves Order: Piciformes)

This group of arboreal birds is most famous for the enlarged bills of its members. Toucans are predominantly South American birds. Most live in the

tropical rainforests. Their bodies are usually black and white, with a colourful breast, and their bills are long, very broad and usually highly coloured. The edges of the bills are serrated, which is thought to help toucans pick up fruit and tear it.

The purpose of the oversized bills is not wholly understood. Since they are actually very lightweight, despite their size, they probably evolved to enable the birds to reach awkwardly positioned fruits hanging from the tree canopy. They use their bills with the utmost dexterity, plucking berries and then tossing them to the back of the throat. It is likely that the colours then evolved because the large bills were a convenient means of visual communication. Toucans commonly live in groups, high in the canopy.

❖ Like their relatives the woodpeckers, barbets and jacamars, toucans have two toes pointing forwards and two backwards. This adaptation helps them to climb up and down tree trunks.

❖ Toucans nest in natural tree cavities and feed on fruit, insects, lizards, small birds and eggs. Small toucans are called 'toucanets'.

➡ *Parrots, Woodpeckers*

TREECREEPERS
(Class: Aves Order: Passeriformes)

The term 'treecreepers' is applied to three families of perching birds. They all share the habit of scuttling around trees, foraging for insects in or under bark. The Australian and New Guinea treecreepers (*Climacteridae*) nest in tree holes and eat a diet mainly of ants. The treecreepers of the family Certhidiidae inhabit woodlands of Europe, Asia, Africa and North and Central America. They invariably climb trees upwards, using a stiffened tail for support. There are two species in the family Rhabdomithidae and these are found in the Philippines where they forage in the tree canopy as well as on bark.

➠ *Nuthatches, Woodpeckers*

TREEFROGS
(Class: Amphibia Order: Anura)

There are about 550 species in the frog family Hylidae, most of which have an arboreal lifestyle and are thus known as treefrogs. Treefrogs are adapted for life in forest canopies and are usually slender and long-limbed. They possess sucker-like pads on the tips of all digits to enable them to grip onto leaves and branches. Treefrogs are found in both temperate and tropical regions. Two species of treefrog inhabit Europe. The European green treefrog (*Hyla arborea*) is the most common of these. Treefrog species vary greatly in size, colour and patterning, although they are most often greenish, as camouflage.

➠ *Frogs, Toads*

ABOVE Treefrogs have sucker-like pads on their toes to help grip onto leaves.
RIGHT Triggerfishes live around coral reefs and are often colourful.

TREE-SHREWS
(Class: Mammalia Order: Scandentia)

Tree-shrews were once believed to be 'primitive' primates because of certain morphological similarities, but they are now placed in their own phylum, Scandetia. They have partial stereoscopic or binocular vision and opposable first digits on their hands and feet, both adaptations for an arboreal lifestyle. They also possess large brains in comparison with terrestrial shrews. They do, though, share the same taste for insects and other invertebrates. A further indication of evolutionary direction is seen in reproduction. They never give birth to more than two offspring, suggesting a bias towards increased parental investment in the nurturing of young.

➠ *Primates*

TRIGGERFISH
(Class: Osteichthyes Order: Tetraodontiformes)

Triggerfish are tropical, marine fish that inhabit shallow water around coral reefs. They are often highly decorated in bright colours and patterns and may reach 60 cm (24 in) in length. Their bodies are round, deep and covered in large scales. Their mouths are small and contain teeth that are modified to crush shells. Triggerfish have three dorsal fin spines, the first two of which have a triggering mechanism that gives the fish their name. These spines can be raised upward and put into a locked position, enabling the fish to secure themselves into small crevices when threatened by predators.

➠ *Bony Fish, Parrot Fish*

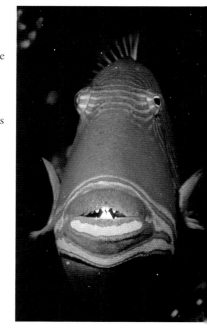

TRIOPS

(Subphylum: Crustacea Class: Branchiopoda)

Triops and Lepidurus are the two genera comprising the notostracans, which are small crustaceans, similar in form to the king crabs. They are an ancient group of animals which are extremely resilient to climatic changes which would kill many other creatures. They live in temporary pools of freshwater. *Triops* species frequent pools in drier, semi-desert regions whilst *Lepidurus* species live around the arctic and in warmer areas. Their eggs are resistant to desiccation and freezing, enabling the animals to live through uncongenial weather for months or even years. The eggs are also extremely small and frequently become airborne among dust particles when wind storms blow up. These eggs can therefore reach obscure habitats, such as mountain lakes or islands where they establish isolated colonies.

Notostracans are omnivores, feeding on whatever organic matter becomes available to them. They gather small particles with a motion of their limbs which directs the food to the mouth. They can also chew off pieces from larger items of food.

❧ Some species of notostracan can grow from egg to adult in just a week or two, so that they can produce new eggs before conditions become too dry for the adults to survive.

➠ *Crustaceans*

TROGONS

(Class: Aves Order: Trogoniformes)

There are 35 species of trogon, most of them in the American tropics. Upper parts of the body are often dark, although sometimes iridescent, while the belly is usually bright red or yellow. Trogons typically have long tails that are square-ended and patterned in black and white underneath. Their bills are short and curved with a wide gape for catching insects in mid-flight. Trogons build their nests in natural tree cavities or holes that they excavate from rotten wood or termite hills. The quetzal (*Pharomachrus mocinno*) has bright green plumage, a red breast, an iridescent crest and long, streaming tail plumes.

➠ *Cuckoos, Orioles*

BELOW Trogons can open their bills wide to catch insects while flying.

TROPIC BIRDS

(Class: Aves Order: Pelecaniformes)

Like their close relatives, the pelicans, darters and frigate birds, the tropic birds are adept fliers. There are three species of these silky, white birds, and they are all confined to the tropics. Their smooth plumage is sometimes tinged with white or pink and they have black markings on their eyes and wings. However the most noticeable physical characteristic of tropic birds is their tail shape. All three species have streaming central tail feathers that are at least as long as the body. Tropic birds usually live in island colonies, swooping into the sea in pursuit of fish or marine invertebrates.

➠ *Darters, Frigate Birds*

TROUT

(Class: Osteichthyes Order: Salmoniformes)

 Like their close relatives, the salmon and pike, trout are native to the Palaearctic – a circumpolar band comprising Europe, Asia and North America – but have been successfully introduced to other countries around the world. They are primarily freshwater fish but some species migrate to the sea when not spawning. Trout are fished for sport and extensively farmed. Trout eat insects, small fish, eggs and other aquatic animals. The rainbow trout (*Salmo gairdneri*) may grow to 1.2 m (4 ft) in length. Their bodies vary in colour from blue to green or brown. They have cream bellies and breeding males have pink shading on their flanks, completing the 'rainbow' colouration.

➡ *Pike, Salmon*

TUATARAS

(Class: Reptilia Order: Rhynchocephalia)

Although similar in appearance to typical lizards, tuataras are sufficiently different to be placed in a separate family. They have stocky bodies and well-developed limbs. The bone structure of their skulls is different to that of familiar lizards and their teeth are part of the jawbone, rather than being inserted into sockets. Tuataras have a long, spiny crest down their backs, which is used in courtship. They reach 60 cm (24 in) in length. Tuataras, or Sphenodons, are found on only 30 small islands off the coast of New Zealand. The two species are *Sphenodon punctatus* and *Sphenodon guntheri*.

While most reptiles are active during the day, when the heat of the sun gives them energy, tuataras are crepuscular animals, active in twilight. They emerge from their burrows on warm evenings to search for insects, snails and other small invertebrates. Tuataras are capable of digging their own burrows but are just as likely to adopt the burrows of birds, if they are made available. Sometimes a bird and a tuatara will share a burrow, but there is always the chance that the reptile may eat the bird's eggs or chicks. Female tuataras lay 8–15 eggs in their burrows, which take up to a year to hatch. Tuataras are the only surviving members of the family Rhynchocephalia, which was a large and common family of reptiles in the Jurassic Period (136–190 million years ago).

❧ Tuataras can slow their metabolism down to such an extent, when basking, that they can survive by taking only one breath every hour. They can also thrive in much lower temperatures than most other reptiles.

❧ Females tuataras do not reach sexual maturity until they are around 20 years old.

❧ Tuataras can survive for several months without any water other than dew.

➡ *Dinosaurs, Reptiles*

ABOVE While basking, tuataras can survive on just one breath every hour. RIGHT Tuna can be found in all oceans and are valued for food.

TUBENOSES

(Class: Aves Order: Procellariiformes)

This order of marine seabirds gets its name from a unique physical characteristic. All members of the group possess tubular nostrils on their upper bills. They are designed as drainage pipes for an organ in the head which extracts salt from seawater, thereby enabling the birds to survive without needing to find freshwater in their oceanic environment. The tubenoses include albatrosses, petrels, shearwaters, storm petrels and the gull-like fulmar (*Fulmarus glacialis*).

It is thought likely that the tubenoses share a common ancestor with the penguins. There are about 90 species. They are all superb and efficient fliers, able to fly continuously over the sea for great distances – a feat they achieve by gliding on up-draughts of wind. They breed on land in very large colonies, often on cliff ledges. They eat fish, squid, plankton and other marine creatures.

❖ The wandering albatross (*Diomedea exulans*) has the greatest wingspan of the birds at 3.5 m (11 ft). They have a very slow rate of reproduction because they breed every other year and a pair only nurtures one chick at a time.

❖ The giant albatross (*Gigantornis*) lived 50 million years ago and had a colossal wingspan of 6 m (20 ft).

➡ *Gulls, Penguins*

TUNA

(Class: Osteichthyes Order: Perciformes)

Tuna, or tunnies, are closely related to mackerel and placed in the same family. Like mackerel, tuna are strong and active swimmers that often undertake long migrations. They inhabit all the world's oceans and live in cool, warm and tropical waters. Tunas are exceptional in that they are able to maintain their body temperature at a higher level than the ambient sea or air temperature. Tunas are normally dark on their dorsal surfaces and flanks but white or silvery underneath. The yellowfin tuna (*Thunnus albacares*) has yellow fins that are edged in black. Tuna are greatly valued as food fish.

➡ *Mackerel, Swordfish*

BELOW Tyrant flycatchers, such as the fork-tailed, often have dull plumage.

TYRANT FLYCATCHERS

(Class: Aves Order: Passeriformes)

This is a large and very diverse group of perching birds that live in the Americas, from Alaska down to the southern tip of Patagonia. Tyrant flycatchers, as their name suggests, generally catch and eat insects on the wing. However as many as a third of the 367 species do not follow this lifestyle. Preferred habitats are also widely diverse. Tyrant flycatchers may live in desert, wetland, riverside, mountainous and rainforest environments. They vary in size from 50–400 mm (2.5–16 in). The smallest is the pygmy tyrant with a wingspan of 35 mm (1.5 in).

Tyrant flycatchers usually have dull plumage – greys, browns, olives above and white, yellow or tan below. Some, however, are black and white and others have yellow or red crests. Generally both sexes are alike. Those birds that catch insects do so by perching in trees and then swooping down on to their prey. Their bills are broad and flattened with bristles at the base to aid in the accurate seizure of flying insects.

❖ The vermillion flycatcher (*Pyrocephalus rubinus*) has a ruby-red body with chocolate-brown wings and tail.

❖ The scissor-tailed flycatcher (*Muscivora forficata*) has long tail feathers, reminiscent of scissor blades.

➡ *Flycatchers, Passerines*

URCHINS

(Phylum: Echinodermata Class: Echinoidea)

Sea urchins are essentially starfish that have adopted a spherical form. They have a shell armed with poisonous spines. This shell reveals a five-sector

radial design when the spines are removed. Like starfish, urchins have tube feet with which they move about the sea floor and catch particles of food. The feet protrude from small holes in the test, between the spines. Most urchins live in shallow waters or on the tide-line of coasts. Their food is both animal and vegetable matter. They have an ability to burrow into rock by abrading the surface, very slowly, with their spines.

➡ *Sea Cucumbers, Starfish*

VAMPIRE SQUID

(Phylum: Mollusca Order: Cephalopoda)

These cephalopods have a web of skin connecting their eight arms to make a cloak-like shape which they use for swimming, by opening and closing it to push themselves against the water. Due to this mode of locomotion they are sometimes called flying squid. Their fifth pair of limbs are quite different from the other squids. They can totally retract them into pockets when not in use. The vampire squid (*Vampyromrpha infernalis*) earned its scientific name due to its 'cloak', its purplish-black colour and its being covered in illuminating organs, which the creature uses for communication in dark, deep waters.

➡ *Octopuses, Squid*

ABOVE The slate pencil urchin is used to make wind chimes.
RIGHT Vertebrates' backbones protect their spinal cords, as in this cat skeleton.

VELVET WORMS

(Phylum: Onychophora)

Despite their worm-like, or rather caterpillar-like, appearance these animals were once classed as arthropods because, although they lack the characteristic tough cuticle – exoskeleton – of typical arthropods, they do share similar internal details. However, velvet worms also share features with segmented worms. They are nocturnal animals that prey on other small invertebrates, especially termites and woodlice, since they move slowly enough for capture. They require moist habitats as they have no defence against desiccation. Velvet worms have an interesting defence mechanism. They spit a milky fluid at enemies, which congeals in contact with air to become very sticky.

Annelid Worms, Arthropods

VERTEBRATES

Vertebrates are animals that have a backbone, spine or spinal column which serves as a conduit for the spinal cord. Vertebrata is a sub-phylum of the phylum Chordata, which contains all animals with at least a notochord – a cartilaginous rod or sheath for protecting the spinal chord – at some stage of their development into adults. There are five major classes of living animals that comprise the vertebrates. They are mammals (Mammalia), birds (Aves), reptiles (Reptilia), amphibians (Amphibia), bony fish (Osteichthyes), and the cartilaginous fish (Chondrichthyes).

The backbone or spinal column comprises a number of vertebrae that are linked together to give the whole

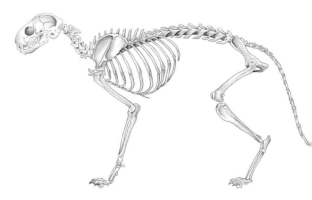

structure some flexibility. As well as protecting the spinal chord from damage the structure provides a central armature for the endoskeleton and muscles. The evolution of the whole skeleton was therefore a seminal progression as it allowed for larger animals to develop, acting as a scaffold. The spine comprises cervical vertebrae (in the neck), thoracic vertebrae (in the thorax), lumber vertebrae (in the abdomen) sacral vertebrae (in the pelvis) and caudal vertebrae (in the tail or coccyx). The number of each type of vertebra varies from species to species.

Vertebrates are also known as craniates (Craniata) because they possess crania (craniums) or skulls. This is the final bone of the spine in effect since it houses the hub of the nervous system – the brain. The first cervical vertebra is attached to the skull, completing the safe passage of the spinal chord along the body.

❧ A characteristic enlargement of the brain, relative to body size, is seen from the lower vertebrates towards humans, but it is important not to think that evolution is leading towards the emergence of humanity.

❧ All vertebrates and invertebrates alive today are at the pinnacle of their own evolutionary journey.

❧ There are far fewer vertebrates than invertebrates.

➠ *Invertebrates*

VIPERS
(Class: Reptilia Order: Squamata)

Vipers are venomous snakes that have hollow fangs positioned towards the front of their upper jaws. The fangs, which are folded back when not in use, inject venom into prey and predators like hypodermic needles. Pit vipers possess small heat-sensitive pits between eyes and nostrils that aid the snakes in detecting and attacking warm-blooded animals. Vipers are reptiles unusually adept at surviving cold conditions and so inhabit both tropical and temperate regions. Some vipers lay eggs but most give birth to live young. The females retain the eggs within their bodies while they develop. This is known as ovoviviparity.

➠ *Adders, Snakes*

BELOW The rhinocerous viper intimidates its prey by hissing loudly. Vipers use their hollow needle-like fangs to administer poison.

VIVIPAROUS REPTILES

Bearing live young is called viviparity. It is a characteristic common to most mammals and some reptiles. Offspring develop within the female's body,

which has obvious advantages for their chances of survival. It does have its disadvantages though, because the female has to invest a greater amount of her energy and time in the development of the young than she would by laying eggs. She is also prevented from producing any more young until her current brood is born.

The term 'viviparous' is used properly in describing animals that are able to provide continuous nourishment – food, gas exchange or both – to the developing embryo via a placenta. This is common in mammals but rare in reptiles. Most reptiles that give birth to live young are actually 'ovoviviparous'. This means that the embryo is receiving protection by being retained by the mother but is not being sustained by nutrients via a placenta. Mother and embryo remain separated by the egg membrane and the embryo receives nourishment solely from the yolk. Boas, which are found mainly in the Americas – with a few species from Africa – are ovoviviparous reptiles. It is believed that a number of extinct reptile species were viviparous or ovoviviparous.

❖ In truly viviparous reptiles there is a close connection

ABOVE Boas are ovoviviparous; they bear live young but inside the mother the embryo receives nutrients from its egg yolk and not through a placenta.

between the mother's tissues and the egg membrane, across which an exchange of gases – oxygen and carbon dioxide – can occur. East Indian brown-sided skinks and the Australian snake *Denisonia superba* are examples.

❖ In some species this 'placenta' is further adapted to allow the additional passage of nutrition to the developing embryo; this happens in the European viper, for example.

❖ In many species, however, the line between viviparity and ovoviviparity is blurred and the degree to which the mother and yolk provide nourishment is yet to be determined.

➡ *Ovoviviparous Reptiles, Reptiles*

VOLES
(Class: Mammalia Order: Rodentia)

Voles are very similar to mice, but have smaller ears and shorter tails. Mice tend to inhabit wooded areas, while voles frequent meadows and woods. They construct tunnel runways for themselves beneath the sward or undergrowth so that they can move about undetected by predators. One species, the southern mole-

vole (*Ellobius fuscocapillus*) has taken to digging tunnels below ground for extra protection. Voles build their nests in spaces beneath tree roots or in similar hideaways. They are plant feeders and multiply rapidly when conditions are favourable. The bank vole (*Clethrionomys glareolus*) is common over most of central Europe and Asia.

➠ *Mice, Rats*

WADERS
(Class: Aves Order: Charadriiformes)

Waders, or shorebirds, are a common sight along beaches and muddy flats around the world. There are 200 species, which are related to gulls and auks. Generally they wade in shallow water, searching for food such as worms and bivalve molluscs. The plumage of waders is commonly white, grey, black or brown. Many have colourful bills, eyes and legs. Waders often have long legs and bills to facilitate their hunt for food. The group contains many diverse birds including avocets, coursers, phalaropes, oystercatchers, plovers, sandpipers, stilts and snipe.

The Eurasian oystercatcher (*Haematopus ostralegus*) is a common sight along shorelines in Europe, parts of Africa and Asia. It has black plumage on its back and head with white underparts and bright red eyes, bill and legs. It feeds on shellfish, cracking mussels and cockles open on rocks. Its razor-sharp, pointed bill can cut the hinge that holds the two halves of the shell together. The bird then consumes the defenceless animal within. The pied avocet (*Recurvirostra avosetta*) is the most common species of avocet. Its white and black body sits on thin bluish legs. Its long, upturned bill is used to sweep the shallow water through which it wades, disturbing small prey.

BELOW The avocet uses its curved bill to sweep the water and disturb its prey.
BELOW LEFT Voles use runways through the undergrowth to conceal themselves.

- ❧ The black-winged stilt (*Himantopus himantopus*) has legs longer in relation to its body than any other bird. This adaptation enables the stilt to feed in deeper waters than other waders.
- ❧ The coursers are unlike most other waders in that they inhabit dry land. In fact they tend to frequent areas with little or no water – deserts.
- ❧ The wrybill (*Aharhynchus frontalis*) is the only bird with a bill that curves to one side, the right. It uses its bill to search for invertebrates beneath pebbles along New Zealand streams. It is a member of the plover family.

➠ *Auks, Gulls*

WAGTAILS
(Class: Aves Order: Passeriformes)

The wagtails are placed in the same family as the pipits. Both are common but the wagtails have a much smaller distribution, being found only in Europe, Asia and Africa. The birds get their name from the incessant habit they have of wagging their tails up and down as they stand. Wagtails often have bright plumage in contrasting colours. They eat insects, which they catch on the ground or while airborne. The pied wagtail (*Motacilla alba*) is commonly seen in Europe. Its distinctive black-and-white plumage and wagging tail make it an attractive visitor to urban gardens and parks.

➠ *Larks, Pipits*

WALL LIZARDS
(Class: Reptilia Order: Squamata)

Wall lizards are related to skinks and whiptails. They belong to the genus Podarcis and demonstrate a considerable variety within the group. The European wall lizard (*Lacerta muralis*) is 15–20 cm (6–8 in) long and mottled brown in appearance. It basks vertically on walls throughout the day. In winter it hibernates in crevices between rocks or bricks in walls. A number of species and sub-species of wall lizard populate the Balearic Islands in the Mediterranean. The Sicilian wall lizard alone has three sub-species that have evolved on three islands. Wall lizards eat small invertebrates but in some instances will turn cannibalistic.

➧ *Lizards, Skinks*

WALLABIES
(Class: Mammalia Order: Diprontodontia)

Wallabies are small kangaroos. To be precise they have to have feet less than 25 cm (10 in) long to qualify. They are no different from kangaroos in habits but their smaller size means that they can live in habitats with heavier plant cover, since they can slip through or beneath it more easily. The natural predator of wallabies was the thylacine, but it is now extinct. They now have to be watchful of introduced predators such as domestic dogs and cats, plus the dingo, which is a semi-wild dog introduced by the aboriginal settlers. There are about 50 wallaby species.

➧ *Kangaroos, Marsupial Mammals*

WARBLERS
(Class: Aves Order: Passeriformes)

There are 300 species of these small birds. They are found in Africa, Asia, Europe and Australia, where they live in woodland, scrubland and open grassland. They sometimes inhabit areas close to water where there are plenty of insects – their main food. Old World warblers differ from the New World variety in their wing structure. They have 10 primary feathers on each wing rather than nine. They are small birds with lengths of 9–26 cm (3.5–10 in). Generally, warblers have dull plumage that is suitably camouflaged for life in the trees. Their bills are thin with long nostrils that have covering flaps.

Warblers are usually good singers, but not as tuneful as thrushes. Most species migrate to warmer climes in winter. willow warblers (*Phylloscopus trochilus*) may travel 12,000 km (7,500 miles) on their migrations. They travel the same distance back in the spring. The greater bush warbler (*Cettia major*) lives in the Himalayas at altitudes approaching 4,000 m (13,200 ft).

♣ One of the most interesting warblers is the long-tailed tailorbird (*Orthotomus sutorius*). It has evolved the remarkable ability of stitching leaves together. It does so to form a cup in which to build its nest, away from predators.

➧ *Birds, Passerines*

ABOVE LEFT Wallabies count domestic dogs and cats among their predators.
ABOVE RIGHT The cuckoo wasp, like many wasps, is brightly coloured.

WASPS

(Class: Insecta Order: Hymenoptera)

There are many types of wasp. They include spider-hunter, potter, mason, social, digger, ruby-tail, velvet, ichneumon and gall wasps. Those most familiar to people are the social wasps, including hornets, which all bear the black and yellow livery to warn predators of their potent stings. Other wasps are brightly coloured too, with red, blue, orange and green against the

black. Wasps are generally carnivorous, preying on a range of other invertebrates, such as caterpillars, spiders, bees and flies. Social wasps have more catholic tastes and will readily feed on fruit pulp and other sweet foods along with carrion.

➡ *Ant, Bees*

WATER FLEAS

(Subphylum: Crustacea Class: Branchiopoda)

The most familiar genus in this order is Daphnia which comprises typical water fleas. They are similar to terrestrial fleas in body shape, but they are not related. They have a laterally compressed, bivalved carapace which contains most of the animal, except its head and branched antennae. Water fleas have the ability

to produce eggs that develop without fertilization, with the result that they can multiply extremely rapidly when conditions are right. They feed on microscopic organisms floating in the water. Water fleas can generate extra haemoglobin in their blood so that they can absorb more oxygen from stagnant water.

➡ *Crustaceans, Invertebrates*

WATER SCORPIONS

(Class: Insecta Order: Hemiptera)

These insects actually resemble mantids far more than scorpions, having evolved a similar design of forelimb for securing their prey. Water scorpions are aquatic bugs that prowl in search of food such as tadpoles, insect larvae and even small fish. Depending on their design, they frequent shallow or deeper water, as some species are short and squat while others are long and thin. They breathe air from the water's surface through a hollow tube attached to the end of the abdomen. Like all bugs they have sucking mouthparts, with which they drain the bodily fluids of their hapless victims.

➡ *Bugs, Insects*

BELOW Water scorpions are aquatic bugs which drain the blood of their victims.

WATERFOWL

(Class: Aves Order: Anseriformes)

 This group of medium to large birds includes the swans, geese, ducks and screamers. They are all at home in aquatic environments – some freshwater, some marine, some brackish, others a combination of the three. They are generally vegetarian, usually feeding on soft greenery, which they will travel inland to find. Many supplement their diets with invertebrates as and when they are available.

Waterfowl are dependent on shoreline vegetation for providing cover and protection for themselves and their nests. The eggs and young of waterfowl may fall prey to many creatures. Foxes, snakes, squirrels, racoons, bullfrogs and other birds may seek out their nests. Waterfowl spend much of their time swimming so their feathers need to be coated in protective oil to keep them waterproof. They acquire the oil from a preen gland at the base of the tail. They typically use their large webbed feet to propel themselves through water, although screamers have only partially webbed feet and are more terrestrial by nature.

The males of many species of duck are much more colourful than the females, especially during the breeding season. Waterfowl are adapted to feeding at different depths, to avoid directly competing with one another for food. Dabbling ducks are essentially surface feeders, while geese and swans can reach through the water with their long necks. Diving ducks can reach farther still. The mergansers are ducks with serrated bills adapted for catching fish.

❧ The eider duck (*Somateria mollissima*) provides people in Scandinavia and Iceland with a living. They collect down from their nests to use for stuffing pillows and duvets.

❧ Short droughts can be advantageous for waterfowl. When a pond or lake dries up fresh vegetation grows. After the water returns, seeds are released into the water which the birds eat. Long droughts, however, can be very detrimental.

➠ *Gulls, Waders*

WAXBILLS

(Class: Aves Order: Passeriformes)

Over 130 species of these tropical, Old World birds are recognized. Their name comes from their conical-shaped bills that are bright red – the colour of sealing wax. Waxbills gather together in large numbers to search through tall grasses for the seed that is the basis of their diet. Their plumage is usually brown or grey with flashes of red, yellow or black. The feathers often

ABOVE Swans use their long necks to reach through the water for food.
RIGHT The beak of the waxbill is the colour of sealing wax.

feature fine barring. Some species are popular as domestic pets. Waxbills build domed nests of grass or they nest in holes in trees. Between four and eight eggs are laid at a time.
➟ *Finches, Passerines*

WAXWINGS

(Class: Aves Order: Passeriformes)

There are three species of these berry-eating birds – the cedar waxwing, Japanese waxwing and the waxwing (*Bombycilla garrulus*). They are found in Europe, Asia and North America. Waxwings get their name from shiny red, wax-like droplets on the secondary wing feathers. Generally they are plump brownish-grey birds with crests, silky plumage and short bills. They are related to silky flycatchers and the hypocolius bird (*Hypocolius ampelinus*). Waxwings congregate in flocks and feed together on berries during the winter months, often stripping trees of their bounty. Flocks of waxwing are known to invade towns and cities in search of berry-laden trees.
➟ *Flycatchers Thrushes*

WEASELS

(Class: Mammalia Order: Carnivora)

The weasel family includes weasels, stoats, martens, badgers, otters, skunks, polecats and the wolverine (*Gulo gulo*) which is a very large and ferocious weasel, capable of killing prey animals as large as the caribou. It does so by leaping from trees and biting the throat of its victim. In fact all members of the family are potentially aggressive and many take prey larger than themselves. The common weasel (*Mustela nivalis*) is typical of the smaller species. It has an elongated, slender body that is never wider than its head so that it can pursue mice and voles along their tunnels.

Martens are weasels that have adapted for an arboreal lifestyle. Like squirrels – their main prey – they have long bushy tails that function as counterbalances and stabilizers when the animals are running and leaping through the branches of trees. Ferrets are domesticated polecats (*Mustela putorius*) that were originally bred to hunt rabbits, by chasing them from their burrows. Hybrids, known as polecat-ferrets, exist in the wild where tame ferrets have become feral and interbred with wild stock.

BELOW The weasel's long, slender body enables it to follow prey into tunnels.

❧ The sable (*Martes zibellina*) has escaped from fur farms into the wild in Britain and Europe, and become a serious predatory pest.
➟ *Badgers, Otters*

WEAVER BIRDS

(Class: Aves Order: Passeriformes)

This is a group of gregarious birds that live in colonies. They are found in woodlands, grassland, wetlands and in towns and cities – mainly in Africa. They are most common in hot, dry regions. Weavers get their name from their ability to build nests from grass and other plant material by weaving the components. The nests are often complex in structure. The breeding males, which are often yellow in colour, build nests that resemble upside-down flasks and then hang from them, calling and flapping their wings in a complex courtship display. Males often breed with more than one female – polygyny. Most weavers eat seeds, although some are insectivorous.

❧ The house sparrow (*Passer domesticus*) is probably the best-known of the weaver family. The social weaver (*Philetairus socius*), of southwestern Africa, makes a communal nest in acacia trees. The nest may reach 3 m (10 ft) in height and contain over 100 chambers. The entrances are all located at the base of the nest.

❧ The whydahs are brood parasitic species of weaver. Like cuckoos, they lay their eggs in other birds' nests. The host parents then incubate and raise their chicks. The paradise whydah (*Vidua paradisaea*) is an example.
➟ *Cuckoos, Sparrows*

WEEVERS

(Class: Osteichthyes Order: Perciformes)

There are four species of weever and they are all bottom-living marine fish. They have venom glands at the base of the spiny rays in their dorsal fins and on their gill covers. Weevers lie on the bottom of the sea in warm coastal regions, waiting for their prey of smaller fish. Since they are well camouflaged, beneath mud and sand, it is easy to stand on a weever. Their venom is so potent and incapacitating that it can cause serious injury to swimmers. The venom can be deactivated, though, by soaking the wound in very hot water for 30 minutes.

➡ *Fish, Scorpionfish*

WHALE SHARKS

**(Class: Chondrichthyes
Order: Orectolobiformes)**

The whale shark (*Rhincodon typus*) reaches a massive 15 m (50 ft) in length and is the largest fish on earth. It is an inhabitant of tropical seas around the world, but its population is considered vulnerable. The whale shark is deep blue or blue-grey on its upper surface and white underneath. Its body is marked with spots and lines like a chequerboard and its head has several characteristic long ridges. The mouth is at the front of the broad snout, rather than below it. Whale sharks have many small teeth and very large gill slits. They do not present any danger to humans.

❖ Whale sharks feed on planktonic organisms that drift the oceans. They coast near to the surface of the water with their wide mouths open. Water enters the mouth and passes through gill rakers. These are specialised organs that filter out the plankton from the water into huge mouthfuls that are then swallowed.

❖ Female whale sharks retain their fertilized eggs inside their bodies until they hatch, then give birth to live young. The young receive all their nutrition from the yolk in the eggs, rather than from a placenta. This process is known as ovoviviparity.

➡ *Cartilaginous Fish, Sharks*

RIGHT The beluga whale's pale colouring provides camouflage in icy regions.
ABOVE The killer whale is a toothed species and eats baby whales and fishes.

WHALES

(Class: Mammalia Order: Cetacea)

Whales are divided into two sub-orders; whalebone whales (Mysticeti) and toothed whales (Odontoceti). The whalebone whales are the right whales, rorqual whales and the grey whale (*Eschrichtius robustus*). The toothed whales are the sperm whales, porpoises, killer

whales, marine dolphins, river dolphins and the narwhal (*Monodon monocerus*). All whales are carnivorous, but their diet varies according to the way they feed.

The whalebone whales are all filter feeders that use a fibrous material called baleen to extract small animals from the water. In this manner they acquire vast

mouthfuls of zooplankton that floats in the oceans. Despite the diminutive size of their prey these whales include the largest animal that has ever lived on earth – the blue whale (*Balaenoptera musculus*), which can grow to 27 m (90 ft). Being so large affords whales certain advantages. For one, they have few, if any, predators. Secondly they have a low surface area to volume ratio, which means they can survive very well in cold oceans.

The toothed whales are all hunters. They feed on a variety of larger animals, including fish, squid, penguins and seals, depending on the species. The largest toothed whale is the sperm whale (*Physeter macrocephalus*), reaching 18 m (60 ft). It specialises in feeding on large, deep-sea squid and is perfectly adapted to dive for them. The killer whale, grampus or orca (*Orcinus orca*) will take all kinds of prey, from baby whales to fish.

❧ Narwhals are unique among whales in having tusks. The male has a modified canine tooth that measures about a metre (3 ft). It is twisted for strength and seems to be used for jousting other males during the breeding season.

❧ Belugas or white whales (*Delphinapterus leucus*) live among the pack ice in arctic waters. Its pale colour provides camouflage protection from polar bears.

➡ *Dolphins, Porpoises, Zooplankton*

BELOW Whip snakes raise their heads when hunting to improve their vision.

WHIP SCORPIONS
(Class: Arachnida Order: Uropygi)

Whip scorpions are so called because they possess a whip-like tail or flagellum at the end of the abdomen. At the base of the tail are two organs which squirt a defensive fluid whenever the whip scorpion is attacked. The fluid contains acetic acid which stings the eyes of predators and smells so strongly that whip scorpions are known as 'vinegaroons' by some populations in the USA. Unlike true scorpions, whip scorpions are not venomous and rely on their strength to overcome prey. They also tend to frequent humid habitats rather than dry ones. Over 70 species are known globally.

➡ *Scorpions, Sun Spiders*

WHIP SNAKES
(Class: Reptilia Order: Squamata)

Whip snakes belong to the genus Masticophis. They inhabit dry and hot regions in North America and Europe. The dark-green whip snake (*Coluber viridiflavus*) is typically long and slender. It is generally green, although covered by an intricate patterning of markings. Whip snakes are active, diurnal or daytime hunters. They eat lizards, small rodents and birds, including their eggs and nestlings. When hunting they will often raise their heads off the ground and wave them from side to side. This technique is called triangulation and it helps them get better depth perception, since they lack three-dimensional, stereoscopic or binocular vision.

➡ *Reptiles, Snakes*

WHITING

(Class: Osteichthyes Order: Gadiformes)

Whiting are closely related to cod, pollock and coley. They inhabit cold and temperate waters, particularly the northern Atlantic Ocean, the North Sea and the Mediterranean Sea. Whiting are olive, sandy-brown or bluish on their dorsal surface and silver, gold or white on their bellies. They grow up to 40 cm (16 in) long. They have three dorsal fins and two anal fins. Whiting live in shallow waters and are more easily caught than either haddock or cod, making them an attractive fish to the commercial fishing industry. Whiting feed on invertebrates and small fish, particularly at dawn and dusk.

➥ *Cod, Pollock*

WOLVES

(Class: Mammalia Order: Carnivora)

Domesticated dogs probably originate from the grey wolf (*Canis lupus*). It is a pack animal with complex hierarchical rules to be observed by each member of the pack. This is why dogs make such obedient pets, for they retain the behavioural instincts of their wild ancestors. The maned wolf (*Chrysocyon brachyurus*) of Brazil and Argentina is quite different from the grey wolf, being a solitary animal that hunts alone. The coyote (*Canis latrans*), of North and Central America is a small wolf that has proved to be highly adaptable to life alongside humans. Its Old World counterparts are the jackals.

➥ *Carnivores, Dogs*

WOMBATS

(Class: Mammalia Order: Diprotodontia)

There are three species of wombat. They are badger-like marsupials that live in burrows which they excavate for themselves. They are long-lived animals that feed on plant matter, especially roots and tubers that they find while digging. The common wombat (*Vombatus ursinus*) is found both in Tasmania and on the Australian mainland. It has dentition similar to rodents, with sharp,

RIGHT It is thought that domestic dogs originated from the grey wolf.
ABOVE RIGHT Wombats are burrowing marsupials and feed on plants.

chisel-lie incisors used for severing plant fibre. They also have molars adapted for masticating green foodstuffs. Wombats have reverse entry pouches, presumably to avoid covering their offspring with soil while burrowing. Only one young is nurtured at a time.

➥ *Mammals, Numbats*

WOODLICE

(Subphylum: Crustacea Class: Malacostraca)

Woodlice are one of only a few groups of crustaceans that have become truly independent of water at all stages of their lifecycle. That is not to say though that they can live without water. Most species are fairly vulnerable to desiccation, so prefer damp habitats.

A few species, such as the pill woodlice (*Armadillidium vulgare*), can venture into open, dry places because they possess defence against both drying out and predation, having armour-like exoskeletons. Woodlice are also called sowbugs and hoglice because their rounded shape is reminiscent of pigs' backs. Woodlice are omnivorous, eating all kinds of organic matter.

➟ *Crustaceans, Slaters*

WOODPECKERS
(Class: Aves Order: Piciformes)

Woodpeckers are related to toucans, puffbirds and jacamars. They are unique amongst birds in their ability to carve holes out of hard wood. Most birds that dig holes only do so in soft or rotten wood. Woodpeckers live almost exclusively in trees – there is only one species of ground-dwelling woodpecker. Like other members of the order Piciformes woodpeckers have two toes facing forwards and two toes facing backwards. This enables them to climb easily up and down tree trunks but makes perching on horizontal branches more difficult. Woodpeckers usually eat insects that they find under the bark of trees, although some also eat berries and fruit. They are found worldwide but are most common in South America and southeast Asia.

❧ Woodpeckers are solitary birds, living singly or in pairs. They can be aggressive towards other members of their own species or even their own mates and offspring.

❧ Males are usually recognized by a splash of colour on their heads. In springtime they may begin territorial behaviour which involves making loud drumming noises on tree trunks. They also display to females by spreading their wings and bobbing their heads. Eggs are laid on the bare floor of a tree cavity.

➟ *Birds, Toucans*

WORM LIZARDS
(Class: Reptilia Order: Squamata)

Amphisbaenids are often given the simpler name 'worm lizards'. While they are closely related to both lizards and snakes, the worm snakes are sufficiently different to warrant being placed in their own family. All worm lizards are long and slender, exactly like snakes.

BELOW Woodpeckers drum on tree trunks to declare their territory.

Their bodies are cylindrical and most have no limbs – although a few species have retained small forelimbs which have claws that can be used for digging. They have simple eyes and hard, smooth heads that are used for burrowing through soil and humus. All worm lizards have a subterranean way of life, searching for insects and worms.

➟ *Lizards, Snakes*

WRASSE
(Class: Osteichthyes Order: Perciformes)

Wrasse belong to the large fish order Perciformes and to the same family as the parrot fish. They are an abundant group with more than 300 species. Wrasse are found in tropical and temperate seas worldwide, particularly around coral reefs. They are mostly carnivorous and feed on small crustaceans and invertebrates. Wrasse characteristically have slender fusiform bodies that are covered with large scales. They have thick lips and prominent teeth in the upper jaw. Colour and patterning of the scales differs considerably between the species. In some instances the colour and patterning varies throughout the lifecycle too. In a number of species a change in colour accompanies a change of sex from female to male.

❧ The cleaner wrasse (*Labroides dimidiatus*) is one of the best-known members of this group. An inhabitant of coral reefs, it is found in small groups that contain several females and one male. Other fish of the reef community that are afflicted with parasites visit the cleaner wrasse group which pick off the parasites. This is known as a symbiotic relationship, as both species of fish benefit. When the male wrasse dies he is replaced by the dominant female. She changes sex by a hormonal process.

➥ *Bony Fish, Parrot Fish*

WRENS
(Class: Aves Order: Passeriformes)

These small, brown birds are characterised by their loud songs, downcurved bills, rounded wings and short, cocked tails. Males and females both have dull plumage that may be finely barred. There is one species of wren found in the Old World – *Troglodytes troglodytes* – which is known simply as the wren. Wrens are commonly found at ground level, searching for insects in thick undergrowth. They inhabit a variety of areas but favour marshes, scrub and woodland. They are common visitors to gardens and parks. The males build the nests, often building more than one to offer the females a choice.

➥ *Flycatchers, Warblers*

ZEBRA-TAILED LIZARDS
(Class: Reptilia Order: Squamata)

The zebra-tailed lizard is a fast-running insectivorous inhabitant of desert flats and plains in North America. It is also known as the gridiron lizard. Both names reflect the pattern of bold, black and white stripes on its belly and tail. Males have a turquoise patch on their chests. The body is flat and slim, legs are long and slender. The zebra-tailed lizard is active during the day and is able to withstand great heat, only seeking shelter during the hottest parts of the day. It can leap several times its own body length off the ground to capture flying insects.

➥ *Lizards, Reptiles*

ABOVE The zebra-tailed lizard can jump in the air to catch flying insects.
LEFT Wrens are small birds, but sing loudly for their size.

feeding sharks, which are equipped with large gaping mouths and filtering structures to extract the animals and plants from the water in huge mouthfuls.

The organisms that make up zooplankton all use the same survival strategy. That strategy is to live in such prodigious numbers that it will always be impossible for predators to eat every last specimen of a single species. It has worked for hundreds of millions of years and will doubtless continue to do so. Living alongside billions of individuals from other species is also an effective way of reducing the odds of being eaten. For larval animals, planktonic life is also a good means of dispersal to other regions, ensuring a healthy flow of genes and giving a chance of establishing colonies in new areas of the oceans.

❧ Although plankton is usually associated with marine environments, freshwater environments can also include plankton.

❧ The word 'plankton' is derived from the Greek 'planktos' which means 'wanderer'.

❧ Planktonic animals cannot swim independently of water currents, but nekton are small waterborne animals that can.

➠ *Invertebrates*

ZOOPLANKTON

(Kingdom: Animalia and Protista)

Zooplankton is the collective term for waterborne animals and protozoans amongst plankton. The waterborne protists are known as phytoplankton. Zooplankton comprises both adult animals, the larval stages of larger animals and protozoans. They drift randomly through the oceans at the surface, where the water is warmest. Many of these zooplankton are plant feeders, but others prey on their neighbours.

Plankton is the foundation of food chains in the world's oceans, and is therefore a very important part of the ecosystem. Flushes of new plankton develop with the seasons in both the northern and southern seas, causing great migrations of larger animals in search of food. As well as feeding small fish and the like, plankton is consumed in vast quantities by baleen whales and filter-

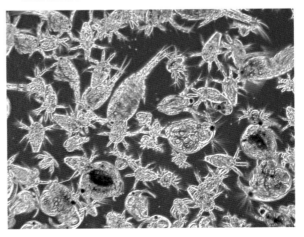

ABOVE Zooplankton live in huge populations to reduce the odds of being eaten.

PREHISTORIC LIFE ON EARTH

The first animals appeared on Earth approximately 2.5 billion years ago and have continued to evolve ever since. Many of the stages in evolution are represented by living species that have remained very much as they were when they first appeared on Earth; others have become extinct or have evolved into the animals we are familiar with today. We know this because of the wealth of fossil and genetic evidence available.

Fossils are formed by the gradual replacement of organic material with minerals, so that a permanent copy of an animal is formed. As the softer parts of organisms tend to decompose rapidly after death, it is usually the harder parts of the body that become fossilised, such as bones, teeth and shells. Nevertheless, these still provide information about the animals from which they came. Genetic evidence provides information about how closely living animals are related to one another.

RIGHT A simple natural history of the Earth

80 MILLION YEARS
Small mammals, such as early relatives of rats, increase in numbers and diversity

147 MILLION YEARS
Birds evolve from some reptiles

65 MILLION YEARS
Dinosaurs die, probably due to the effects of a meteorite impact

400 MILLION YEARS
Fish, the first vertebrates, dominate the oceans

545 MILLION YEARS
Invertebrates, such as trilobites, emerge

340 MILLION YEARS
Plants spread across the land masses

c. 4.6 BILLION YEARS
Earth forms

150 MILLION YEARS
Dinosaurs dominate the land masses

260 MILLION YEARS
Amphibians, lizard-like creatures, evolve from fish and popluate the land masses

3.75 BILLION YEARS
Bacteria emerge

5–6 MILLION YEARS
First humans evolve from an ape-like ancestor

2006
There are an estimated 6 billion people on Earth

EVOLUTION OF LIFE ON EARTH

During the 1830s an Englishman, Charles Darwin, went on a worldwide expedition as naturalist aboard HMS *Beagle*. In 1859 he published his book *On the Origin of Species by Means of Natural Selection*. He was prompted to finally publish after receiving a letter from fellow naturalist Alfred Russel Wallace which outlined the very same idea. Darwin's work revolutionized the way life on earth was understood, and 'evolution' became the new watchword.

The wildlife of the Galapagos Islands was central to Darwin's inspiration. The islands were home to varieties of finch and tortoise that had clearly evolved from single points of origin, to fill the various econiches available. They demonstrated perfectly how natural selection promotes evolutionary divergence and, therefore, the creation of new species. It is now recognized that evolution is a complex phenomenon, but the fundamental mechanism by which it is driven is described as the Darwinian Principle.

RIGHT The 14 different species of Galapagos finch have all evolved differently.
FAR RIGHT Galapagos tortoises are adapted to store food in a harsh environment.
ABOVE RIGHT Wildlife on the Galapagos inspired Charles Darwin.

EVOLUTION OF LIFE

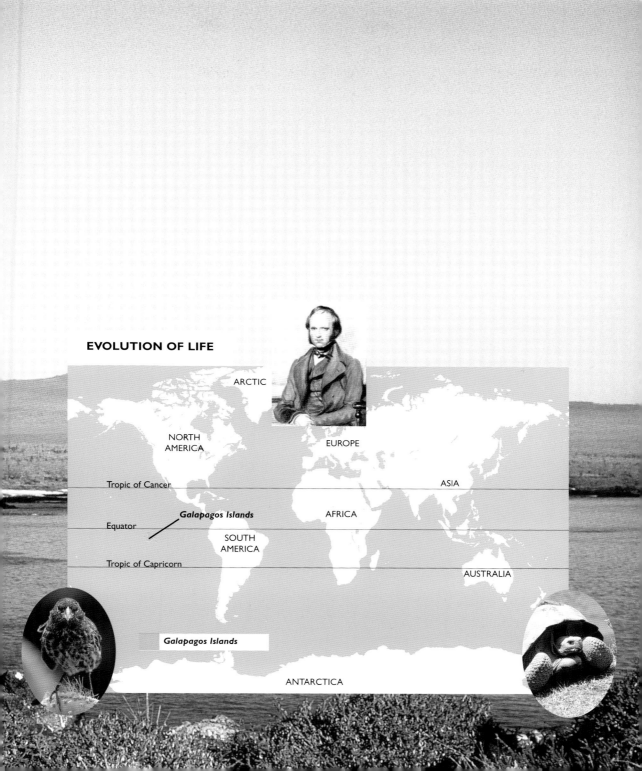

ARCTIC

NORTH
AMERICA

EUROPE

Tropic of Cancer

ASIA

Galapagos Islands

AFRICA

Equator

SOUTH
AMERICA

Tropic of Capricorn

AUSTRALIA

Galapagos Islands

ANTARCTICA

FAMILY: HOMINIDS

Australopithecines

Several species of small ape-like creatures, able to walk bipedally.

Homo habilis

First Homo species, and able to fashion basic tools from stone and organic materials.

Homo erectus

The species which takes humanity over the Old World and invents culture.

Millions of Years Ago

| 4 | 3.5 | 3 | 2.5 | 2 | 1.5 | 1 |

Homo sapiens

Refined intellect, developed language.

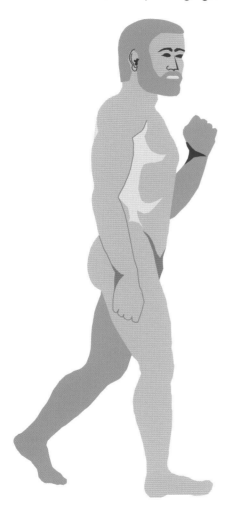

NATURAL HISTORY OF HUMANS

Human beings, like all life forms, have evolved from prehistoric ancestors. It became clear to Charles Darwin that fossils of ape-like people must have been our forebears, so he published his *Descent of Man* to explain his theory. Since then a great deal of work has been done to find out more about the evolution of humans or *Homo sapiens* (wise human) – our species' name. The scientists doing this work are called physical anthropologists.

It now seems likely that there were originally several kinds of prototype human living simultaneously. They are called the australopithecines (southern apes). Eventually one line evolved into the first species in our genus – *Homo habilis* (handy human) – 2–4 million years ago. *Homo erectus* (upright human) was the next stage and saw people moving to new areas from Africa. Since then the Homo genus has been through a series of refinements, resulting in modern humans – *Homo sapiens.*

Millions of Years Ago

0.5   0

CAMOUFLAGE

For all animals it is necessary to increase their chances of survival, whether they are predators, prey or both, so that they can breed and produce a new generation. In all environment there are animals that have evolved colours, patterns, shapes or movements to make them blend in with their backgrounds so that they go unseen by their adversaries. This is called camouflage.

Camouflage creates the illusion of invisibility. Humans have very discerning eyesight so it is often easier for us to isolate the outlines of camouflaged creatures than it is for the creatures' natural enemies. The type of camouflage adopted by species is typical to their environment, so forest creatures will imitate the colours and shapes of foliage, for example, while desert creatures will need to imitate rocks and sand. Many animals take a short cut by covering themselves in objects found in their environment.

RIGHT A common stargazer waiting for prey.
ABOVE RIGHT A cicada from Indonesia blends into the bark of a tree.
MAIN A lioness lies camouflaged against the background of the Masai Mara.

MIMICRY

Although camouflage is the most common type of mimicry, there are occasions where animals imitate others species specifically rather than attempting to hide themselves within their environment. Many harmless species have evolved to look similar to dangerous species so that predators leave them alone. This is called Batesian mimicry. Good examples are hover flies that imitate bees and wasps for protection. There are also many moths and butterflies that mimic poisonous varieties for the same reason.

Although most mimics use their resemblance to other animals for protection from predators, there are others that use mimicry to catch prey or access food. The caterpillar of the large blue butterfly (*Maculinea arion*) pretends to be an ant grub so that it is carried into an ants' nest, where it feeds on real ant grubs. There are several spiders that mimic ants in order to approach and prey on unsuspecting flies.

RIGHT The clear-winged moth mimics a wasp.
ABOVE RIGHT The caterpiller of a hawkmoth imitates a snake in its defensive position.
MAIN A leaf-imitating katydid from the Brazilian rainforest.

LOCOMOTION

Most animals respond to stimuli by moving – this may be to acquire food or to avoid predators. It may be also to find a mate or to avoid inclement weather. Animal locomotion takes many forms, depending on whether they travel through air, on water, underwater, overland, underground or through forests. Methods of movement are described as terrestrial (on land), subterranean (underground), aquatic (on or in water), aerial (through air), and arboreal (through trees) locomotion.

For terrestrial animals walking and running are most common, but some hop while others slither and underground species burrow. Waterborne animals paddle or use the wind to sail along. Those underwater swim by means of fins, body movements or thrust from water jets. Others merely drift in the currents. Arboreal animals climb and jump through trees. Airborne animals fly, glide, or ride thermals.

RIGHT A little owl clutches its insect prey mid-flight.
ABOVE RIGHT Red kangaroo uses its powerful hind legs to transport itself.
MAIN Polar bears have feet that are designed both to grip ice and to swim.

MIGRATION

When animals move regularly from one place to another it is described as their migration. Migrations may cover thousands of kilometres, whatever the mode of locomotion. Other migrations may only be a few kilometres. The reasons for migrations occurring are typically related to seasonal changes and availability of food.

Apart from keeping themselves alive, animals need to migrate to places where there is a bounty of food so that they have a reasonable chance of rearing offspring, thereby producing the next generation. Otherwise there species would simply cease to exist. There are mammal, bird, reptile, amphibian, fish, cephalopod, crustacean and insect species that are known to migrate to and from places for this reason. Their movements occur each and every year without fail.

RIGHT Wildebeest migrating across the Masai Mara, Kenya, Africa.
ABOVE RIGHT Migrating western sandpipers from Washington, USA.
MAIN Canada geese migrating over the Teton Mountains, Wyoming, USA.

ENDANGERED SPECIES

Throughout prehistory there have been species of animal that have become extinct. This happens whenever species are unable to evolve quickly enough to cope with changes in their environment. The earth itself is constantly changing and the momentum of so many species of plant and animal evolving at the same time brings about unpredictable changes in habitats. So, the animals that are around today, including people, are simply the ones that had ancestors lucky enough to survive.

However, the activities of people are now the main cause of animals becoming endangered or extinct. Humans are so successful that they have altered environments far more rapidly than would usually happen naturally. There are some well documented examples of extinction attributed to humans. Perhaps the most remarkable and telling though is that of the passenger pigeon, which was hunted to extinction from an original population in its tens of millions.

RIGHT These ring-tailed lemurs are counted as a species under threat.
FAR RIGHT The Siberian tiger is also an endangered species.
MAIN Jaguar skins are prized and have resulted in dwindling populations.

HABITATS OF THE WORLD

To understand the distribution of animals over the globe it is necessary to know about how the world is divided into habitats. These are largely dictated by the position of lands and seas in relation to the equator and the two poles. The earth has been subjected to a series of ice ages and catastrophic natural events that have affected these habitats over time. The map to the right shows the division of the world's surface into typical habitat types.

Type of Habitat

Tundra & ice
Coniferous forest
Broadleaf forest
Mediterranean scrub
Grassland
Savannah
Sub tropical forest
Dry tropical scrub & thorn forest
Monsoon forest
Tropical rain forest
Scrub, steppe & semi-desert
Desert
Ocean & lakes

TAXONOMIC INFORMATION

One hundred years before Charles Darwin published his theory of evolution, scientists were beginning to classify animals and plants according to their similarities – their taxonomy. Because different countries had their own common or colloquial names for identical species it became necessary to invent scientific names (nomenclature) that were universally recognized. The rules were set in 1758 by the '*Code of the International Commission on Zoological Nomenclature*'. The chosen language used for scientific names was a combination of Latin and Greek.

The chart below shows how surviving life forms are currently grouped. It stops at 'class' because orders, sub-orders, families, genera, species and sub-species combined number in their millions. The classification of species is fraught with contention between scientists with differing opinions, but this table provides a generally accepted view of the important groups.

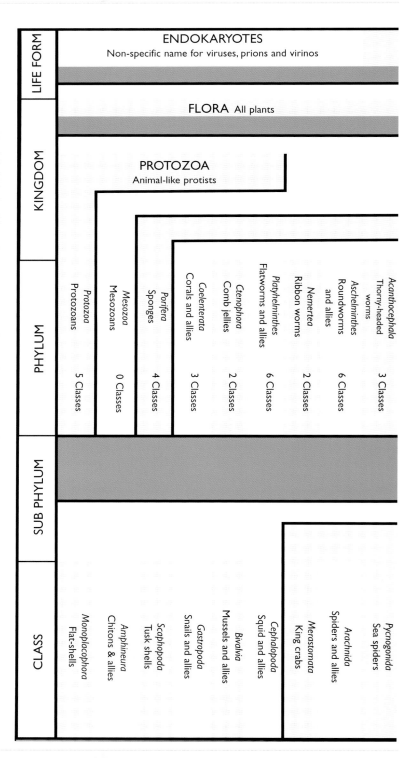

LIFE FORM

ENDOKARYOTES — Non-specific name for viruses, prions and virinos

FLORA All plants

KINGDOM

PROTOZOA — Animal-like protists

PHYLUM

Phylum	Common name	Classes
Protozoa	Protozoans	5 Classes
Mesozoa	Mesozoans	0 Classes
Porifera	Sponges	4 Classes
Coelenterata	Corals and allies	3 Classes
Ctenophora	Comb jellies	2 Classes
Platyhelminthes	Flatworms and allies	6 Classes
Nemertea	Ribbon worms	2 Classes
Aschelminthes	Roundworms and allies	6 Classes
Acanthocephala	Thorny-headed worms	3 Classes

SUB PHYLUM

CLASS

Class	Common name
Monoplacophora	Flat-shells
Amphineura	Chitons & allies
Scaphopoda	Tusk shells
Gastropoda	Snails and allies
Bivalvia	Mussels and allies
Cephalopoda	Squid and allies
Merostomata	King crabs
Arachnida	Spiders and allies
Pycnogonida	Sea spiders

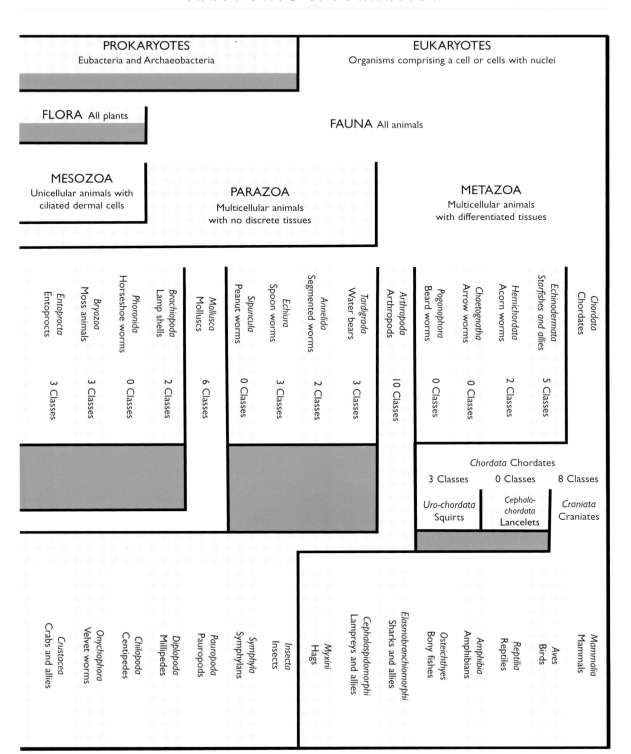

GLOSSARY

AESTIVATION
Period of dormancy similar to hibernation but usually carried out during the summer months to survive times of drought.

AIRBORNE
Carried through the air by flying, gliding or floating.

AMPHIBIAN
Cold-blooded vertebrate with limbs, typically with gill-breathing, aquatic larvae and lung-breathing terrestrial adults.

ANTARCTICA
Zoogeographical region comprising the Antarctic continent, the Southern Ocean and the islands within.

AFRICA
Zoogeographical region comprising the African continent and divided from Asia by the Sinai desert.

AQUATIC
Living in water – saltwater, brackish water or freshwater.

ARBOREAL
Living among trees.

ASIA
Zoogeographical region comprising the Middle East, Far East and southeast Asia. Separated from Europe by the Carpathian Mountains and Black Sea. Separated from Africa by the Sinai Desert and from Australasia by the Wallace's line.

AUSTRALASIA
Zoogeographical region comprising Australia, New Zealand, neighbouring Pacific islands and islands to the north of Australia as far as Wallace's line.

BRACHIATION
Method of locomotion in apes by swinging from arm to arm.

BRACKISH
Water that is a mixture of saltwater and freshwater, typically at an estuary.

CARNIVORE
Animal that eats the flesh of another animal.

CLASS
Taxonomic grouping of species above order and below phylum.

CONVERGENT EVOLUTION
When unrelated animals happen to evolve in very similar ways because they live in identical, though usually separate, habitats.

DESERT
Environment characterised by low rainfall and general aridity – maybe hot or cold.

DIURNAL
Animal that sleeps at night and is active by day.

ECONICHE
Specific niche within a habitat that a species has adapted to fill.

ENDANGERED
To have a population in decline or so small that sustainability is in question.

ENVIRONMENT
Type of living space, usually larger than a habitat and smaller than a region.

EURASIA
Double zoogeographical region comprising Europe and Asia.

EUROPE
Zoogeographical region divided from Asia by the Carpathian Mountains and Black Sea. Includes Scandinavia to the north and the Mediterranean islands.

EXTANT
Species with a viable population in existence.

EXTINCT
Species that no longer survives.

FAMILY
Taxonomic grouping of species above genus and below class.

FOLIVORE
Vegetarian animal that specifically eats leaves.

FOODCHAIN
Hierarchical sequence of species that consume one another for food.

FRESHWATER
Any water that is not contaminated by salt – sodium chloride.

FRUGIVORE
Vegetarian animal that specifically eats fruits.

GENUS
Taxonomic grouping above species and below family.

HABITAT
Specific and immediate surroundings of a species.

HERBIVORE
An animal that feeds on plant matter.

HIBERNATION
Dormant phase spent during the winter months to conserve energy.

HOMEOSTASIS
Maintenance of equilibrium in bodily processes – especially body warmth.

INSECTIVORE
Animal that eats insects and other invertebrates.

INVERTEBRATE
Animal that lacks vertebrae, although it may still posses a spinal chord.

MAMMAL
Warm-blooded animal with fur or hairs. Three types – placental, marsupial and monotreme.

MARINE
Environment characterised by saltwater or brackish water.

MOUNTAINOUS
Habitat surrounding mountains – from the foothills up to the snowline.

NEW WORLD
Double zoogeographical region comprising North America and South America.

NOCTURNAL
Animal characterised by activity at night.

NORTH AMERICA
Zoogeographical comprising Alaska, Canada, Greenland, USA and Mexico as far south as the Sierra Madre Mountains.

OCCIDENTAL
The Western World – technically all that is west of the Greenwich meridian – Europe and North America.

OLD WORLD
Triple zoogeographical region comprising Europe, Asia and Africa.

OMNIVORE
Animal that feeds on both animal and plant matter.

ORDER
Taxonomic grouping above family and below class.

ORIENTAL
The Eastern World – Asia.

PALAEARCTIC

Circumpolar zoogeographical region comprising North America, Europe and Asia.

PHYLUM

Taxonomic grouping above class and below kingdom.

POLAR

Habitat characterized by its proximity with the two poles – north and south.

PREDATOR

Animal that kills prey animals for food.

PREY

Animal that is killed by a predator for food.

RAINFOREST

Forest in tropical regions, characterized by high levels of rainfall generated by microclimates.

REPTILE

Cold-blooded vertebrate with limbs and scales.

SOUTH AMERICA

Zoogeographical region separated from North America by the Sierra Madre Mountains.

SPECIES

Taxonomic classification below genus and above subspecies.

SUBSPECIES

Variety of a species that can interbreed with other varieties of the same species.

SUBTERRANEAN

Animals that live below ground.

TEMPERATE

Climate characterised by seasonal change.

TERRESTRIAL:

Living on land – encompassing ground living, arboreal and flying animals.

TROPICAL

Climate characterized by warm, humid conditions.

WALLACE'S LINE

Theoretical boundary that divides Southeast Asia from Australiasia in zoogeographical terms.

WATERBORNE

Carried on or in water.

AUTHOR BIOGRAPHIES

GERARD CHESHIRE
Author and General Editor

Gerard began his career as a naturalist at an early age, having been bought up on the outskirts of the New Forest in Hampshire, England. He is a graduate of University College London and has written and edited a wide variety of projects relating to natural history and the sciences. He also works as a field ecologist.

CAMILLA DE LA BÉDOYÈRE
Contributor

After leaving university with a degree in zoology, Camilla de la Bédoyère taught biology and chemistry in Kenya. She has written books on natural history often specializing on the examination of life on Earth and the ethical questions posed by our relationship with its other inhabitants.

PICTURE CREDITS

Colin Varndell: 19, 43 (r), 52, 66 (bl), 70, 73 (r), 83, 131, 145 (t), 164, 188, 193, 194 (b), 206 (b)

Foundry Arts: 1, 3, 5, 6, 7, 10 (r), 24 (t), 25, 35, 66 (t), 82 (t), Shahriar Coupal 137, 166 (b), 198 (bl), 182 (b), 200–1, 218

Science Photo Library/David Scharf: 40 (r)

Still Pictures: Nigel J Dennis 8 (t), 23 (r), 137 (r); John Cancalosi 8 (b), 49, 59, 78 (r), 81, 89, 99, 111 (t), 123 (t), 125 (b), 165, 180, 182, 210–11; Nicholas Granier 202–3; Kevin Schafer 9, 16, 36 (l), 75, 106 (b), 132 (b), 190 (b); Roland Seitre 10 (l), 11, 14 (b), 22, 29, 34, 53 (t), 98 (l), 108, 114, 117 (b), 118, 132 (t), 135, 140 (r), 186, 192 (t); Norbert Wu 12 (l), 26 (r), 141 (l), 151, 182 (t); Secret Sea Visions 12 (r), 48 (b), 86, 106 (t); Cyril Ruoso 13, 14 (t), 107, 113 (r), 119 (b); Remy Amann 15; M & C Denis-Huot 17 (t), 57; Denis Bringard 17 (b); Michael J Doolittle 18 (t); Carl R Sams II 18 (b), 87 (t); Robert Bergerot 20; Doug Cheeseman 21 (bl) & (tr); Marilyn Kazmers 21 (br), 190 (t); Thomas D Mangelsen 23 (l), 71 (t), 129 (r), 208–9; Luiz C Marigo 24 (b), 79, 96 (t), 130 (l), 204–5; R Andrew Odum 27, 76 (r), 150 (t), 159 (r); Pascal Kobeh 28 (t), 44 (t), 181 (b); W Fischer 28 (b); Sea Studios Inc 30 (l); Hans Pfeltschinger 30 (r), 58 (r), 101 (t), 162, 187 (tr) & (br), 205 (t) & (b); Kjell B Sandved 31; Martin Wendler 32 (t); Bruno Pambour 32 (b), 88 (l), 129 (l); Michel Gunther 33, 62 (t), 134 (b), 161 (b); Brunner-Unep 35 (l); Fred Bavendam 26 (l), 36 (r), 80 (b), 96 (b), 154 (l), 156, 158, 203 (b); Christian Testu 38; Tristan Lafranchis 39 (t); Yvette Tavernier 39 (b), 128, 146 (r), 175 (l); Xavier Eichaker 40 (l), 154 (b); Edward Parker 42, 116 (r); Rafel Al Ma'ary 43 (t), 58 (l), 178 (r); Bojan Brecelj 44 (b), 122 (l); Mark Carwardine 45, 100, 147, 157; Bengt Lundberg 46 (l); Martin Gilles 46 (r); Franck Deschandol 47, 150 (bl); Mark Edwards 48 (t); Nicole Duplaix 53 (b); Fabrice Cahez 54 (t); J J Alcalay 54 (b); O Gautier 55; John R MacGregor 56 (t), 150 (br), 194-195 (t); Daniel Heuclin 56 (b), 74 (r), 77, 85 (t), 145 (b), 160, 184 (t); Jean Cassou 60; Chin Fah Shin 61 (t); C Allen Morgan 61 (b); Kelvin Aitken 62 (b), 104 (t), 146 (l), 168 (r); Bruno P Zehnder 63; Dave Watts 71 (b), Fritz Polking 74 (l), 76 (l), 87 (b), 90 (t), 110, 130 (l), 142 (l), 148 (br), 209 (b); Robert Henno 78 (l); Emile Barbelette 82 (b), 124 (b); Jeffrey Rotman 84, 143; Manfred Danegger 85 (b); Jean-Luc & F Ziegler 88 (r), 140 (l); Muriel Nicolotti 90 (b); Yann Arthus-Bertrand 91; Thierry Montford 94 (l); Alain Compost 94 (r), 173 (t); James Gerholdt 95, 183; Yves Lefevre 97, 109, 122 (r), 123 (b), 155; G Verhaegen 98 (r), 169; Michel Ribette 101 (b); Gregory Talvy 102; Thierry Thomas 211 (r); Hubert Klein 103 (l), 111 (b), 113 (l), 133, 138, 173 (b), 176, 211 (l); Olivier Langrand 103 (r); Dominique Halleux 105, 116 (l); Schafer & Hill 117 (t); M & C Photography 112; B Stein 115 (l); Patricia Jordan 115 (r); Ed Reschke 119 (t); Thier Vanbaelinghem 124 (t); Patric Sabonnadiere 125 (t); Kim Heacox 134 (t); Gerard Lacz 136 (l), 149, 189 (t); Michel Roggo 136 (r); Paul Springett 139 (t); David Cavagnaro 139 (b), 144; Georges Lopez 141 (r); Steve Kaufman 142 (r), 189 (b); H Willocx 148 (t); Jany Sauvenet 148 (bl), 163, 171 (b); Mazquiaran-Unep 159 (l); Regis Cavignaux 161 (t), 181 (t); Paul Glendell 166 (t); Malcolm Watson 167; Gunter Ziesler 16 (t), 168 (l); Claude Thouvenin 170; Franco/Bonnard 171 (t); Michael Sewell 172, 177, 178 (l), 191; Don Riepe 174; Guy Piton 175 (r); Neckles-Unep (179); Rene Krekels 184 (b); Guy Bortolato 185; Michel Rauch 187 (l); Lynn Rogers 192 (b); Roland Birke 195 (b)

Topham Picture Library: 41, 199 (t)

INDEX